SEVEN SEAS ENT[ER]

The Danger

story and art by **NORIO SAKURAI**

VOLUME 2

TRANSLATION
Nan Rymer

LETTERING
Arbash Mughal

COVER DESIGN
Hanase Qi

EDITOR
Peter Adrian Behravesh

PREPRESS TECHNICIAN
Rhiannon Rasmussen-Silverstein

PRODUCTION ASSOCIATE
Christa Miesner

PRODUCTION MANAGER
Lissa Pattillo

MANAGING EDITOR
Julie Davis

ASSOCIATE PUBLISHER
Adam Arnold

PUBLISHER
Jason DeAngelis

THE DANGERS IN MY HEART. VOLUME 2
© Norio Sakurai 2019
Originally published in Japan in 2019 by Akita Publishing Co., Ltd.
English translation rights arranged with Akita Publishing Co., Ltd.
through TOHAN CORPORATION, Tokyo.

Seven Seas press and purchase enquiries can be sent to Marketing Manager Lianne Sentar at press@gomanga.com. Information regarding the distribution and purchase of digital editions is available from Digital Manager CK Russell at digital@gomanga.com.

Seven Seas and the Seven Seas logo are trademarks of Seven Seas Entertainment. All rights reserved.

ISBN: 978-1-64827-443-5
Printed in Canada
First Printing: September 2021
10 9 8 7 6 5 4 3 2 1

///// READING DIRECTIONS /////

This book reads from *right to left*, Japanese style. If this is your first time reading manga, you start reading from the top right panel on each page and take it from there. If you get lost, just follow the numbered diagram here. It may seem backwards at first, but you'll get the hang of it! Have fun!!

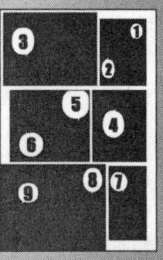

Follow us online: www.SevenSeasEntertainment.com

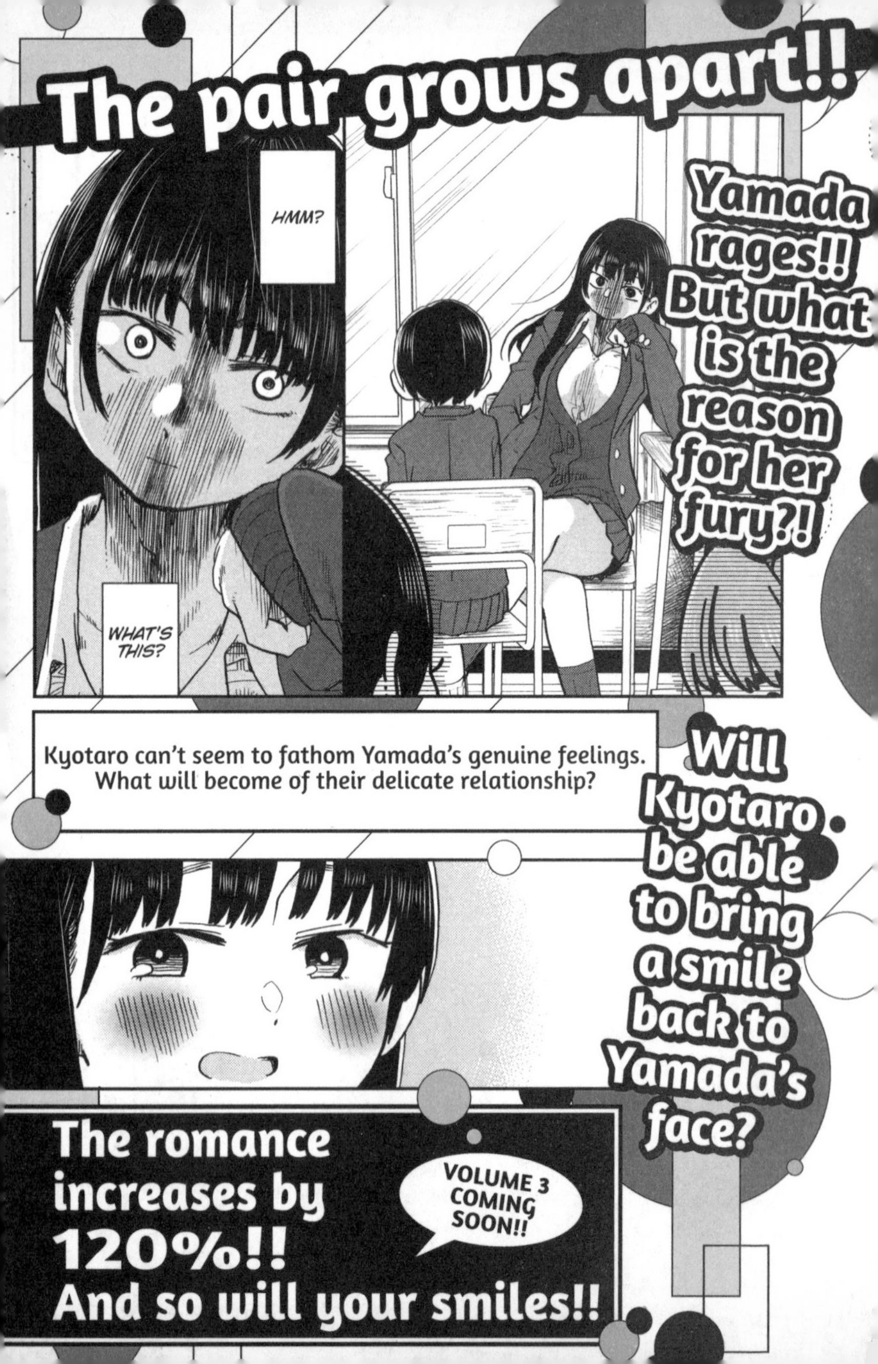
The pair grows apart!!
Yamada rages!! But what is the reason for her fury?!
HMM?
WHAT'S THIS?
Kyotaro can't seem to fathom Yamada's genuine feelings. What will become of their delicate relationship?
Will Kyotaro be able to bring a smile back to Yamada's face?
The romance increases by 120%!! And so will your smiles!!
VOLUME 3 COMING SOON!!

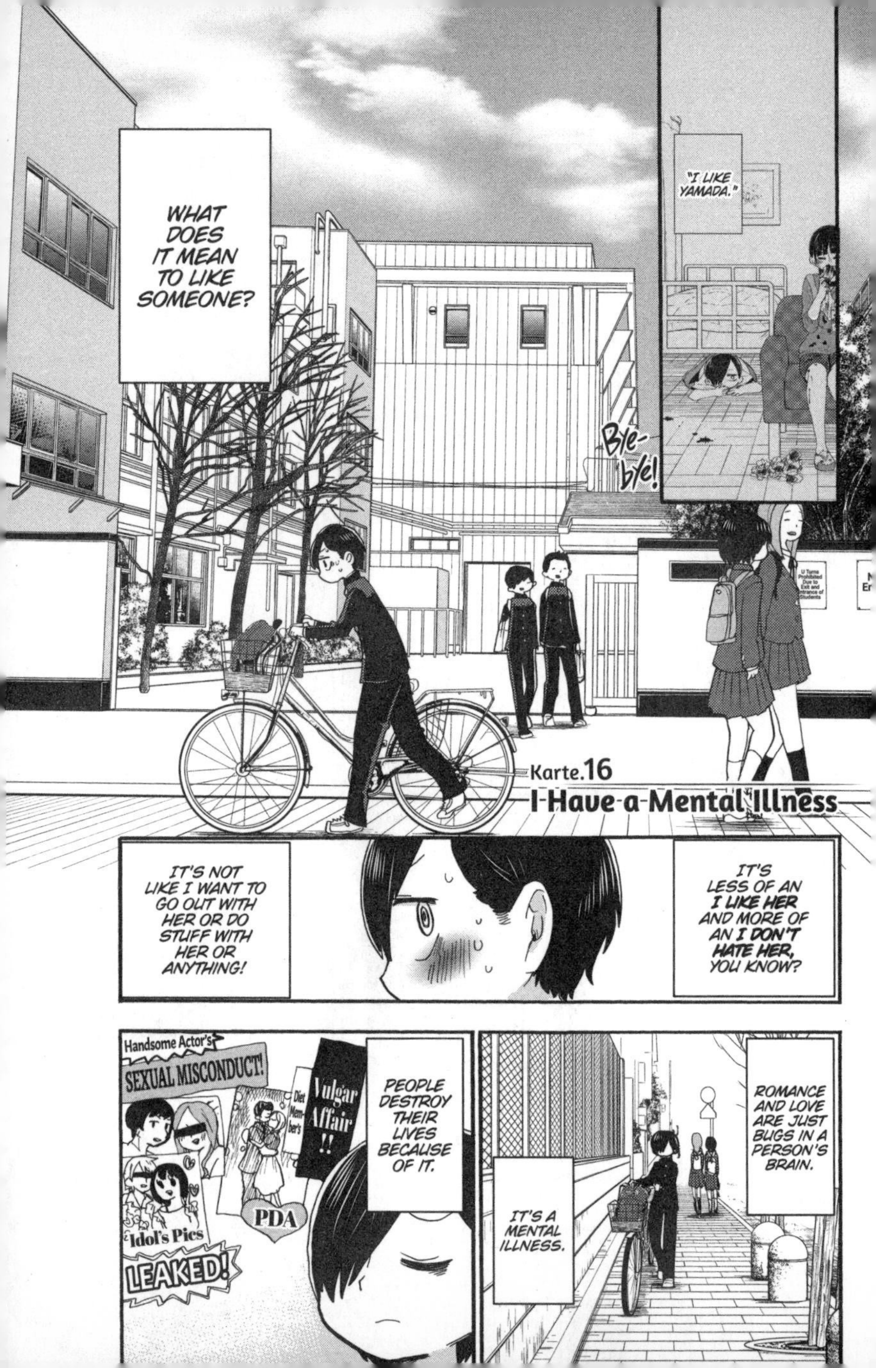
"I LIKE YAMADA."
Bye-bye!
WHAT DOES IT MEAN TO LIKE SOMEONE?
Karte.16
I Have a Mental Illness
IT'S LESS OF AN I LIKE HER AND MORE OF AN I DON'T HATE HER, YOU KNOW?
IT'S NOT LIKE I WANT TO GO OUT WITH HER OR DO STUFF WITH HER OR ANYTHING!
ROMANCE AND LOVE ARE JUST BUGS IN A PERSON'S BRAIN.
IT'S A MENTAL ILLNESS.
PEOPLE DESTROY THEIR LIVES BECAUSE OF IT.
Vulgar Affair!!
Diet Member's
Handsome Actor's
SEXUAL MISCONDUCT!
PDA
Idol's Pics
LEAKED!

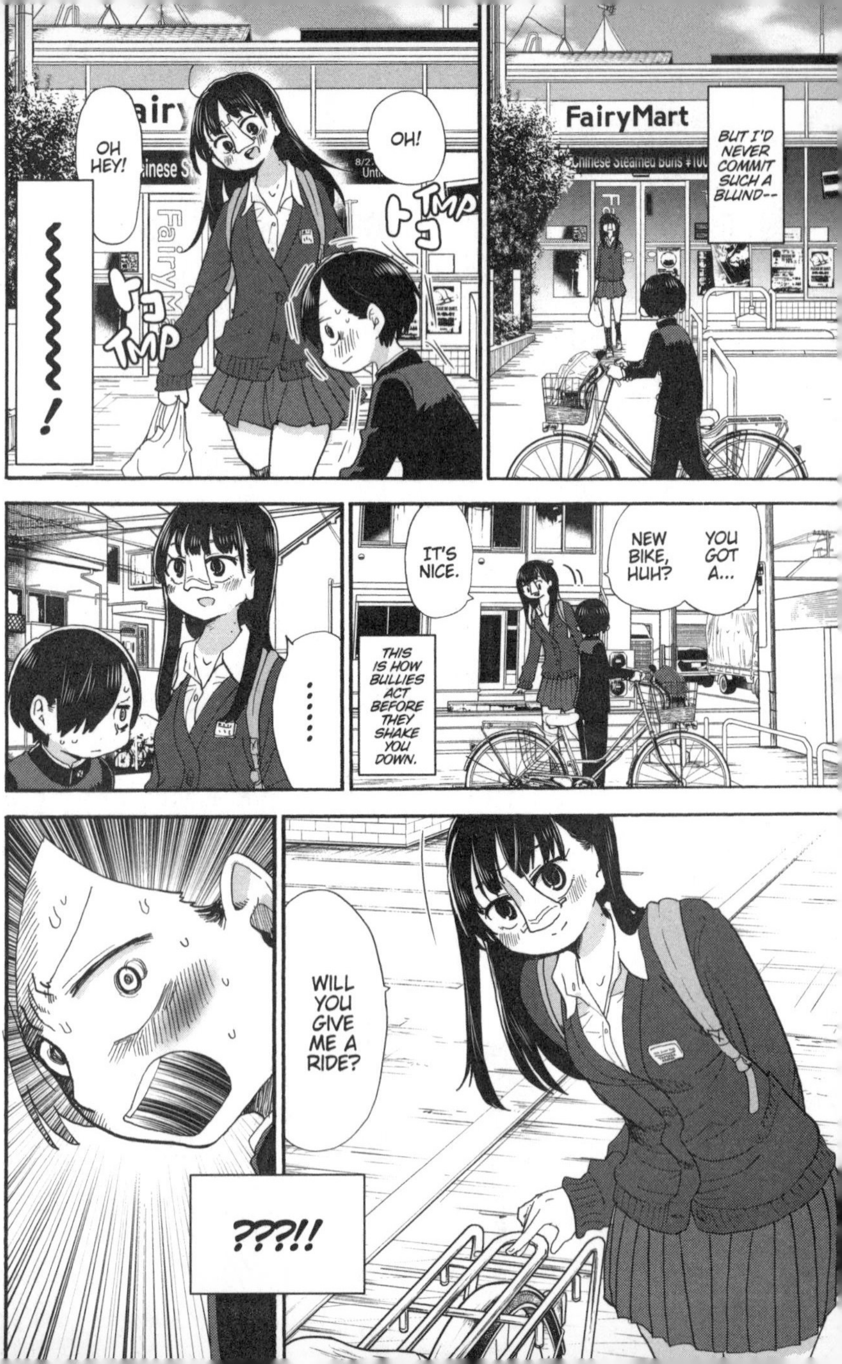
FairyMart
Chinese Steamed Buns ¥100
BUT I'D NEVER COMMIT SUCH A BLUND--
OH!
TMP
OH HEY!
~~~~~!
TMP
YOU GOT A...
NEW BIKE, HUH?
IT'S NICE.
THIS IS HOW BULLIES ACT BEFORE THEY SHAKE YOU DOWN.
......
WILL YOU GIVE ME A RIDE?
???!!
~~~~~

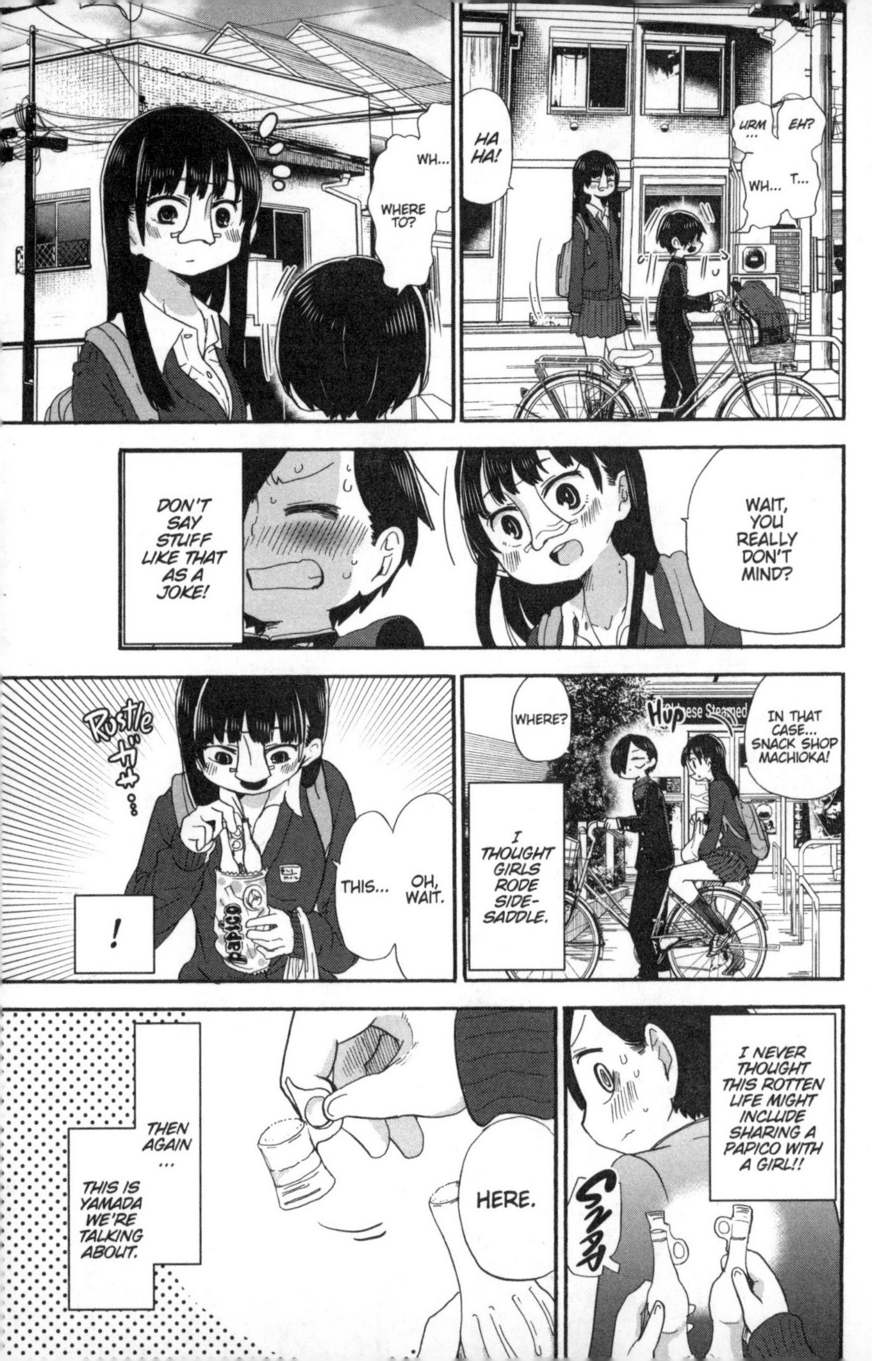

EH?
URM ...
T...
WH...
HA HA!
WH...
WHERE TO?
WAIT, YOU REALLY DON'T MIND?
DON'T SAY STUFF LIKE THAT AS A JOKE!
IN THAT CASE... SNACK SHOP MACHIOKA!
Hup
WHERE?
I THOUGHT GIRLS RODE SIDE-SADDLE.
Rustle
OH, WAIT.
THIS...
papico
!
I NEVER THOUGHT THIS ROTTEN LIFE MIGHT INCLUDE SHARING A PAPICO WITH A GIRL!!
SNAP
HERE.
THEN AGAIN ... THIS IS YAMADA WE'RE TALKING ABOUT.

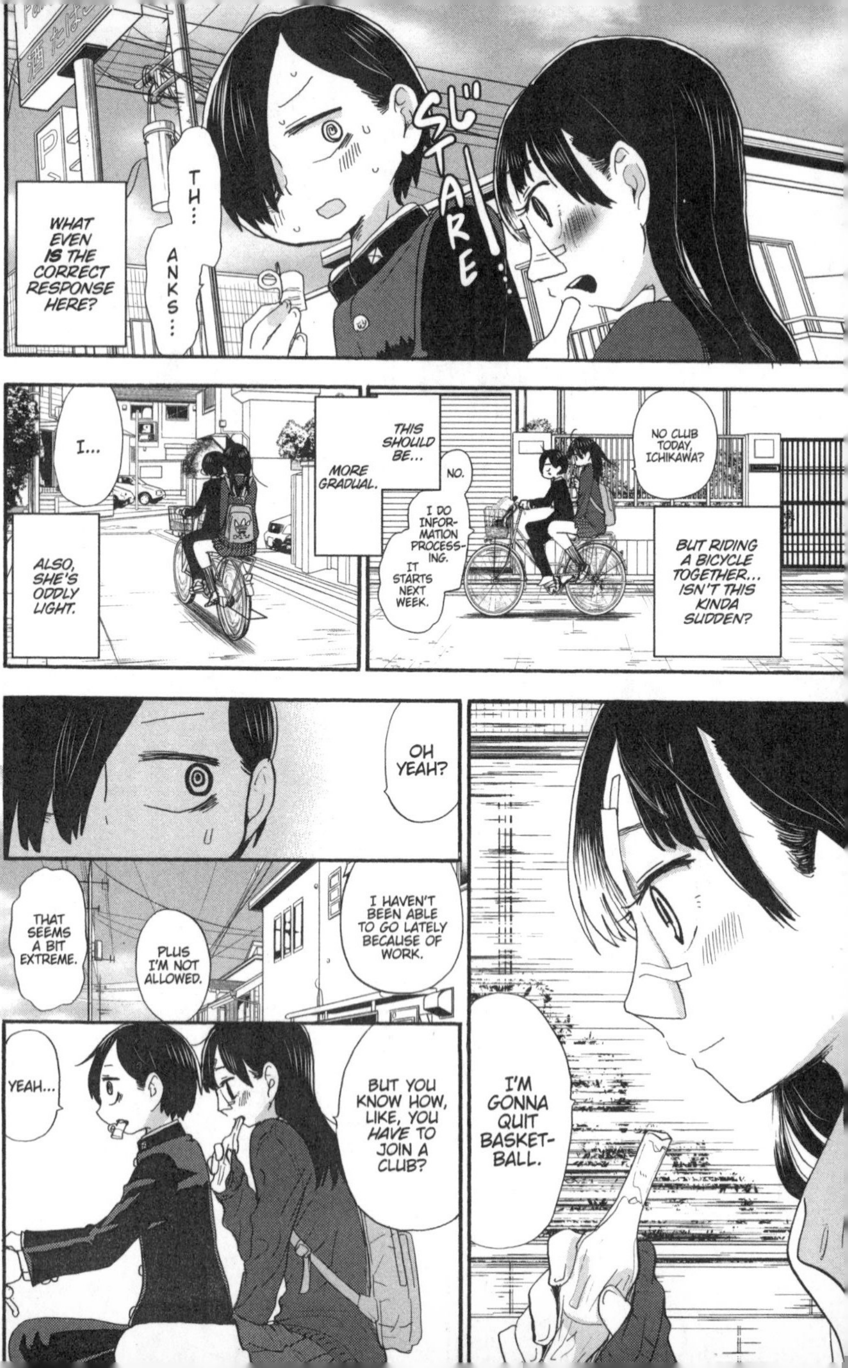

じ STARE
TH... ANKS...
WHAT EVEN IS THE CORRECT RESPONSE HERE?
NO CLUB TODAY, ICHIKAWA?
BUT RIDING A BICYCLE TOGETHER... ISN'T THIS KINDA SUDDEN?
NO.
I DO INFORMATION PROCESSING.
IT STARTS NEXT WEEK.
THIS SHOULD BE... MORE GRADUAL.
I...
ALSO, SHE'S ODDLY LIGHT.
I'M GONNA QUIT BASKETBALL.
OH YEAH?
I HAVEN'T BEEN ABLE TO GO LATELY BECAUSE OF WORK.
PLUS I'M NOT ALLOWED.
THAT SEEMS A BIT EXTREME.
BUT YOU KNOW HOW, LIKE, YOU HAVE TO JOIN A CLUB?
YEAH...

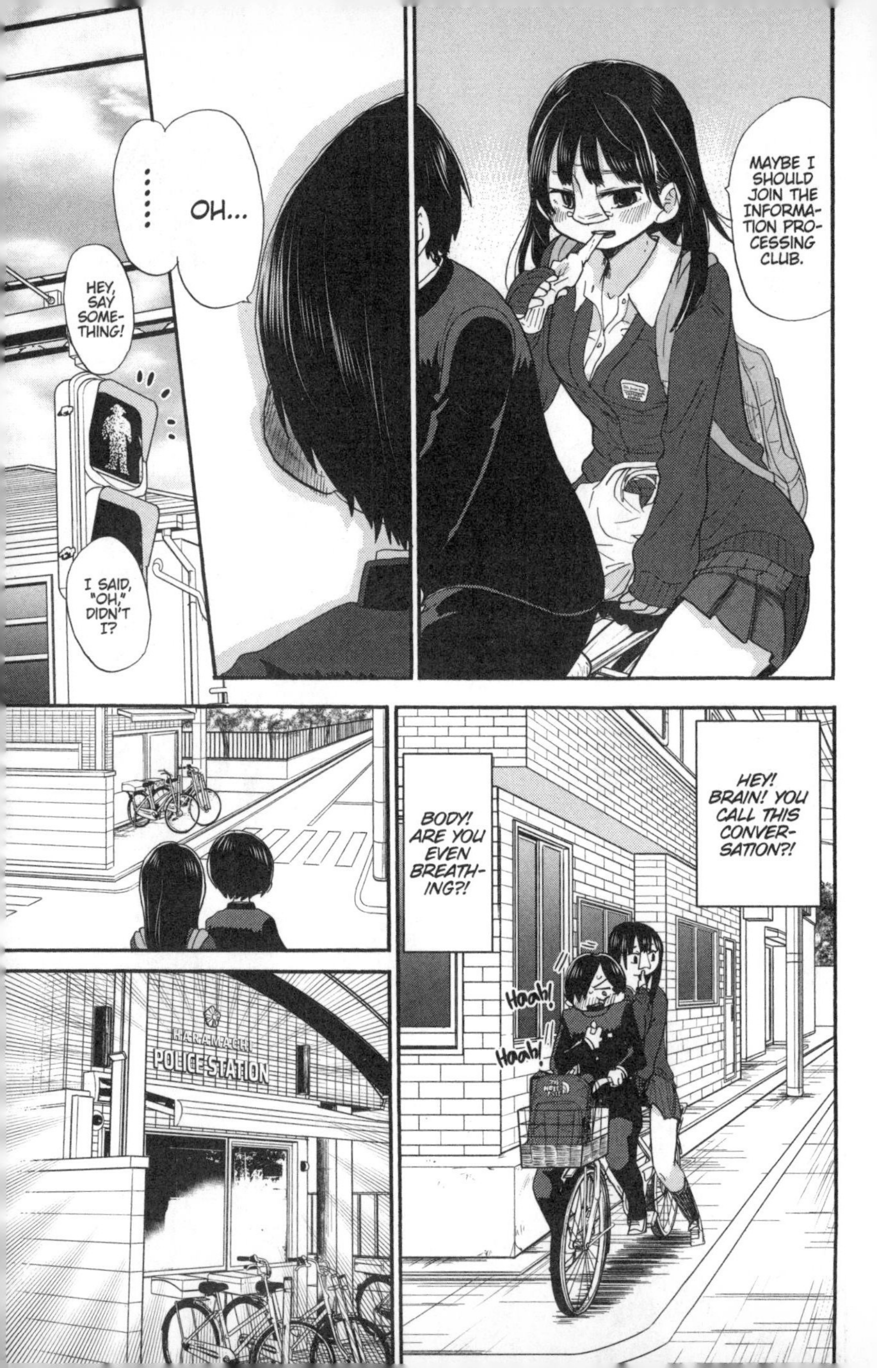
MAYBE I SHOULD JOIN THE INFORMATION PROCESSING CLUB.
OH...
......
HEY, SAY SOMETHING!
I SAID, "OH," DIDN'T I?
HEY! BRAIN! YOU CALL THIS CONVERSATION?!
BODY! ARE YOU EVEN BREATHING?!
Haah!
Haah!
HARAMACHI
POLICE STATION

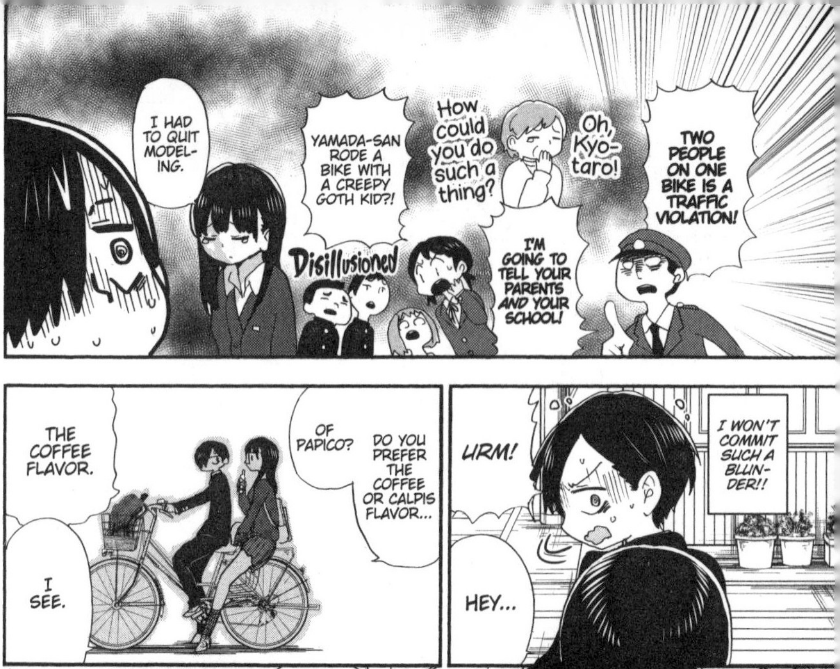
TWO PEOPLE ON ONE BIKE IS A TRAFFIC VIOLATION!
I'M GOING TO TELL YOUR PARENTS AND YOUR SCHOOL!
Oh, Kyo-taro!
How could you do such a thing?
YAMADA-SAN RODE A BIKE WITH A CREEPY GOTH KID?!
Disillusioned
I HAD TO QUIT MODELING.
I WON'T COMMIT SUCH A BLUNDER!!
URM!
HEY...
DO YOU PREFER THE COFFEE OR CALPIS FLAVOR...
OF PAPICO?
THE COFFEE FLAVOR.
I SEE.

※ *More accurately, the White Sour flavor.*

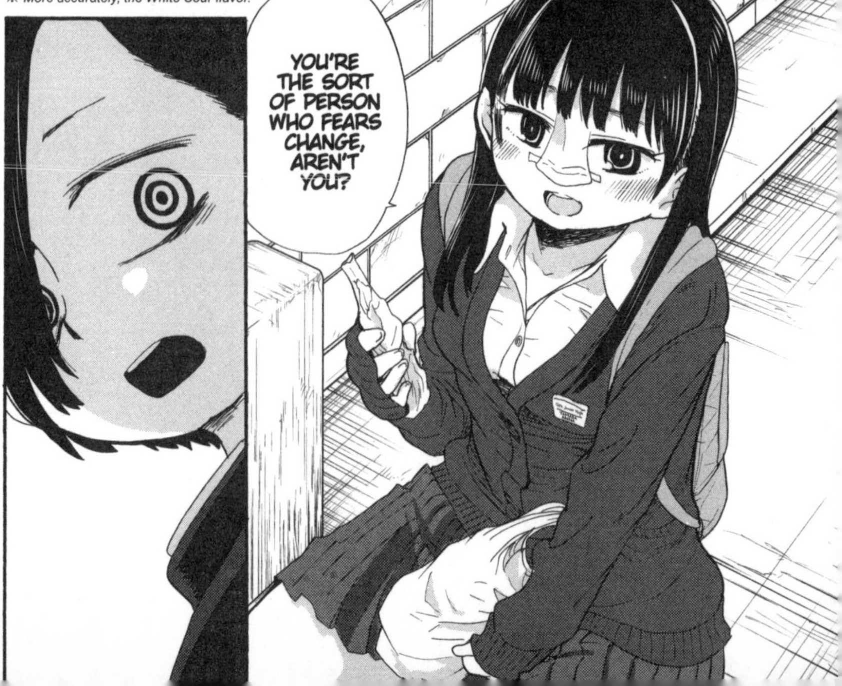
YOU'RE THE SORT OF PERSON WHO FEARS CHANGE, AREN'T YOU?

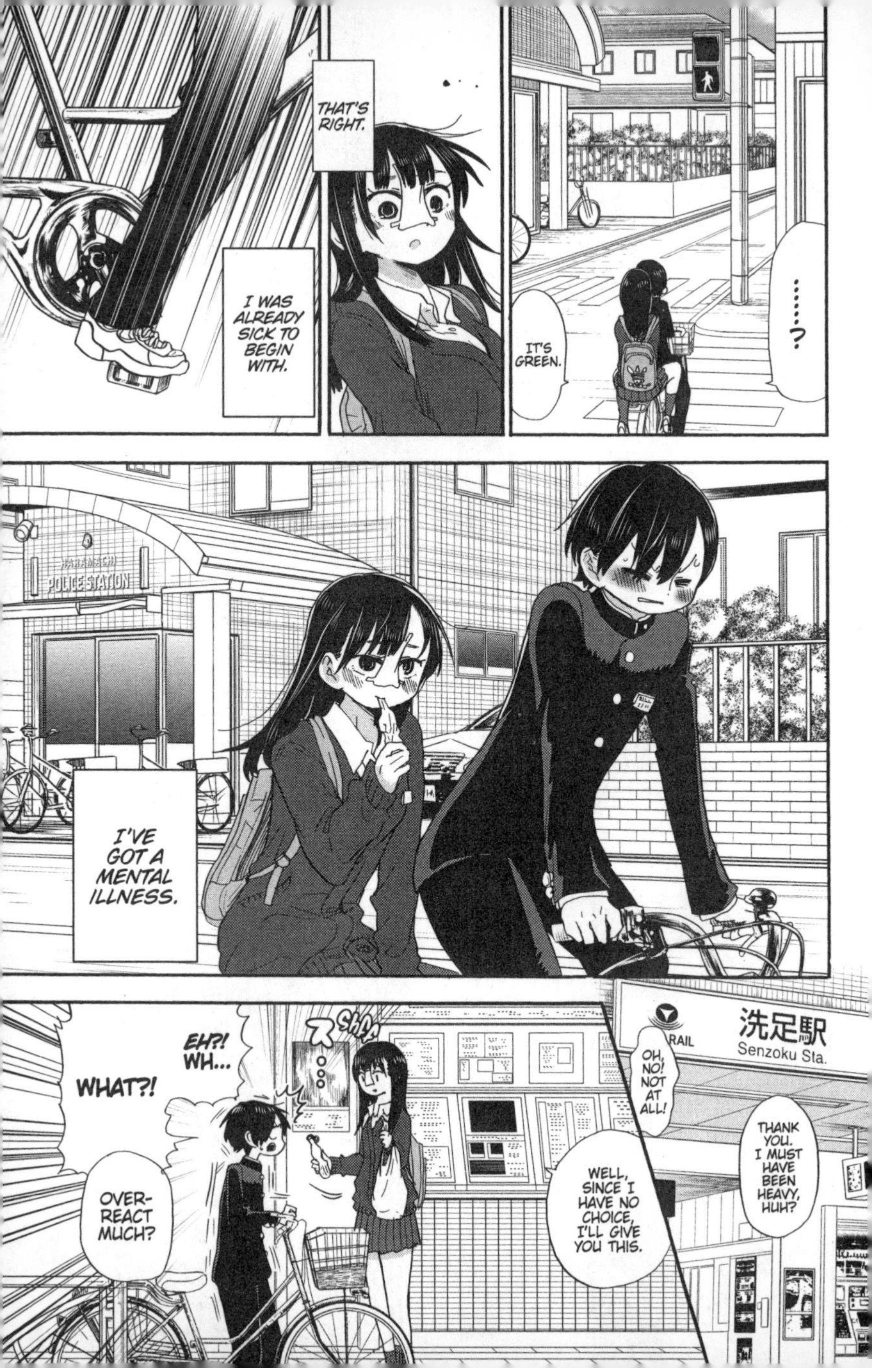
......?
IT'S GREEN.
THAT'S RIGHT.
I WAS ALREADY SICK TO BEGIN WITH.
POLICE STATION
I'VE GOT A MENTAL ILLNESS.
洗足駅
Senzoku Sta.
RAIL
THANK YOU. I MUST HAVE BEEN HEAVY, HUH?
OH, NO! NOT AT ALL!
WELL, SINCE I HAVE NO CHOICE, I'LL GIVE YOU THIS.
EH?! WH...
WHAT?!
OVER-REACT MUCH?

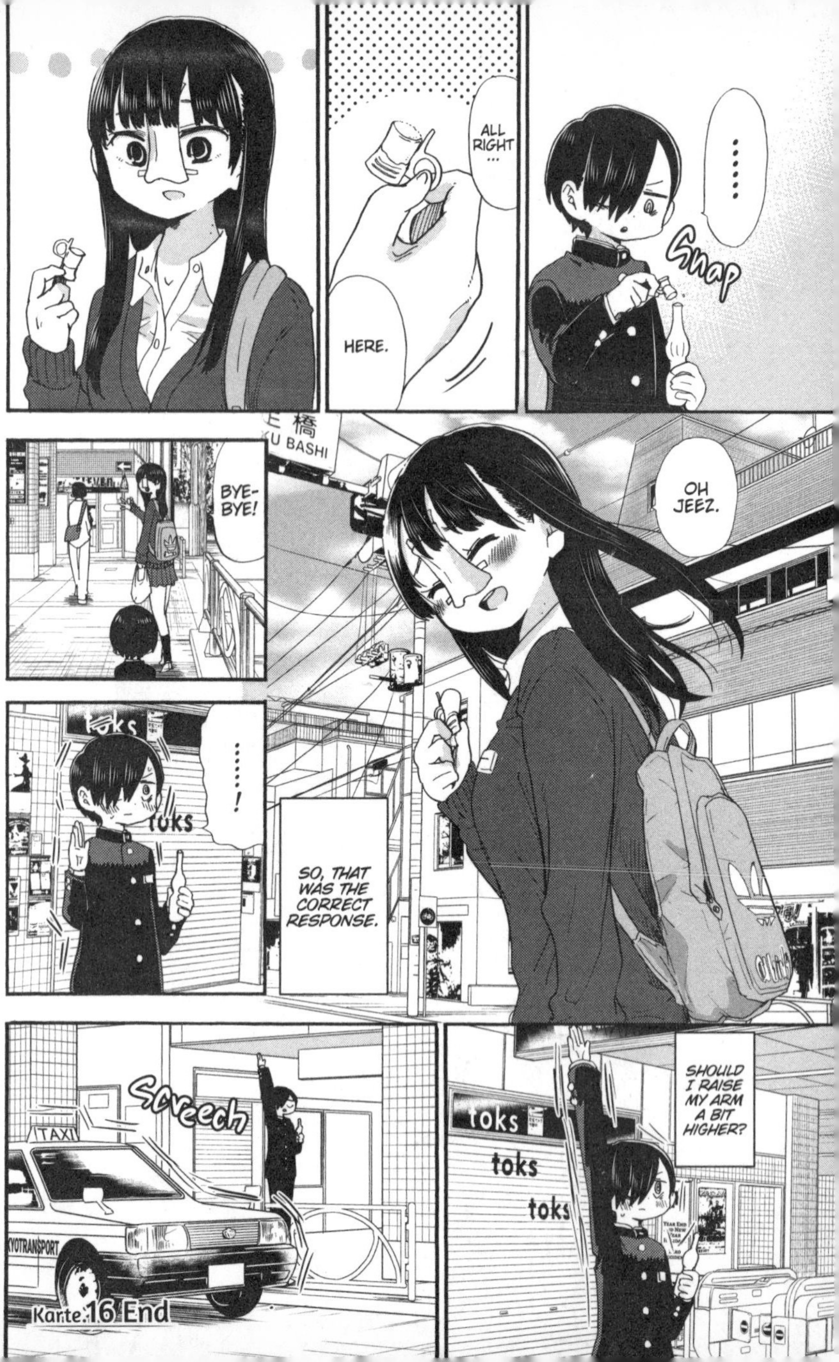
......
Snap
ALL RIGHT ...
HERE.
OH JEEZ.
SO, THAT WAS THE CORRECT RESPONSE.
BYE-BYE!
......!
toks
SHOULD I RAISE MY ARM A BIT HIGHER?
toks
toks
toks
Screech
TAXI
Karte.16 End

Extra

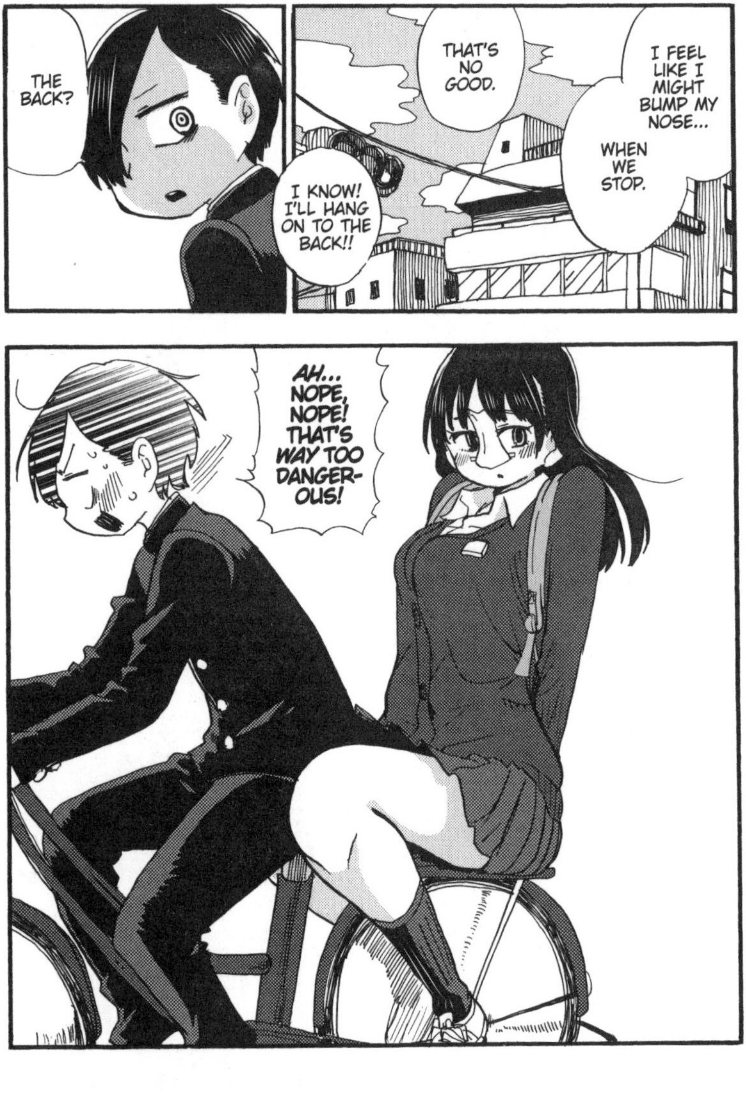

I FEEL LIKE I MIGHT BUMP MY NOSE...
WHEN WE STOP.
THAT'S NO GOOD.
I KNOW! I'LL HANG ON TO THE BACK!!
THE BACK?
AH... NOPE, NOPE! THAT'S WAY TOO DANGER-OUS!

The Dangers in My Heart

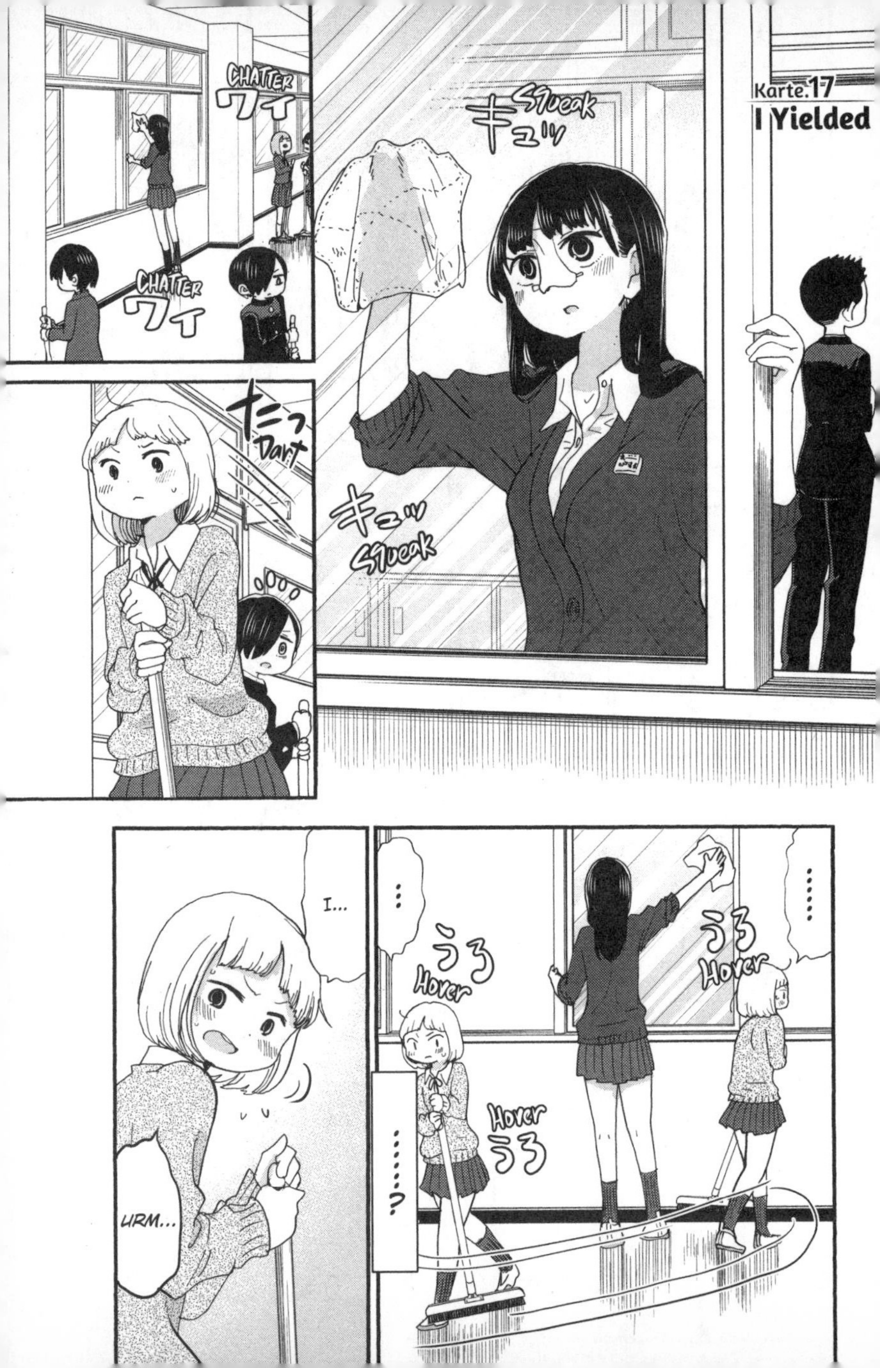

Karte.17
I Yielded
キュッ
Squeak
キュッ
Squeak
CHATTER
ワイ
CHATTER
ワイ
Dart
......
......
うろ
Hover
うろ
Hover
Hover
うろ
......?
I...
URM...

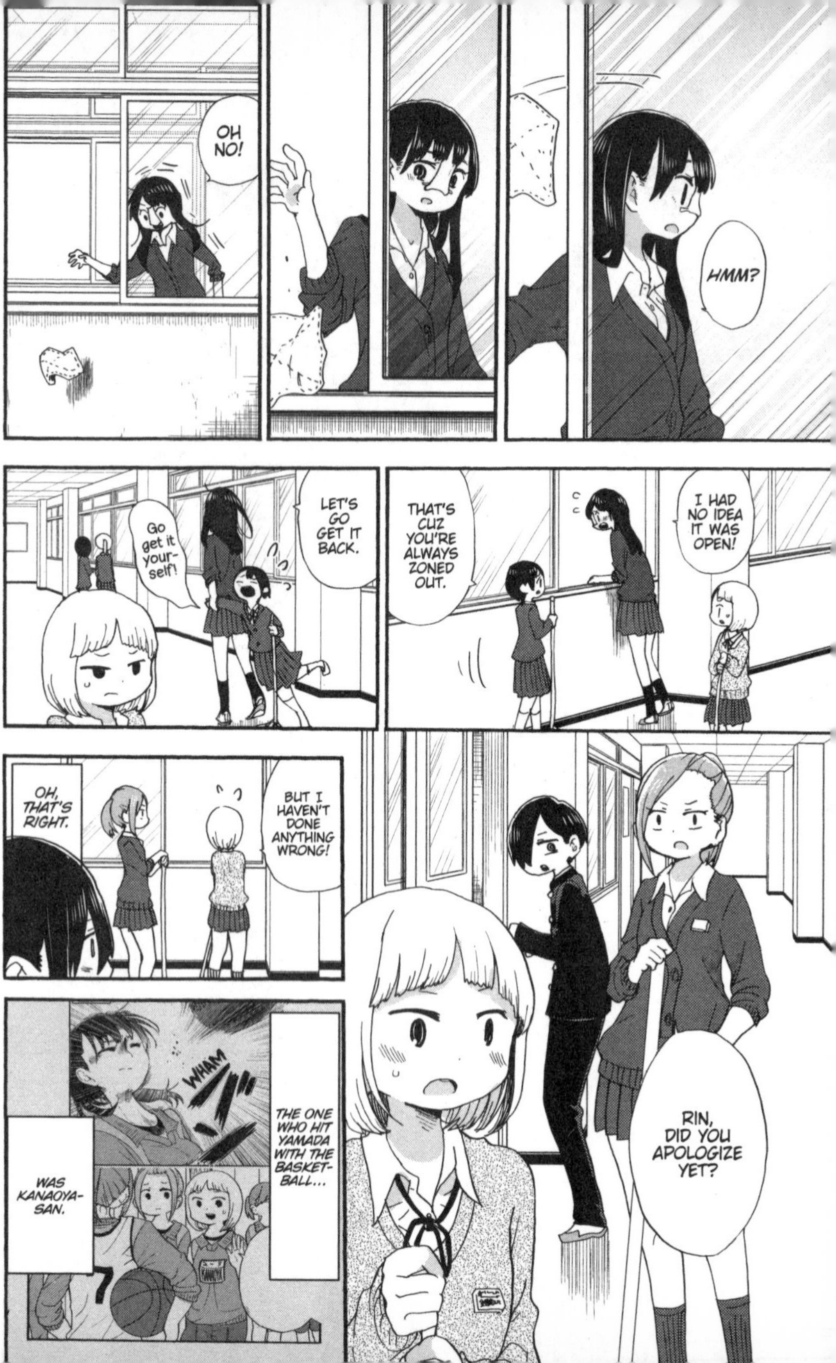
HMM?
OH NO!
I HAD NO IDEA IT WAS OPEN!
THAT'S CUZ YOU'RE ALWAYS ZONED OUT.
LET'S GO GET IT BACK.
Go get it your-self!
RIN, DID YOU APOLOGIZE YET?
BUT I HAVEN'T DONE ANYTHING WRONG!
OH, THAT'S RIGHT.
THE ONE WHO HIT YAMADA WITH THE BASKET-BALL...
WHAM
WAS KANAOYA-SAN.

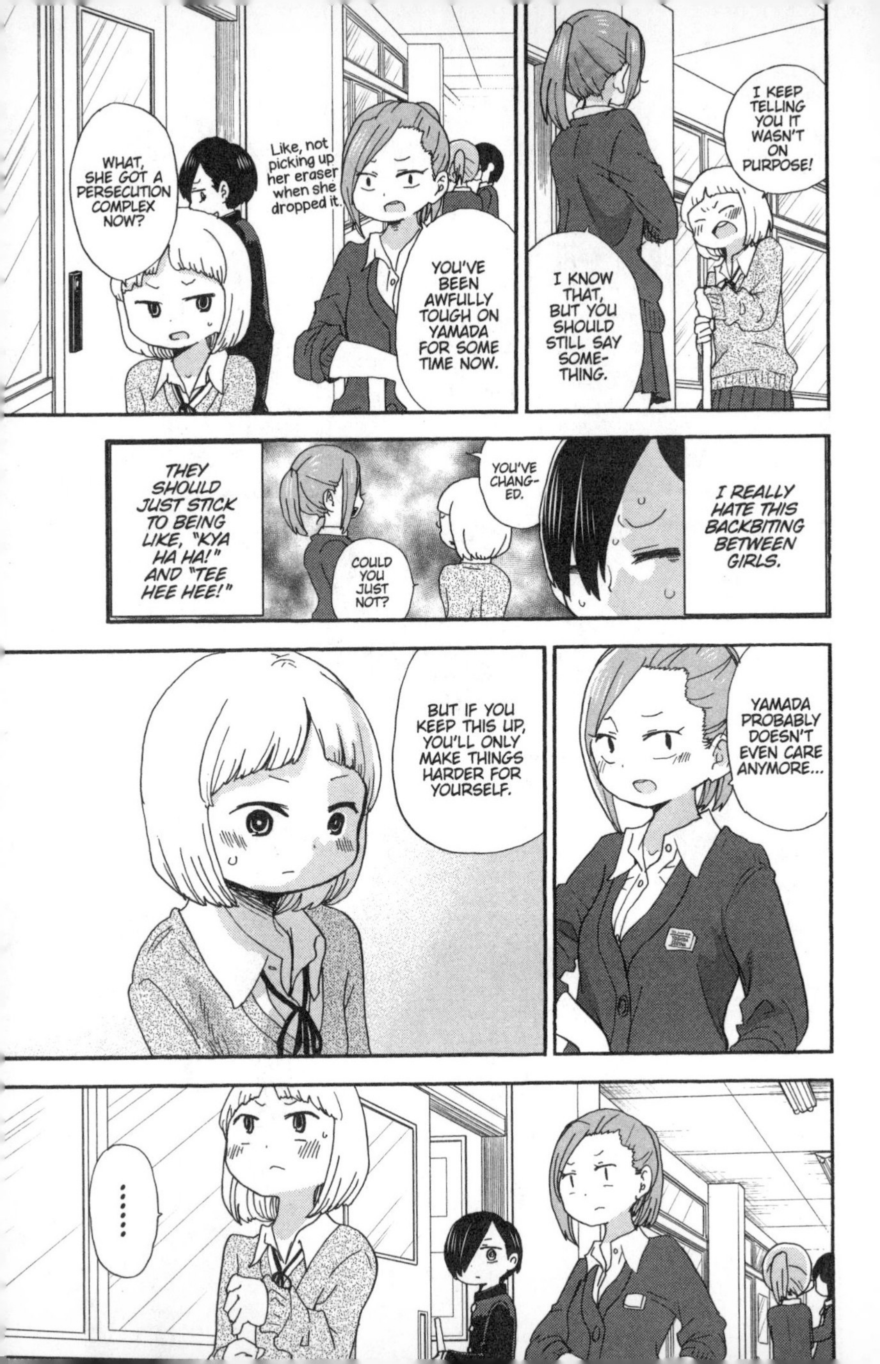
I KEEP TELLING YOU IT WASN'T ON PURPOSE!
I KNOW THAT, BUT YOU SHOULD STILL SAY SOMETHING.
YOU'VE BEEN AWFULLY TOUGH ON YAMADA FOR SOME TIME NOW.
Like, not picking up her eraser when she dropped it.
WHAT, SHE GOT A PERSECUTION COMPLEX NOW?
I REALLY HATE THIS BACKBITING BETWEEN GIRLS.
YOU'VE CHANGED.
COULD YOU JUST NOT?
THEY SHOULD JUST STICK TO BEING LIKE, "KYA HA HA!" AND "TEE HEE HEE!"
YAMADA PROBABLY DOESN'T EVEN CARE ANYMORE...
BUT IF YOU KEEP THIS UP, YOU'LL ONLY MAKE THINGS HARDER FOR YOURSELF.
......

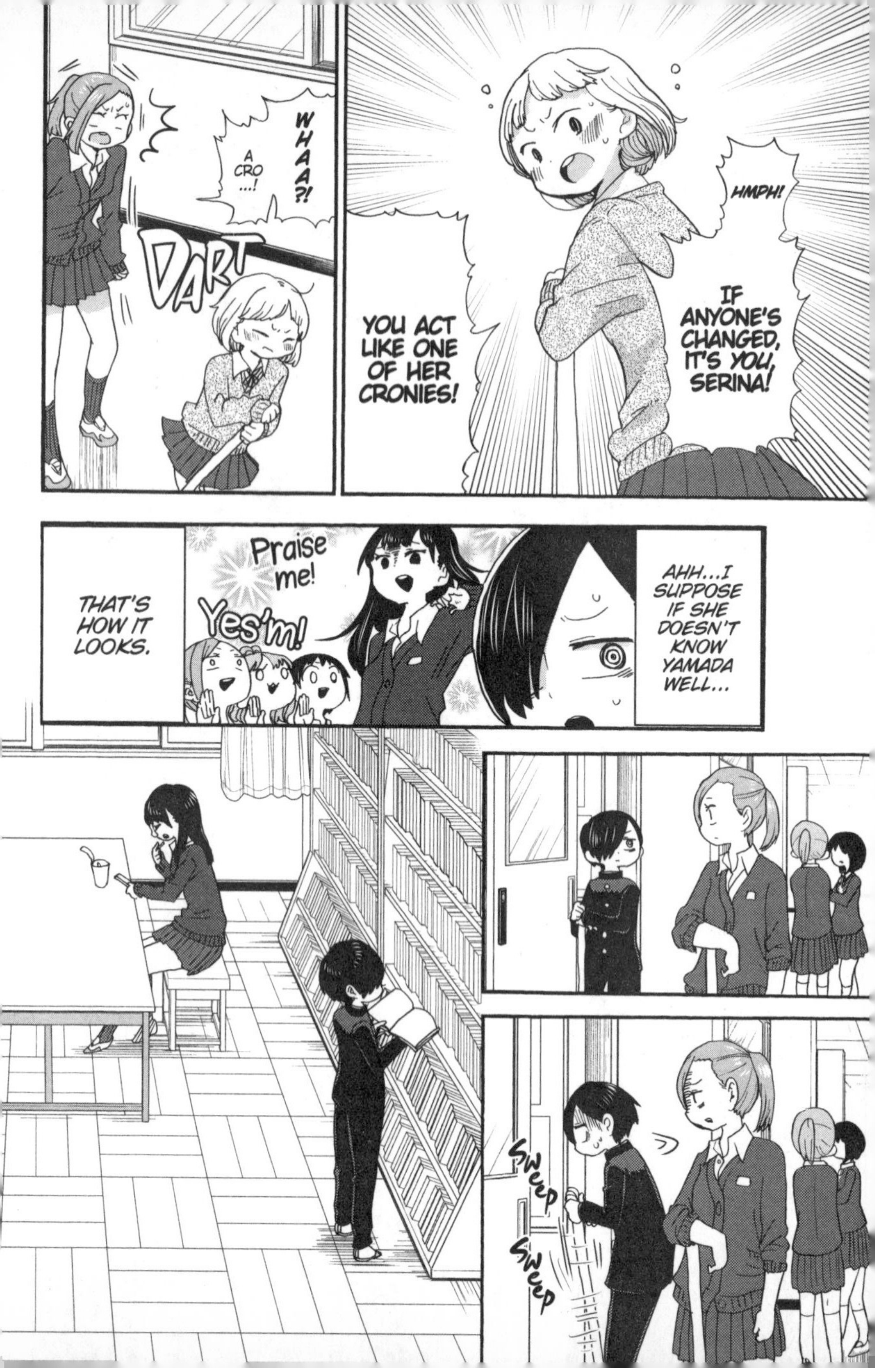
HMPH!
IF ANYONE'S CHANGED, IT'S YOU, SERINA!
YOU ACT LIKE ONE OF HER CRONIES!
WHAAA?!
A CRO...!
DART
AHH...I SUPPOSE IF SHE DOESN'T KNOW YAMADA WELL...
Praise me!
Yes'm!
THAT'S HOW IT LOOKS.
Sweep
Sweep

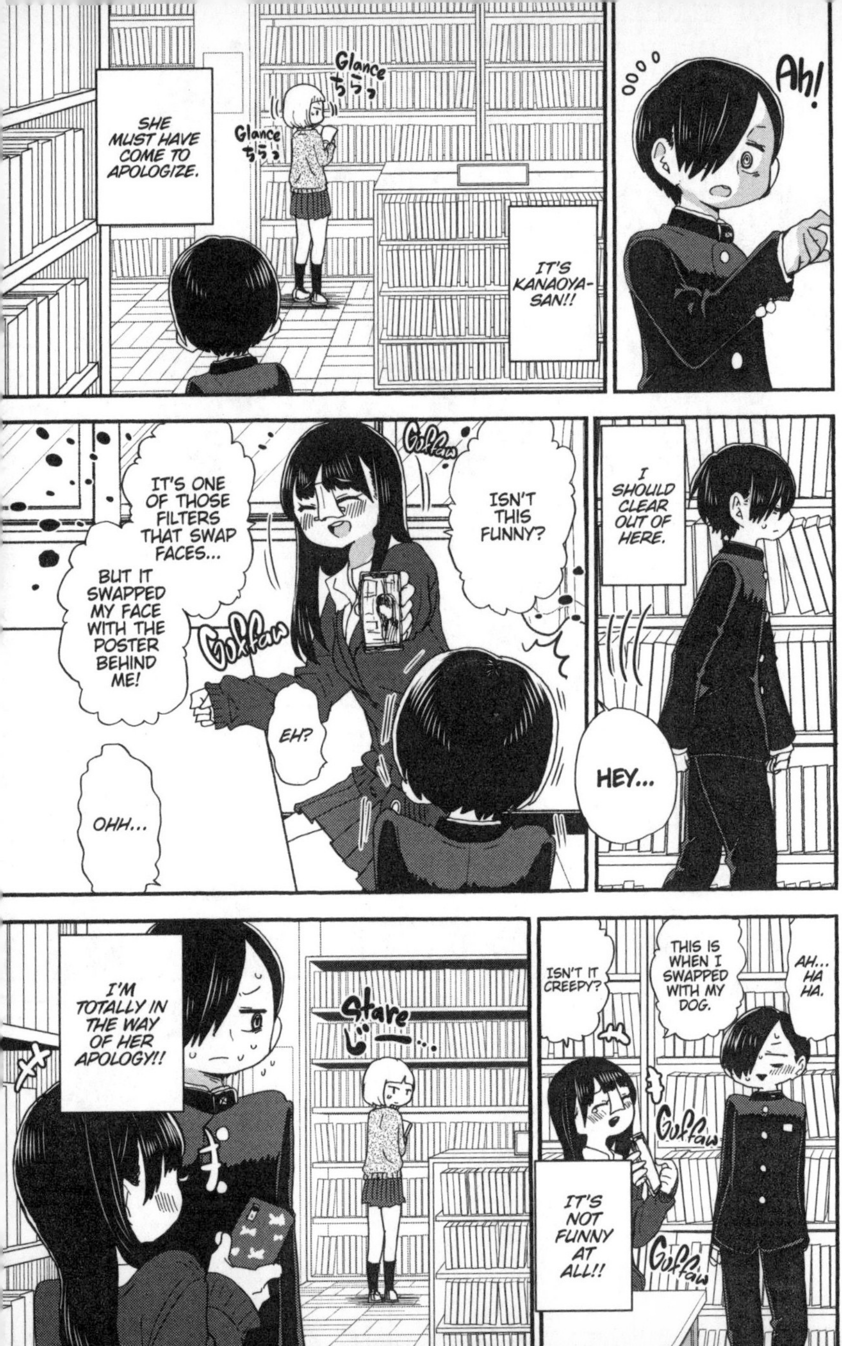

Ah!
IT'S KANAOYA-SAN!!
Glance ちらっ
Glance ちらっ
SHE MUST HAVE COME TO APOLOGIZE.
I SHOULD CLEAR OUT OF HERE.
HEY...
Guffaw
ISN'T THIS FUNNY?
IT'S ONE OF THOSE FILTERS THAT SWAP FACES...
BUT IT SWAPPED MY FACE WITH THE POSTER BEHIND ME!
Guffaw
EH?
OHH...
AH... HA HA.
THIS IS WHEN I SWAPPED WITH MY DOG.
ISN'T IT CREEPY?
Guffaw
IT'S NOT FUNNY AT ALL!!
Guffaw
I'M TOTALLY IN THE WAY OF HER APOLOGY!!
Stare じーー…

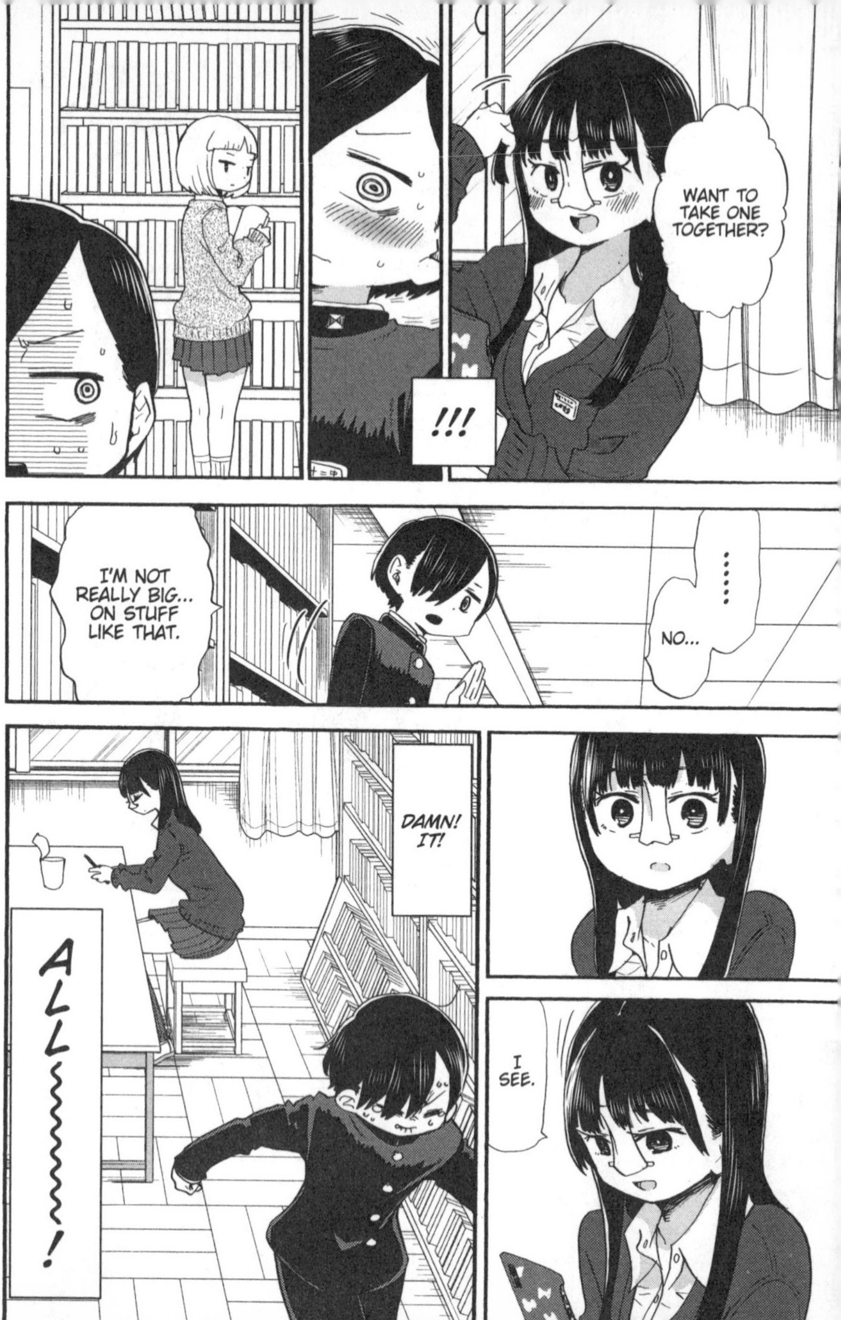
WANT TO TAKE ONE TOGETHER?
!!!
......
NO...
I'M NOT REALLY BIG... ON STUFF LIKE THAT.
I SEE.
DAMN! IT!
ALL~~~~~!

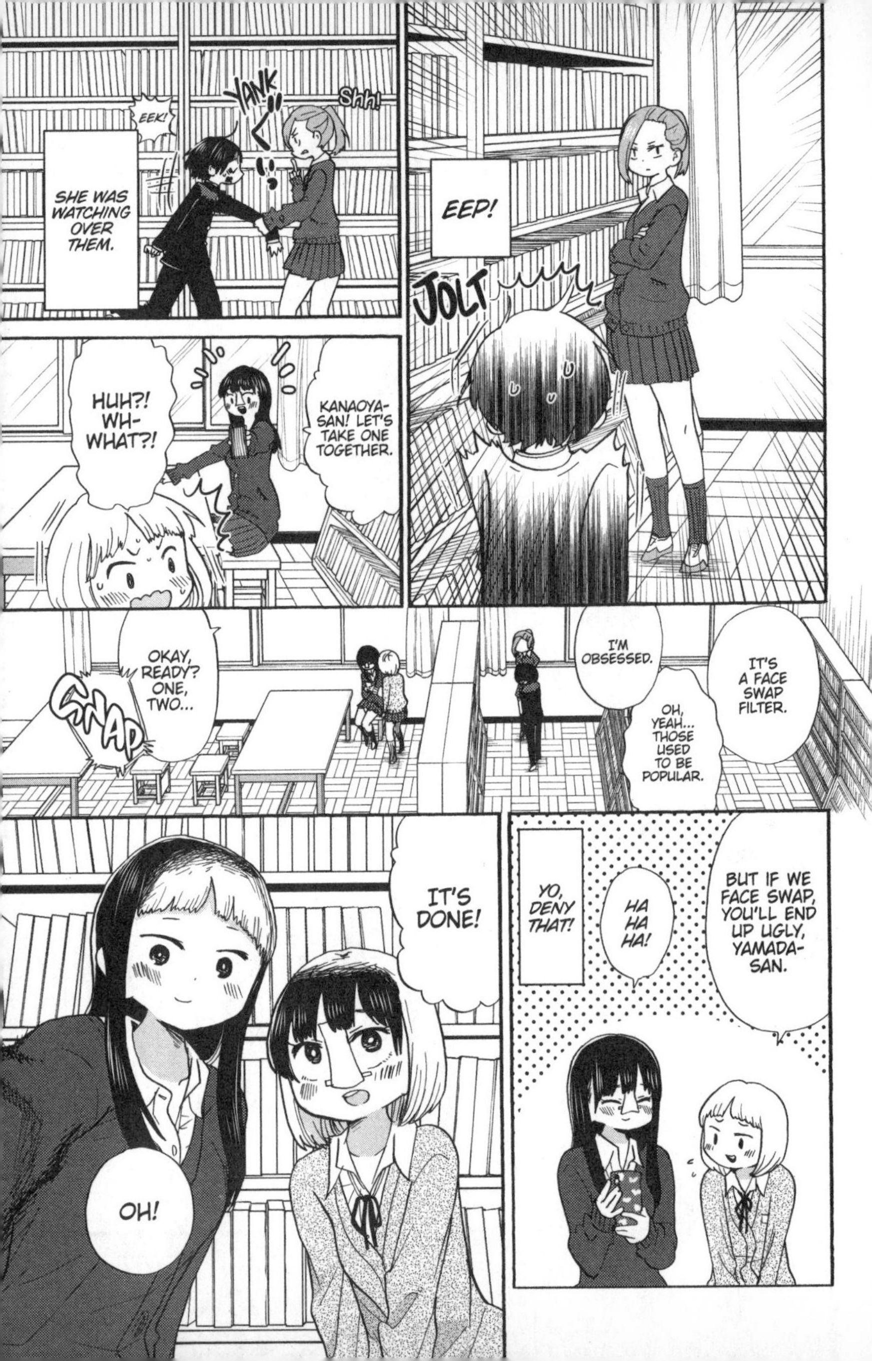
EEP!
JOLT
Shh!
YANK
EEK!
SHE WAS WATCHING OVER THEM.
KANAOYA-SAN! LET'S TAKE ONE TOGETHER.
HUH?! WH-WHAT?!
IT'S A FACE SWAP FILTER.
I'M OBSESSED.
OH, YEAH... THOSE USED TO BE POPULAR.
OKAY, READY? ONE, TWO...
SNAP
BUT IF WE FACE SWAP, YOU'LL END UP UGLY, YAMADA-SAN.
HA HA HA!
YO, DENY THAT!
IT'S DONE!
OH!

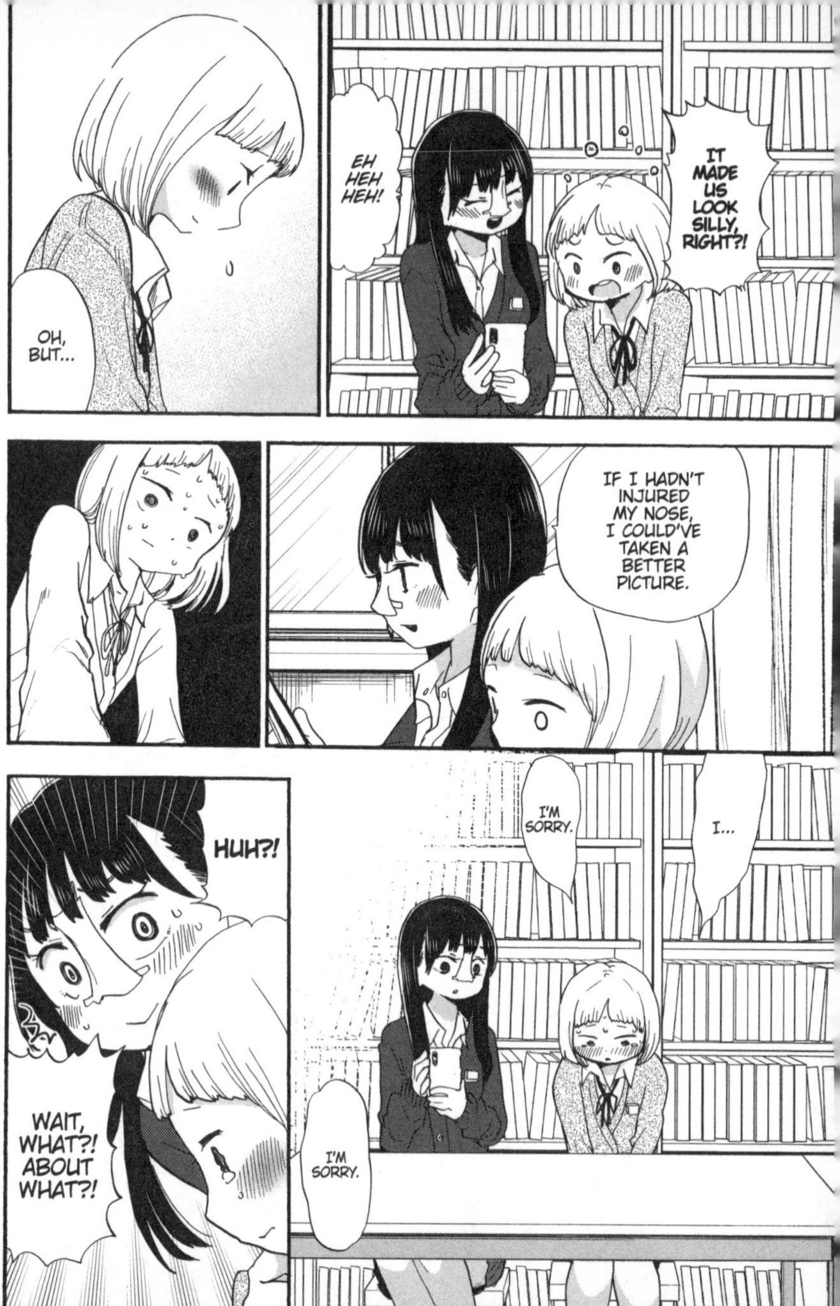
IT MADE US LOOK SILLY, RIGHT?!
EH HEH HEH!
OH, BUT...
IF I HADN'T INJURED MY NOSE, I COULD'VE TAKEN A BETTER PICTURE.
I...
I'M SORRY.
I'M SORRY.
HUH?!
WAIT, WHAT?! ABOUT WHAT?!

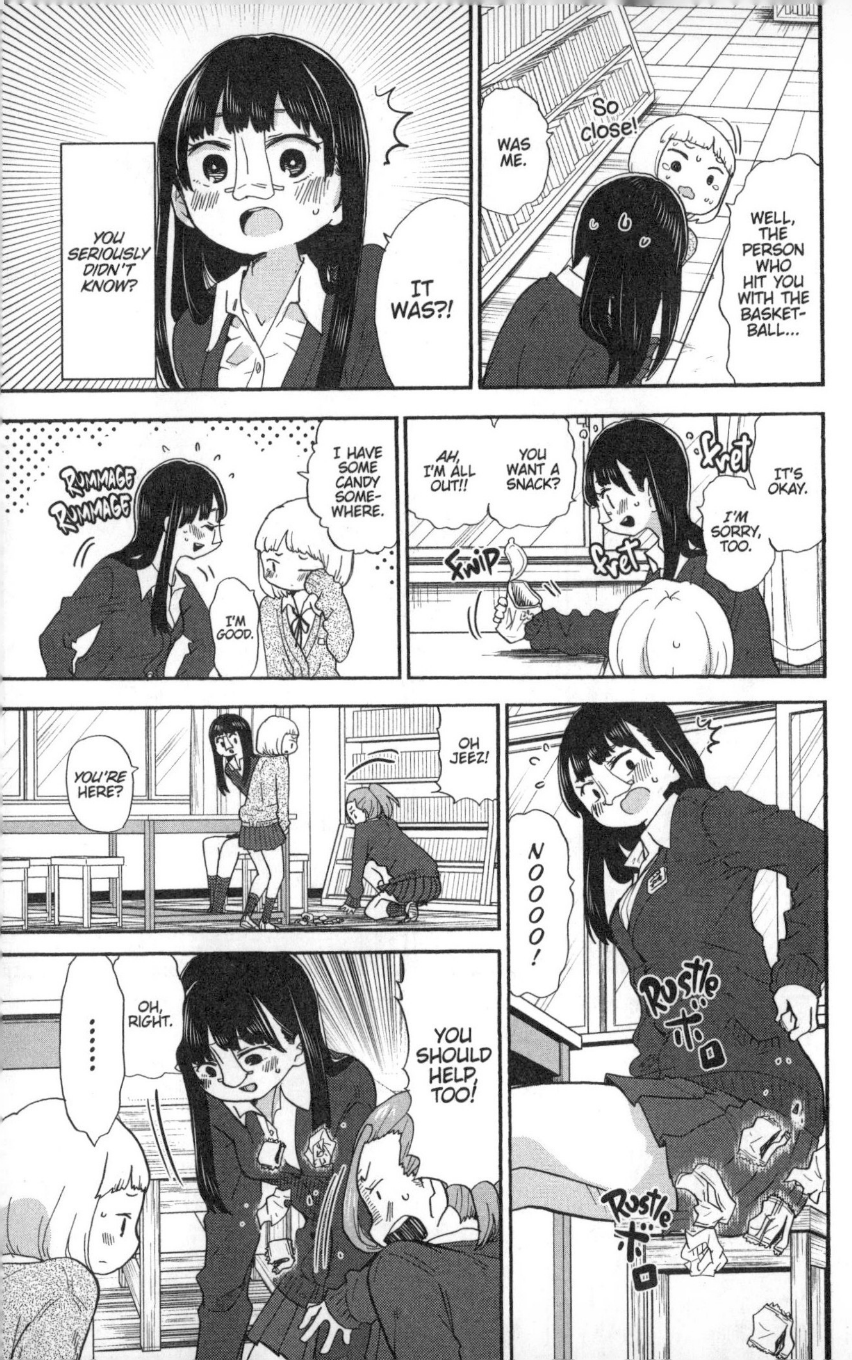

WELL, THE PERSON WHO HIT YOU WITH THE BASKET-BALL...
WAS ME.
So close!
IT WAS?!
YOU SERIOUSLY DIDN'T KNOW?
Fret
IT'S OKAY.
I'M SORRY, TOO.
Fret
YOU WANT A SNACK?
AH, I'M ALL OUT!!
FWIP
I HAVE SOME CANDY SOME-WHERE.
RUMMAGE RUMMAGE
I'M GOOD.
NOOOOO!
Rustle
Rustle
OH JEEZ!
YOU'RE HERE?
YOU SHOULD HELP, TOO!
OH, RIGHT.
......

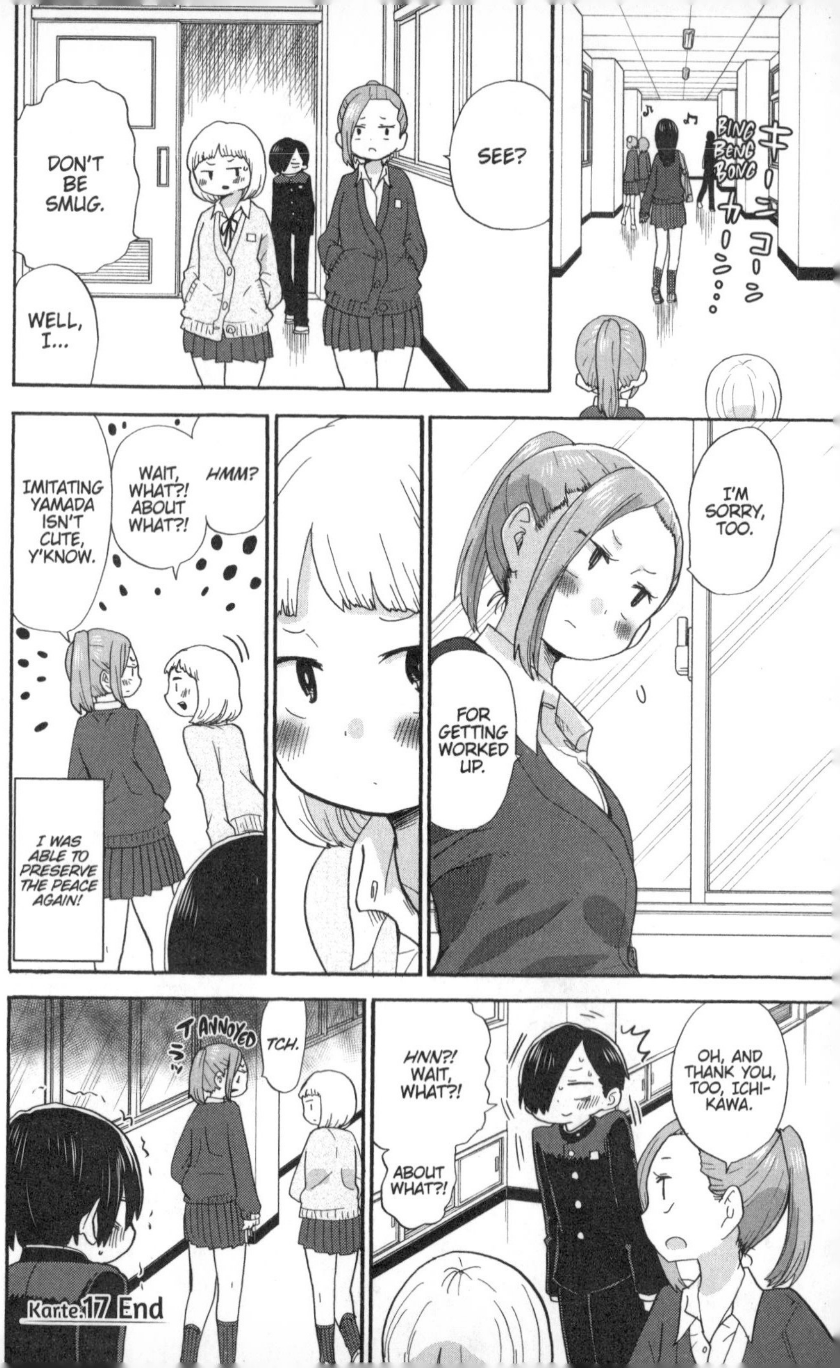
BING BENG BONG
SEE?
DON'T BE SMUG.
WELL, I...
I'M SORRY, TOO.
FOR GETTING WORKED UP.
HMM?
WAIT, WHAT?! ABOUT WHAT?!
IMITATING YAMADA ISN'T CUTE, Y'KNOW.
I WAS ABLE TO PRESERVE THE PEACE AGAIN!
OH, AND THANK YOU, TOO, ICHI-KAWA.
HNN?! WAIT, WHAT?!
ABOUT WHAT?!
ANNOYED
TCH.
Karte.17 End

Moe 4-koma

YOU TWO WERE GOOD FRIENDS BACK IN ELEMENTARY SCHOOL, RIGHT?
Same Elementary School
WELL, WE WERE IN THE SAME CLASS.
YOU AND NYAH WERE LIVING THE "PLEASED TO BEAT YOU" LIFE, SO IT WAS HARD TO APPROACH YOU.
You even dyed your hair blonde back then.
WHAT DO YOU MEAN, "PLEASED TO BEAT YOU"?
SHE CALLS YOU "NYAH"?!
Serina → Serinya → Nyah
JUST LET IT GO.

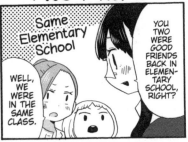

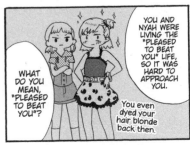

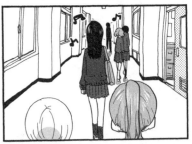

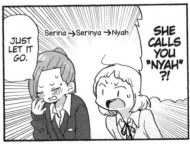

The
Dangers
in My
Heart

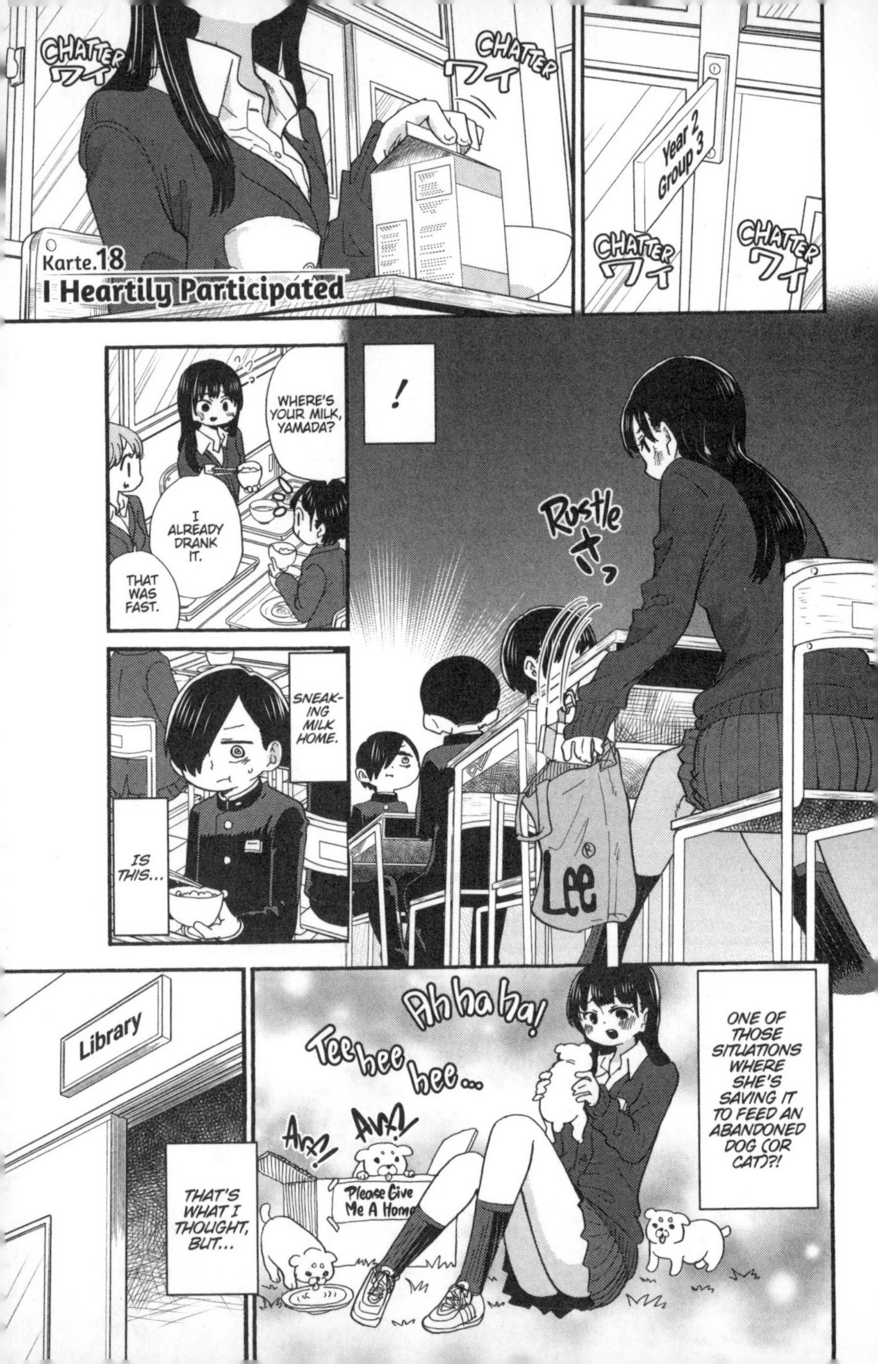
Year 2 Group 3
CHATTER ワイ
CHATTER ワイ
CHATTER ワイ
CHATTER ワイ
Karte.18
I Heartily Participated
!
Rustle さっ
WHERE'S YOUR MILK, YAMADA?
I ALREADY DRANK IT.
THAT WAS FAST.
SNEAKING MILK HOME.
IS THIS...
ONE OF THOSE SITUATIONS WHERE SHE'S SAVING IT TO FEED AN ABANDONED DOG (OR CAT)?!
Ah ha ha!
Tee hee hee...
Arf!
Arf!
Please Give Me A Home
THAT'S WHAT I THOUGHT, BUT...
Library

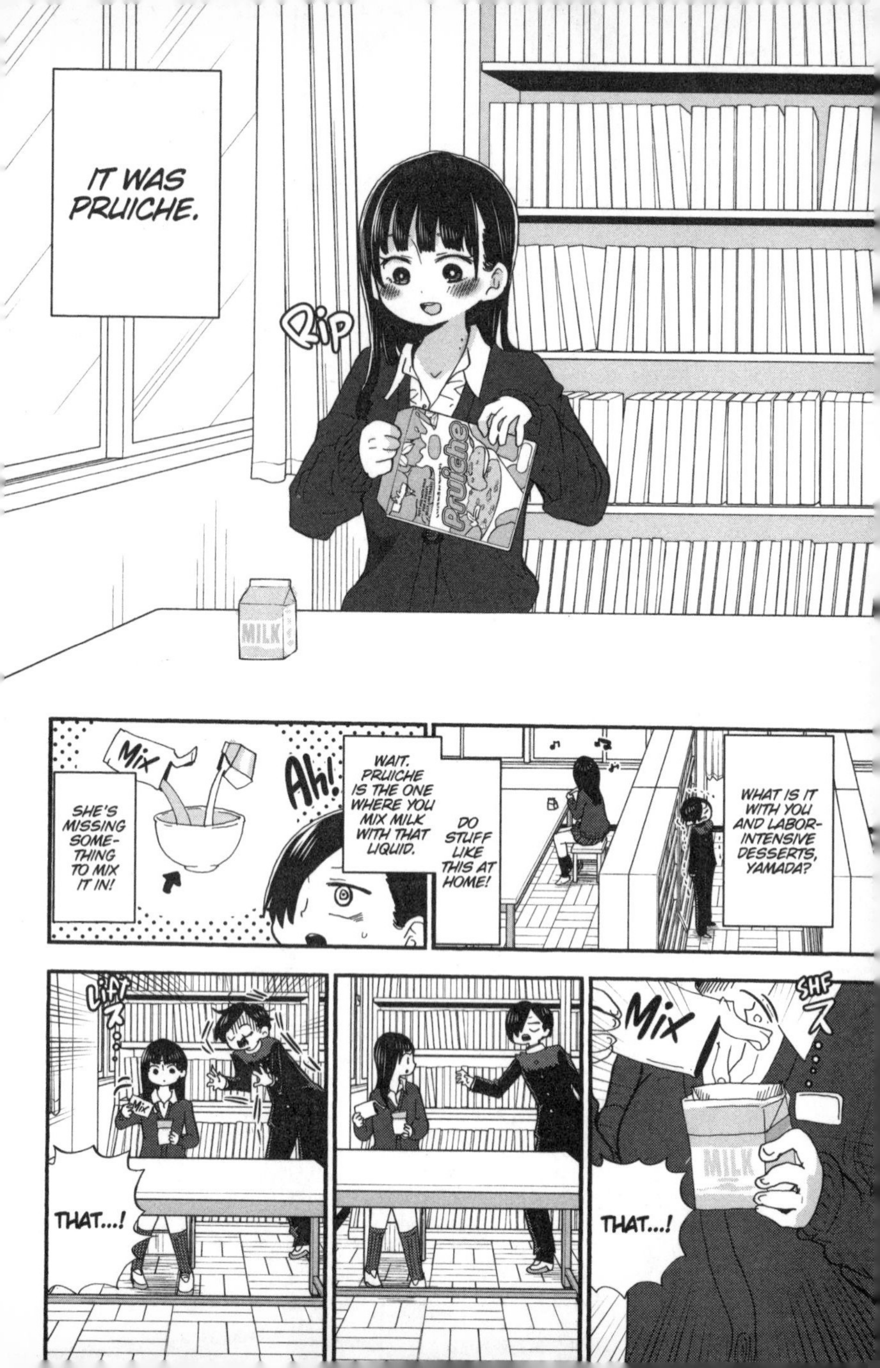
IT WAS PRUICHE.
Rip
Pruiche
MILK
WHAT IS IT WITH YOU AND LABOR-INTENSIVE DESSERTS, YAMADA?
WAIT. PRUICHE IS THE ONE WHERE YOU MIX MILK WITH THAT LIQUID.
DO STUFF LIKE THIS AT HOME!
Ah!
Mix
SHE'S MISSING SOME-THING TO MIX IT IN!
SHF
Mix
MILK
THAT...!
Lift
Mix
THAT...!

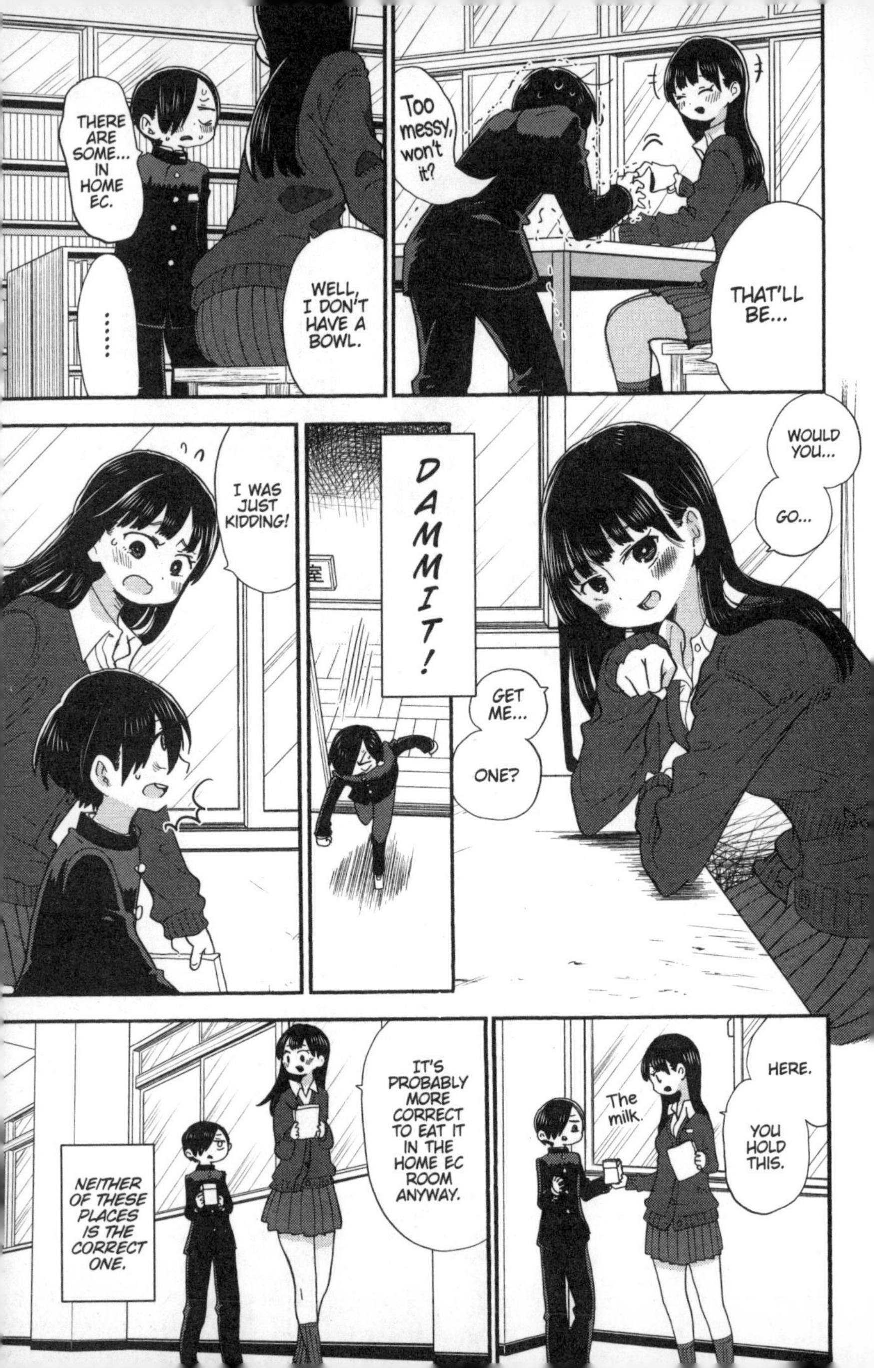
THAT'LL BE...
Too messy, won't it?
WELL, I DON'T HAVE A BOWL.
THERE ARE SOME... IN HOME EC.
......
WOULD YOU...
GO...
GET ME...
ONE?
DAMMIT!
I WAS JUST KIDDING!
HERE.
YOU HOLD THIS.
The milk.
IT'S PROBABLY MORE CORRECT TO EAT IT IN THE HOME EC ROOM ANYWAY.
NEITHER OF THESE PLACES IS THE CORRECT ONE.

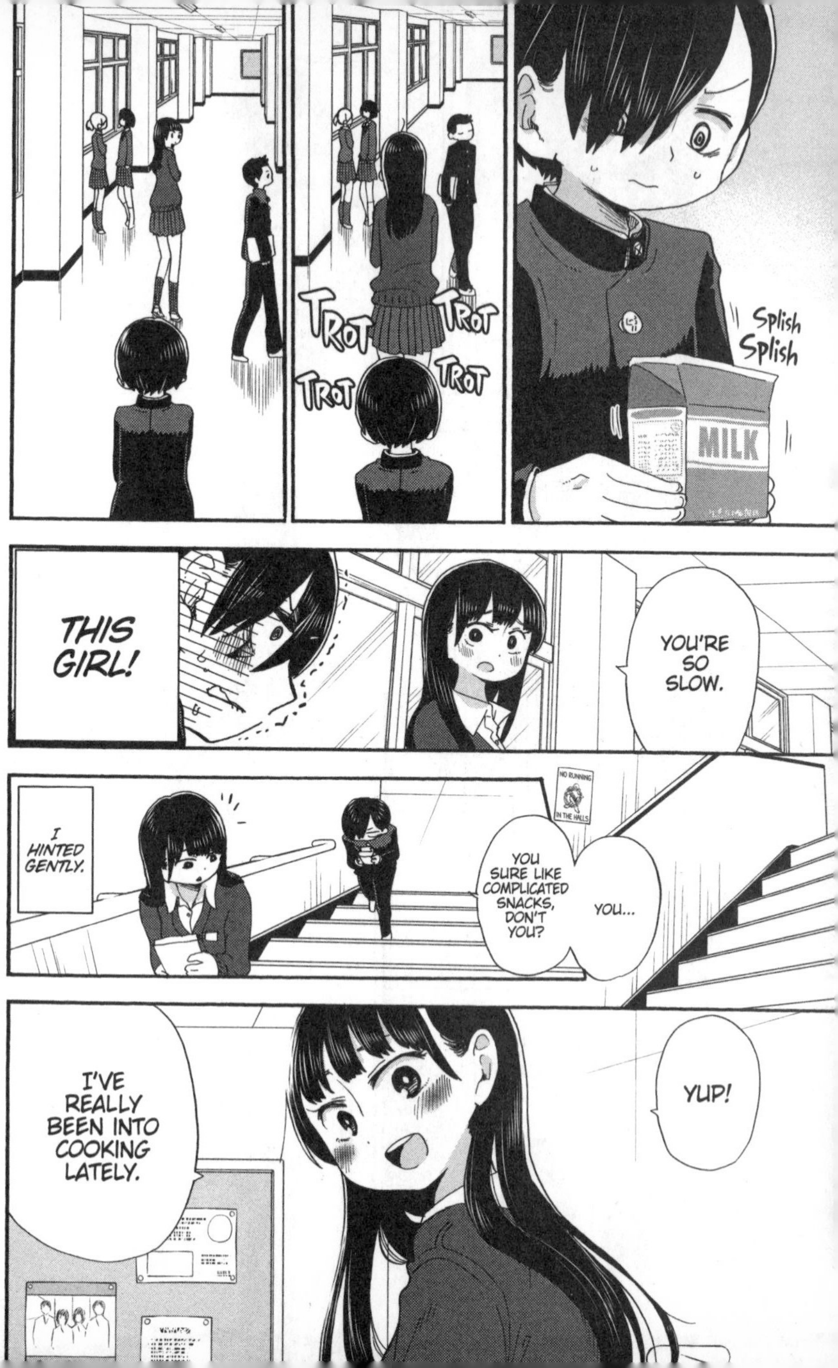
Splish
Splish
MILK
TROT
TROT
TROT
TROT
YOU'RE SO SLOW.
THIS GIRL!
YOU...
YOU SURE LIKE COMPLICATED SNACKS, DON'T YOU?
NO RUNNING IN THE HALLS
I HINTED GENTLY.
YUP!
I'VE REALLY BEEN INTO COOKING LATELY.

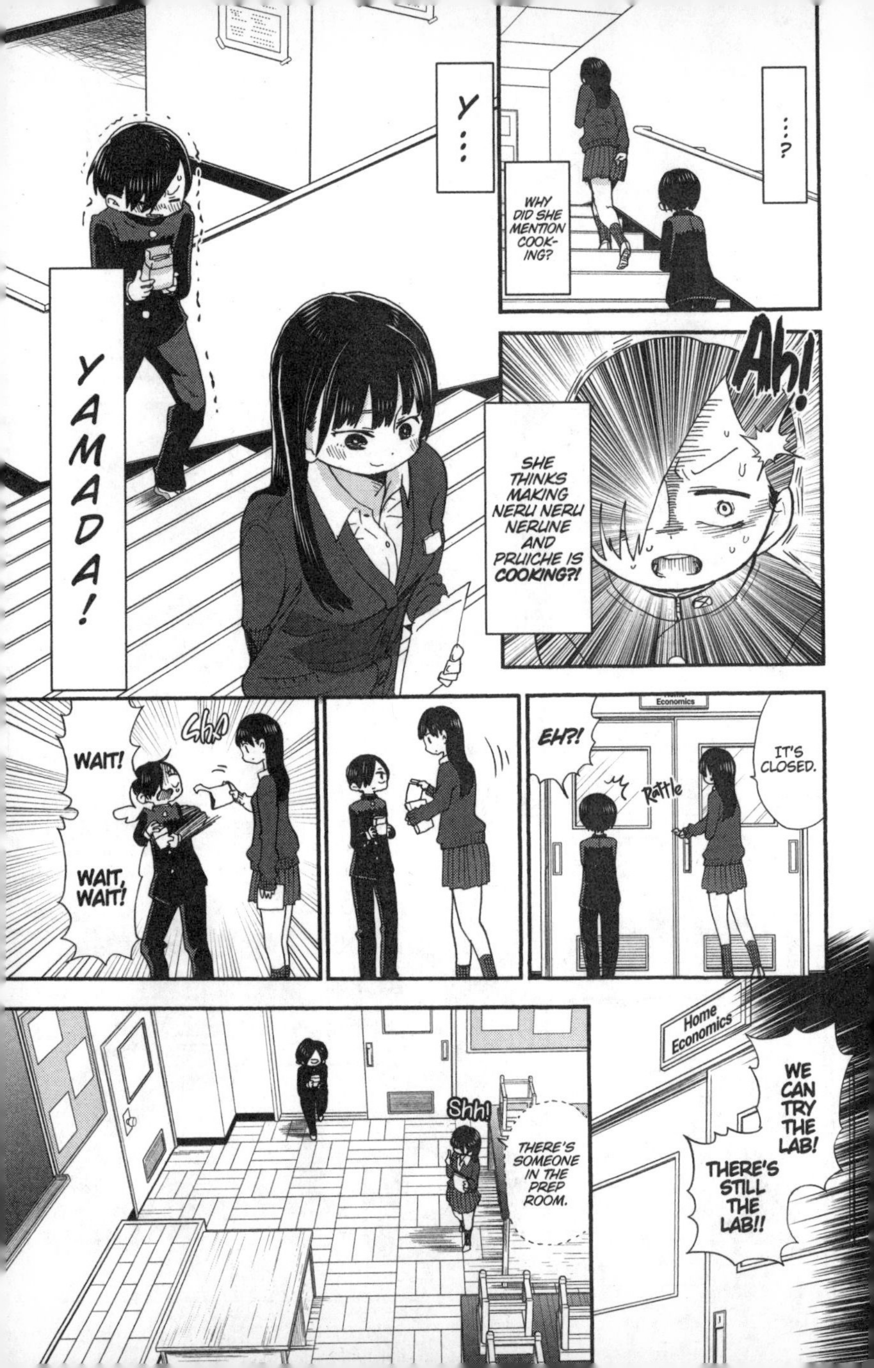
...?
WHY DID SHE MENTION COOK-ING?
Ah!
SHE THINKS MAKING NERU NERU NERUNE AND PRUICHE IS COOKING?!
Y...
YAMADA!
Home Economics
IT'S CLOSED.
Rattle
EH?!
Shk
WAIT!
WAIT, WAIT!
Home Economics
WE CAN TRY THE LAB!
THERE'S STILL THE LAB!!
Shh!
THERE'S SOMEONE IN THE PREP ROOM.

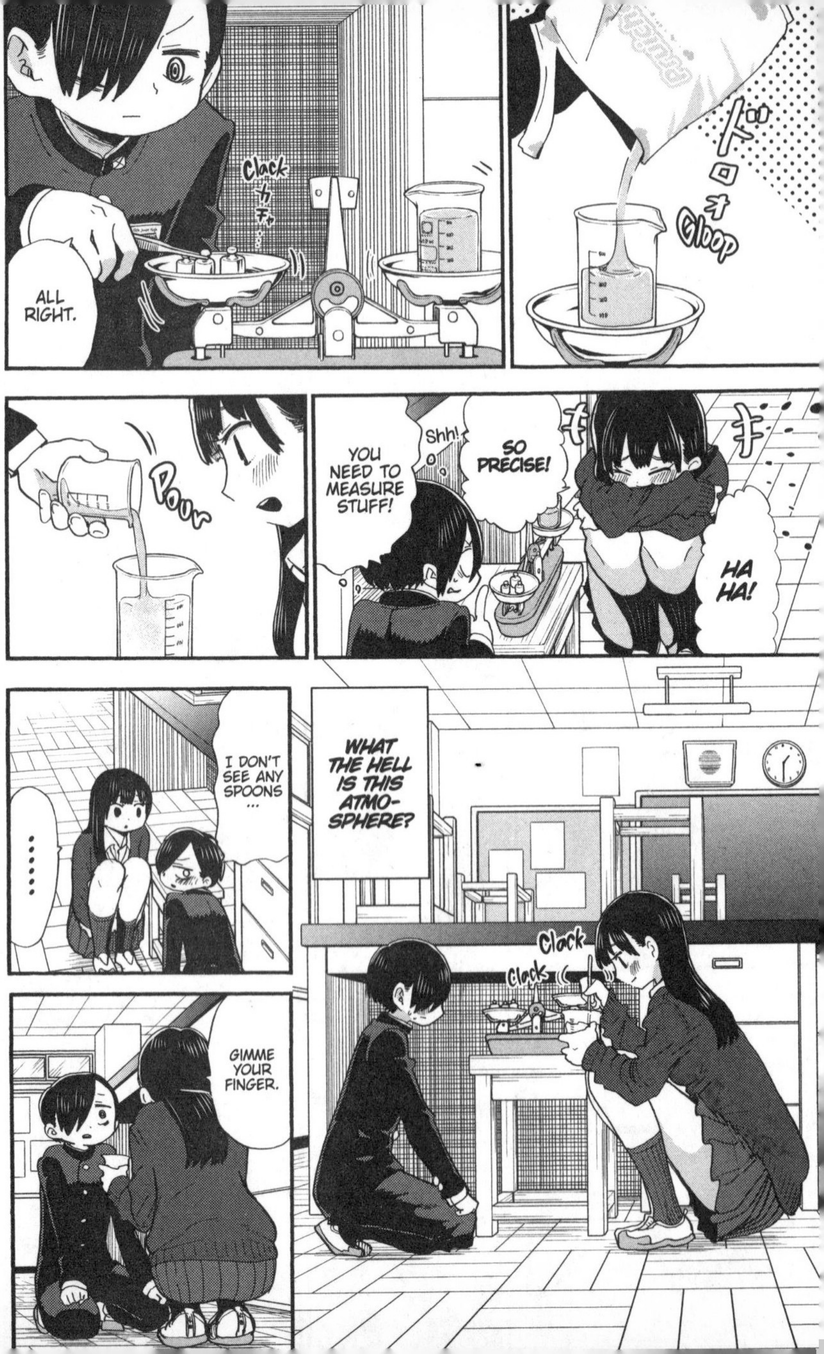
ドロオ
Gloop
Clack
カチャ…
ALL RIGHT.
キ
キ
SO PRECISE!
Shh!
YOU NEED TO MEASURE STUFF!
HA HA!
Pour
WHAT THE HELL IS THIS ATMO-SPHERE?
Clack
Clack
I DON'T SEE ANY SPOONS…
……
GIMME YOUR FINGER.

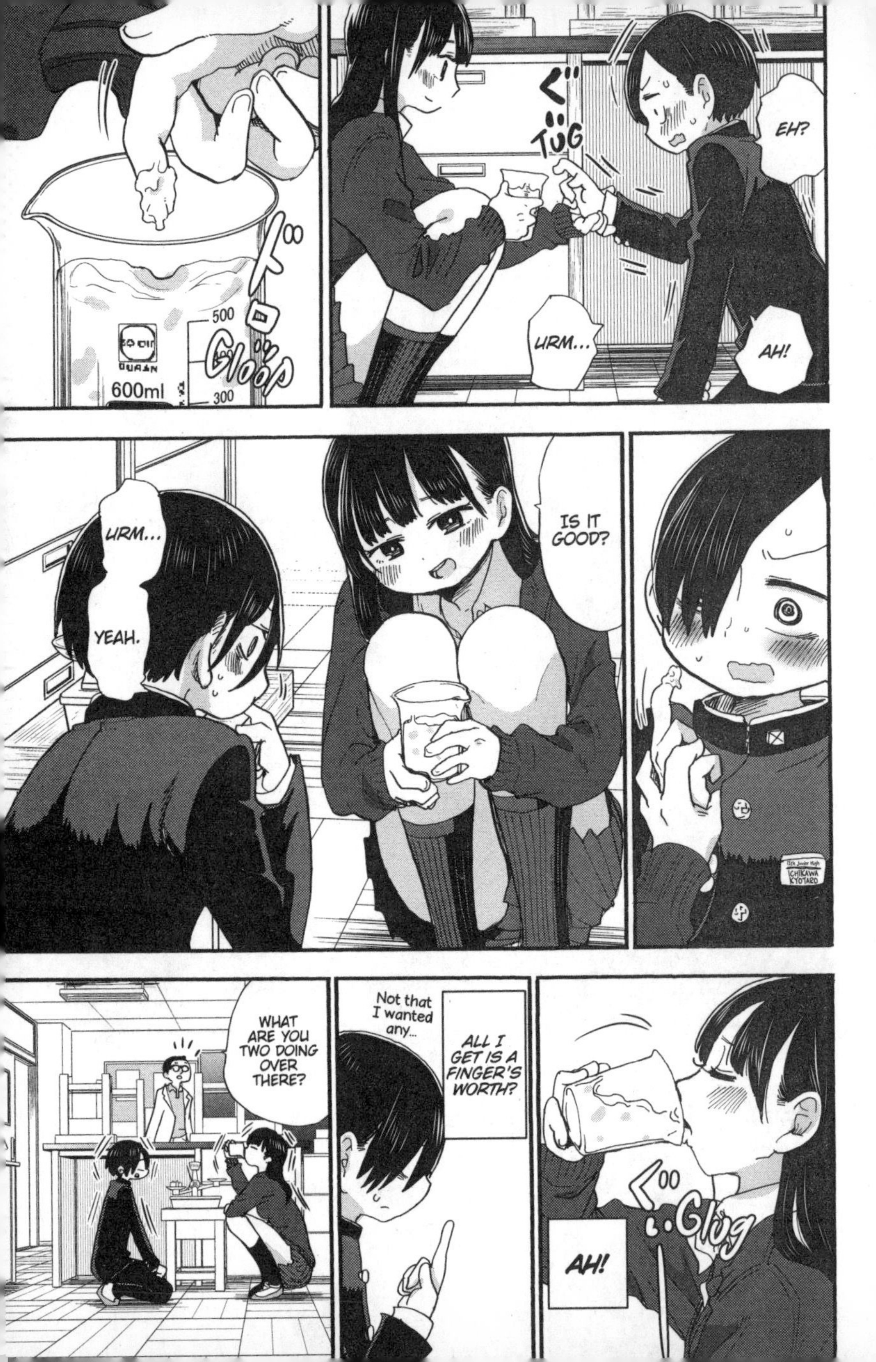
ぐ"
TUG
EH?
URM...
AH!
ド
ロ
Gloop
500
600ml
300
ICHIKAWA KYOTARO
IS IT GOOD?
URM...
YEAH.
く
Glug
AH!
Not that I wanted any...
ALL I GET IS A FINGER'S WORTH?
WHAT ARE YOU TWO DOING OVER THERE?

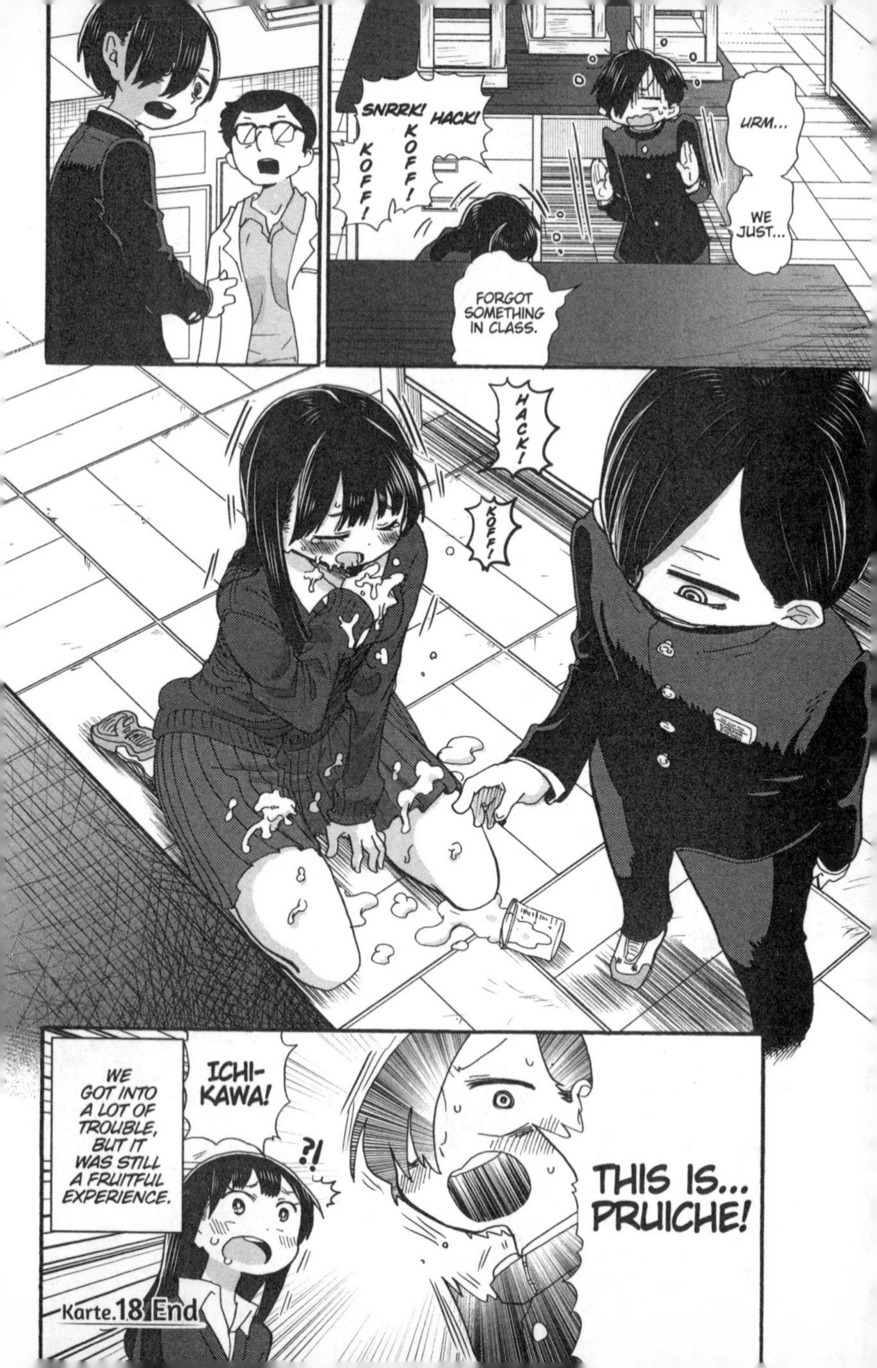
URM...
WE JUST...
HACK!
KOFF!
SNRRK!
KOFF!
FORGOT SOMETHING IN CLASS.
HACK!
KOFF!
THIS IS... PRUICHE!
?!
ICHI-KAWA!
WE GOT INTO A LOT OF TROUBLE, BUT IT WAS STILL A FRUITFUL EXPERIENCE.
Karte.18 End

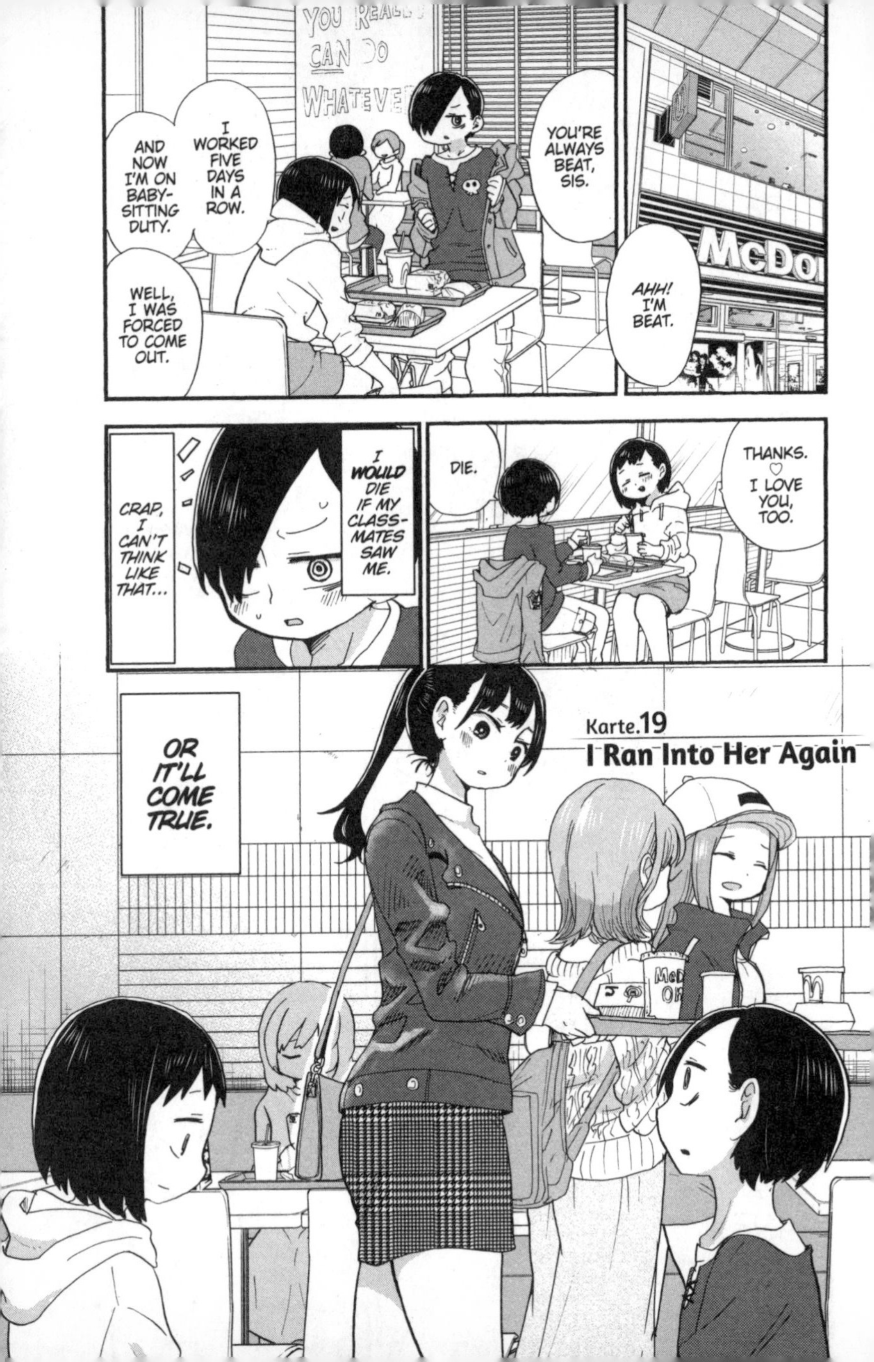
AHH! I'M BEAT.
YOU'RE ALWAYS BEAT, SIS.
I WORKED FIVE DAYS IN A ROW.
AND NOW I'M ON BABY-SITTING DUTY.
WELL, I WAS FORCED TO COME OUT.
THANKS. ♡ I LOVE YOU, TOO.
DIE.
I WOULD DIE IF MY CLASS-MATES SAW ME.
CRAP, I CAN'T THINK LIKE THAT...
Karte.19
I Ran Into Her Again
OR IT'LL COME TRUE.

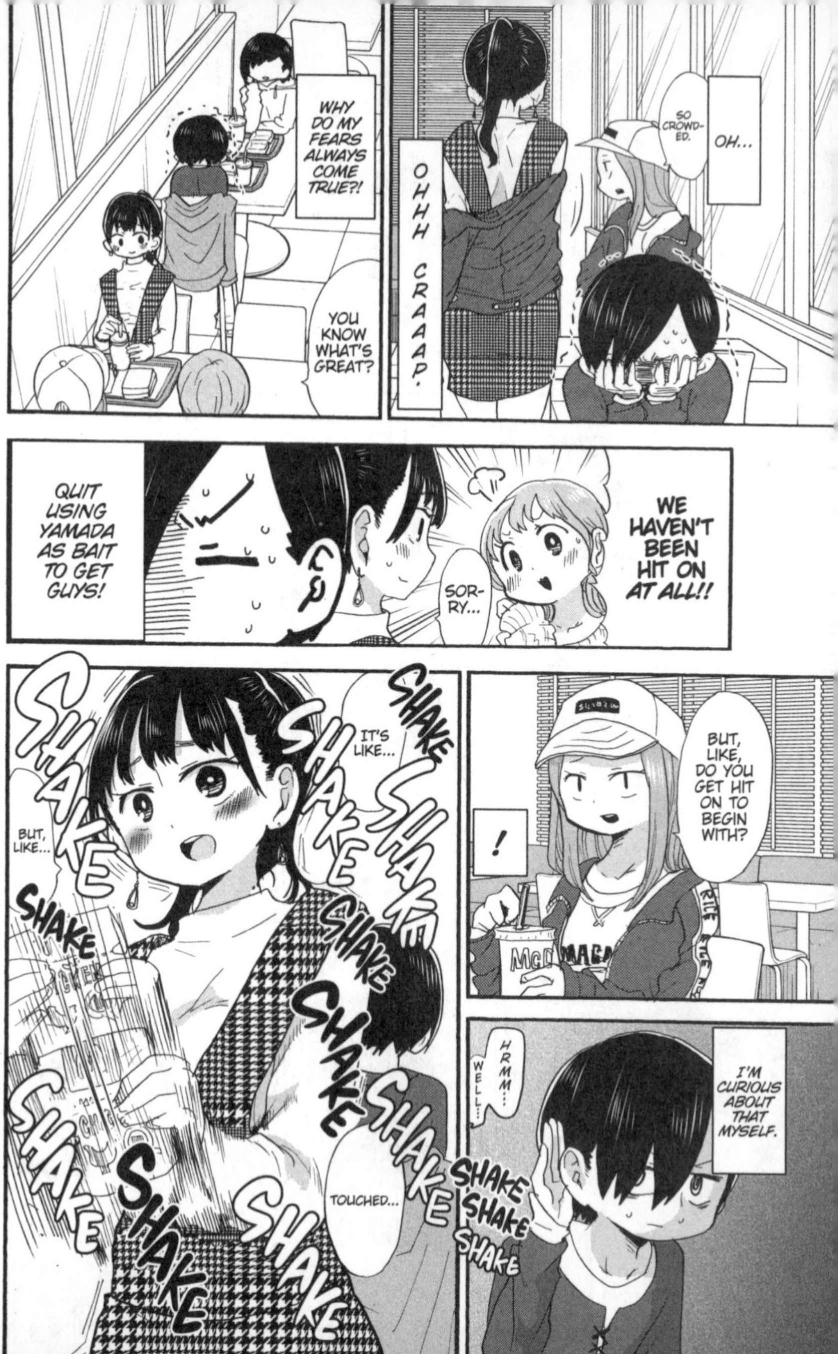
OH...
SO CROWDED.
OHHH CRAAAP.
WHY DO MY FEARS ALWAYS COME TRUE?!
YOU KNOW WHAT'S GREAT?
WE HAVEN'T BEEN HIT ON AT ALL!!
SORRY...
QUIT USING YAMADA AS BAIT TO GET GUYS!
BUT, LIKE, DO YOU GET HIT ON TO BEGIN WITH?
!
I'M CURIOUS ABOUT THAT MYSELF.
HRMM...
WELL...
SHAKE
SHAKE
SHAKE
SHAKE
IT'S LIKE...
SHAKE
SHAKE
SHAKE
SHAKE
BUT, LIKE...
SHAKE
TOUCHED...
SHAKE
SHAKE
SHAKE
SHAKE
SHAKE

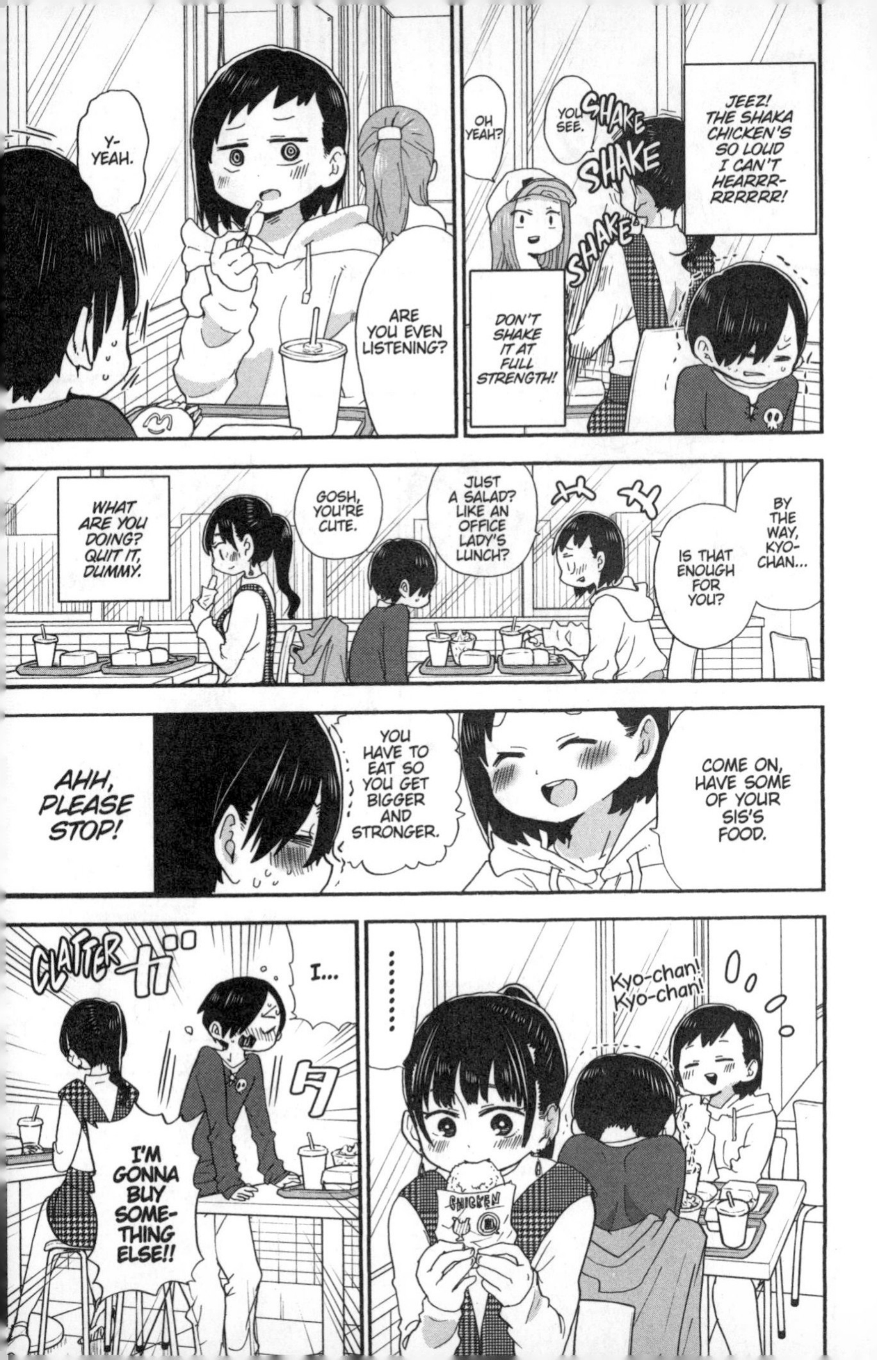
JEEZ! THE SHAKA CHICKEN'S SO LOUD I CAN'T HEARRR-RRRRRR!
YOU SEE.
SHAKE SHAKE SHAKE
OH YEAH?
DON'T SHAKE IT AT FULL STRENGTH!
ARE YOU EVEN LISTENING?
Y-YEAH.
BY THE WAY, KYO-CHAN...
IS THAT ENOUGH FOR YOU?
JUST A SALAD? LIKE AN OFFICE LADY'S LUNCH?
GOSH, YOU'RE CUTE.
WHAT ARE YOU DOING? QUIT IT, DUMMY.
COME ON, HAVE SOME OF YOUR SIS'S FOOD.
YOU HAVE TO EAT SO YOU GET BIGGER AND STRONGER.
AHH, PLEASE STOP!
Kyo-chan! Kyo-chan!
....
I...
CLATTER
I'M GONNA BUY SOME-THING ELSE!!
CHICKEN

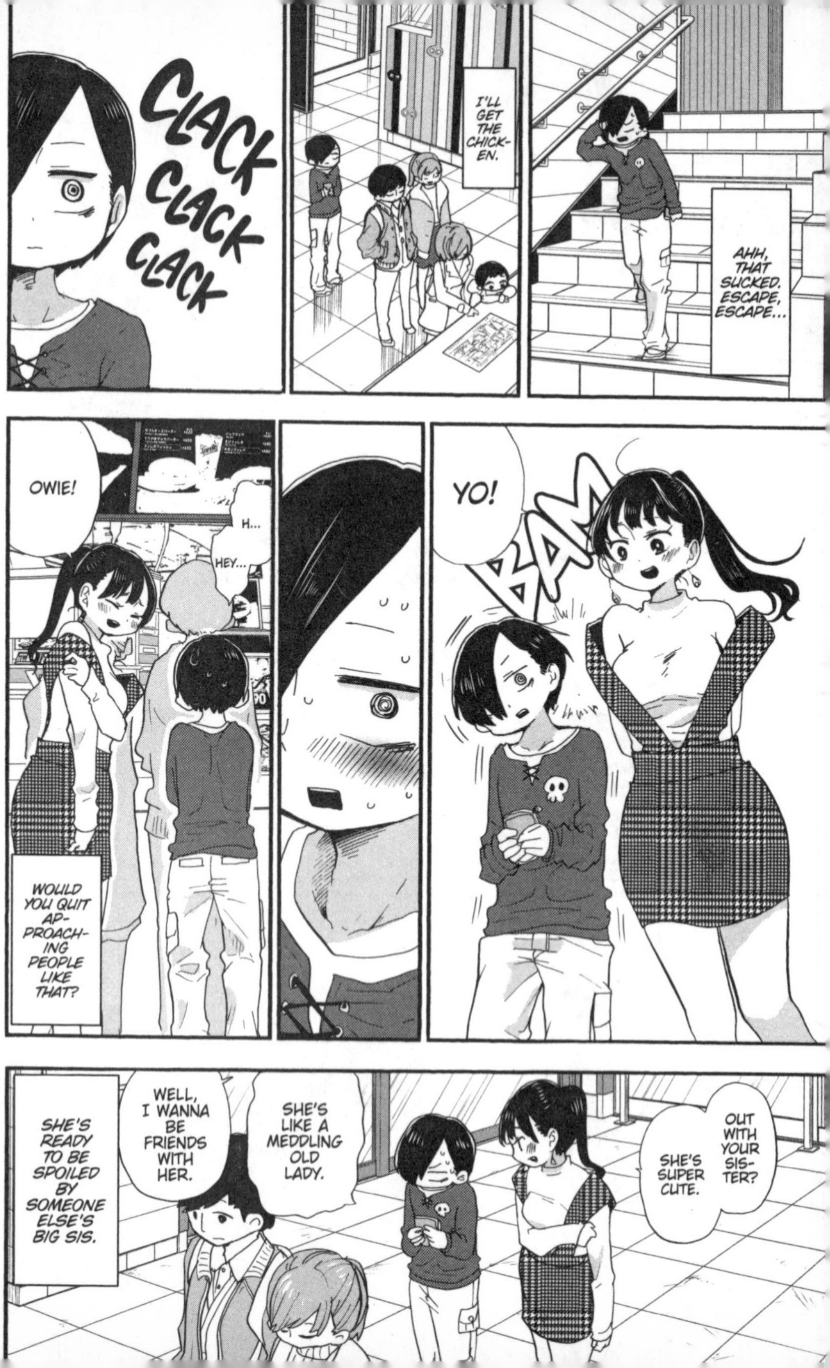
AHH, THAT SUCKED. ESCAPE, ESCAPE...
I'LL GET THE CHICK-EN.
CLACK CLACK CLACK
YO!
BAM
OWIE!
H...
HEY...
WOULD YOU QUIT AP-PROACH-ING PEOPLE LIKE THAT?
OUT WITH YOUR SIS-TER?
SHE'S SUPER CUTE.
SHE'S LIKE A MEDDLING OLD LADY.
WELL, I WANNA BE FRIENDS WITH HER.
SHE'S READY TO BE SPOILED BY SOMEONE ELSE'S BIG SIS.

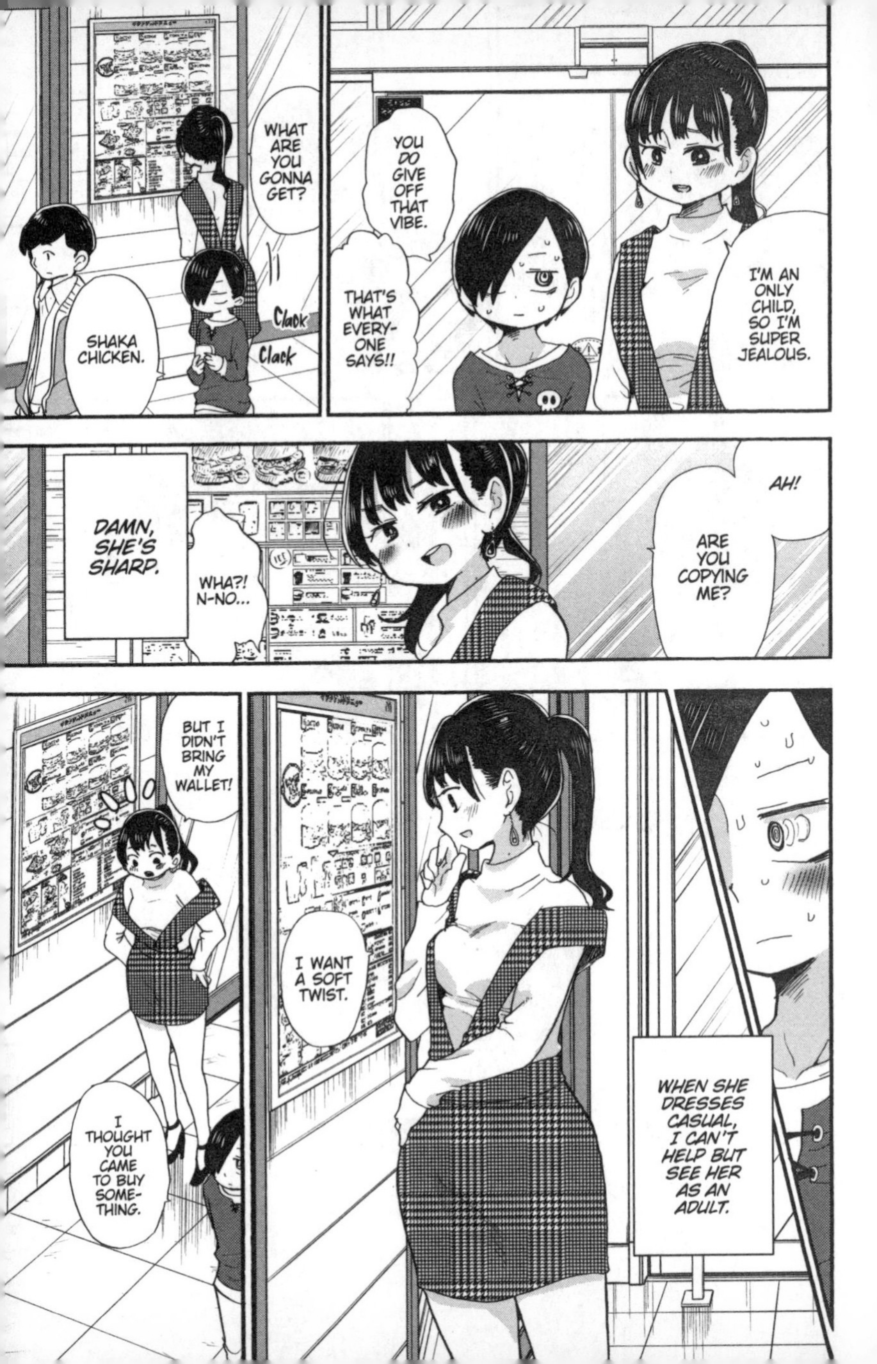
I'M AN ONLY CHILD, SO I'M SUPER JEALOUS.
YOU DO GIVE OFF THAT VIBE.
THAT'S WHAT EVERY-ONE SAYS!!
WHAT ARE YOU GONNA GET?
Clack
Clack
SHAKA CHICKEN.
AH!
ARE YOU COPYING ME?
WHA?! N-NO...
DAMN, SHE'S SHARP.
WHEN SHE DRESSES CASUAL, I CAN'T HELP BUT SEE HER AS AN ADULT.
I WANT A SOFT TWIST.
BUT I DIDN'T BRING MY WALLET!
I THOUGHT YOU CAME TO BUY SOME-THING.

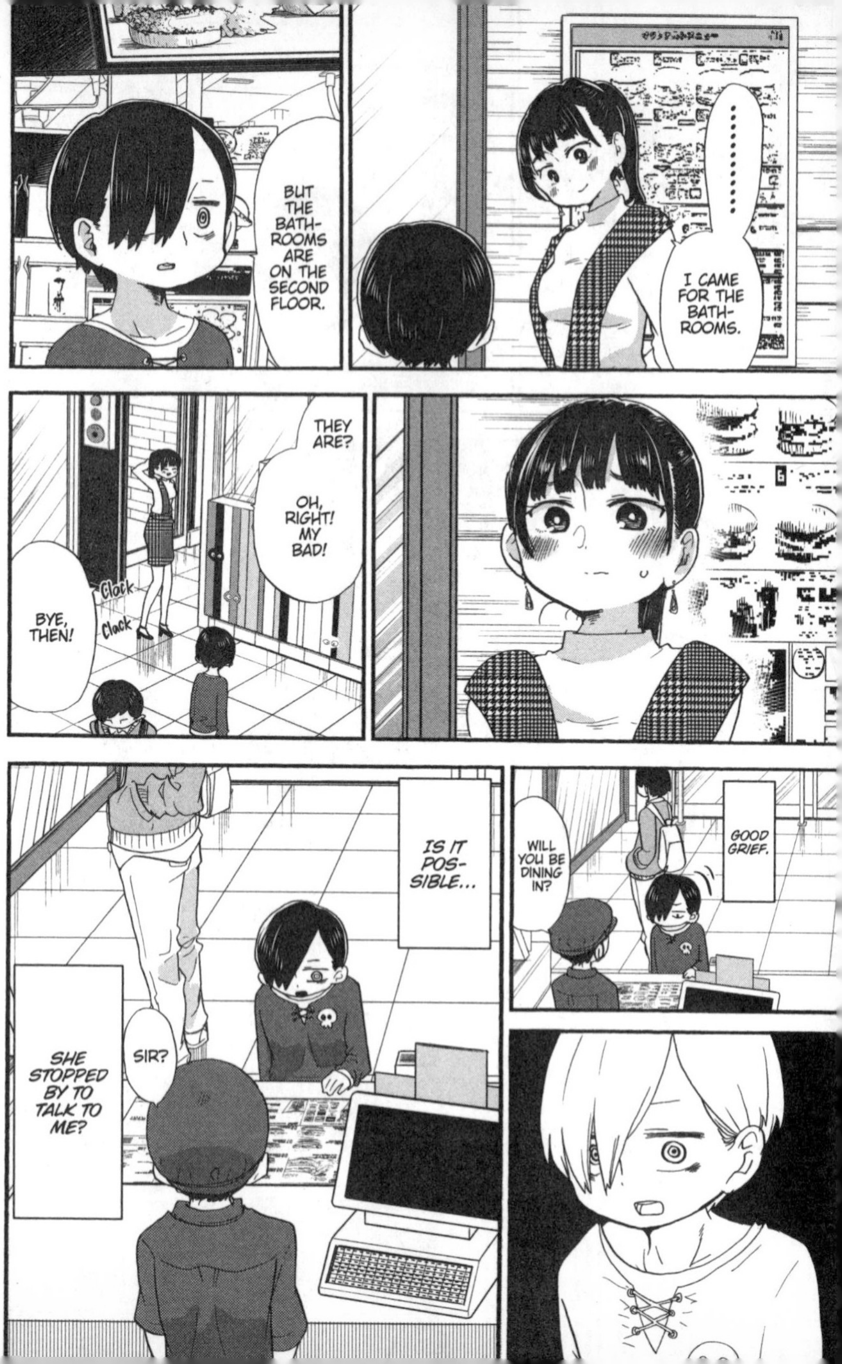
......
I CAME FOR THE BATH-ROOMS.
BUT THE BATH-ROOMS ARE ON THE SECOND FLOOR.
THEY ARE?
OH, RIGHT! MY BAD!
BYE, THEN!
Clack
Clack
GOOD GRIEF.
WILL YOU BE DINING IN?
IS IT POS-SIBLE...
SIR?
SHE STOPPED BY TO TALK TO ME?

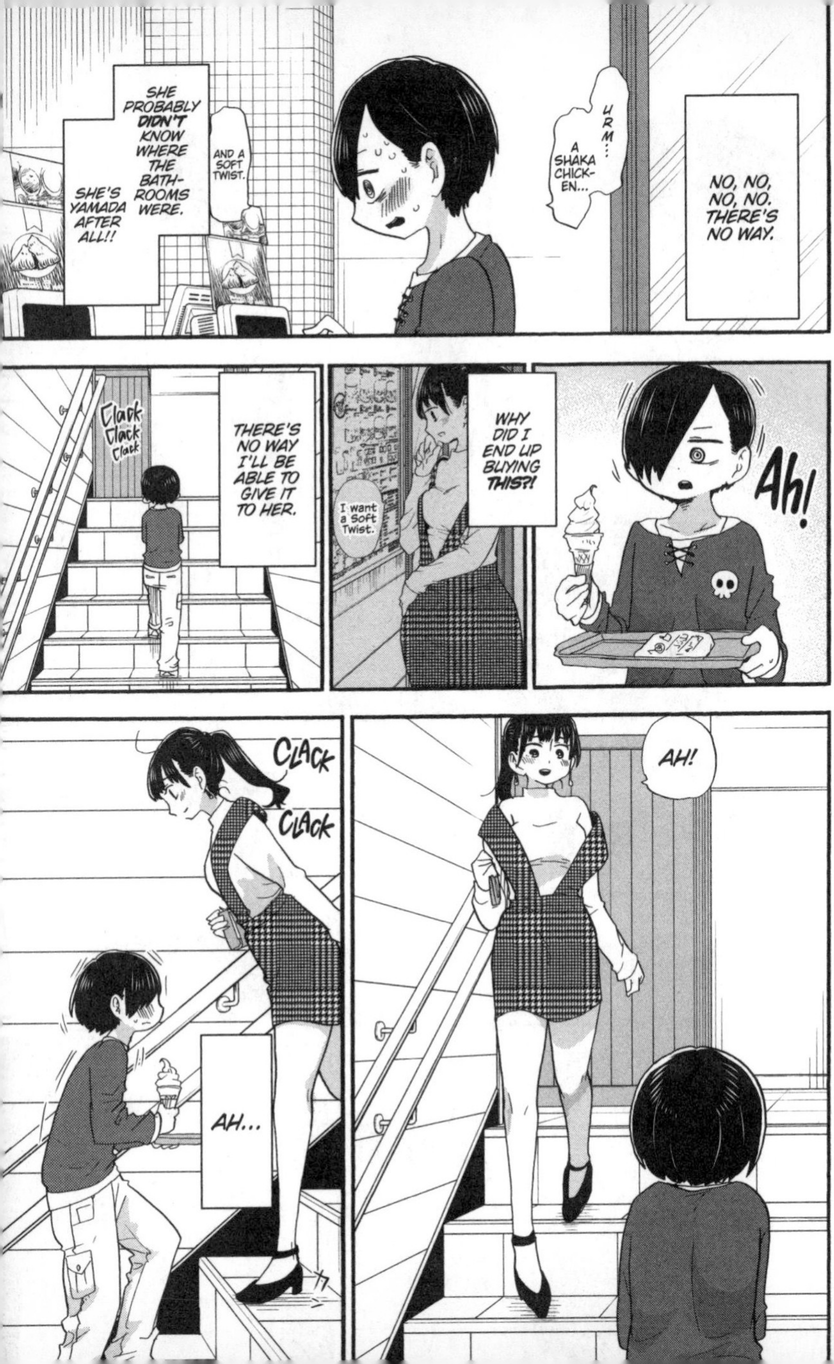
NO, NO, NO, NO. THERE'S NO WAY.
URM... A SHAKA CHICKEN...
AND A SOFT TWIST.
SHE PROBABLY DIDN'T KNOW WHERE THE BATHROOMS WERE.
SHE'S YAMADA AFTER ALL!!
AH!
WHY DID I END UP BUYING THIS?!
I want a Soft Twist.
THERE'S NO WAY I'LL BE ABLE TO GIVE IT TO HER.
Clack Clack Clack
AH!
CLACK
CLACK
AH...

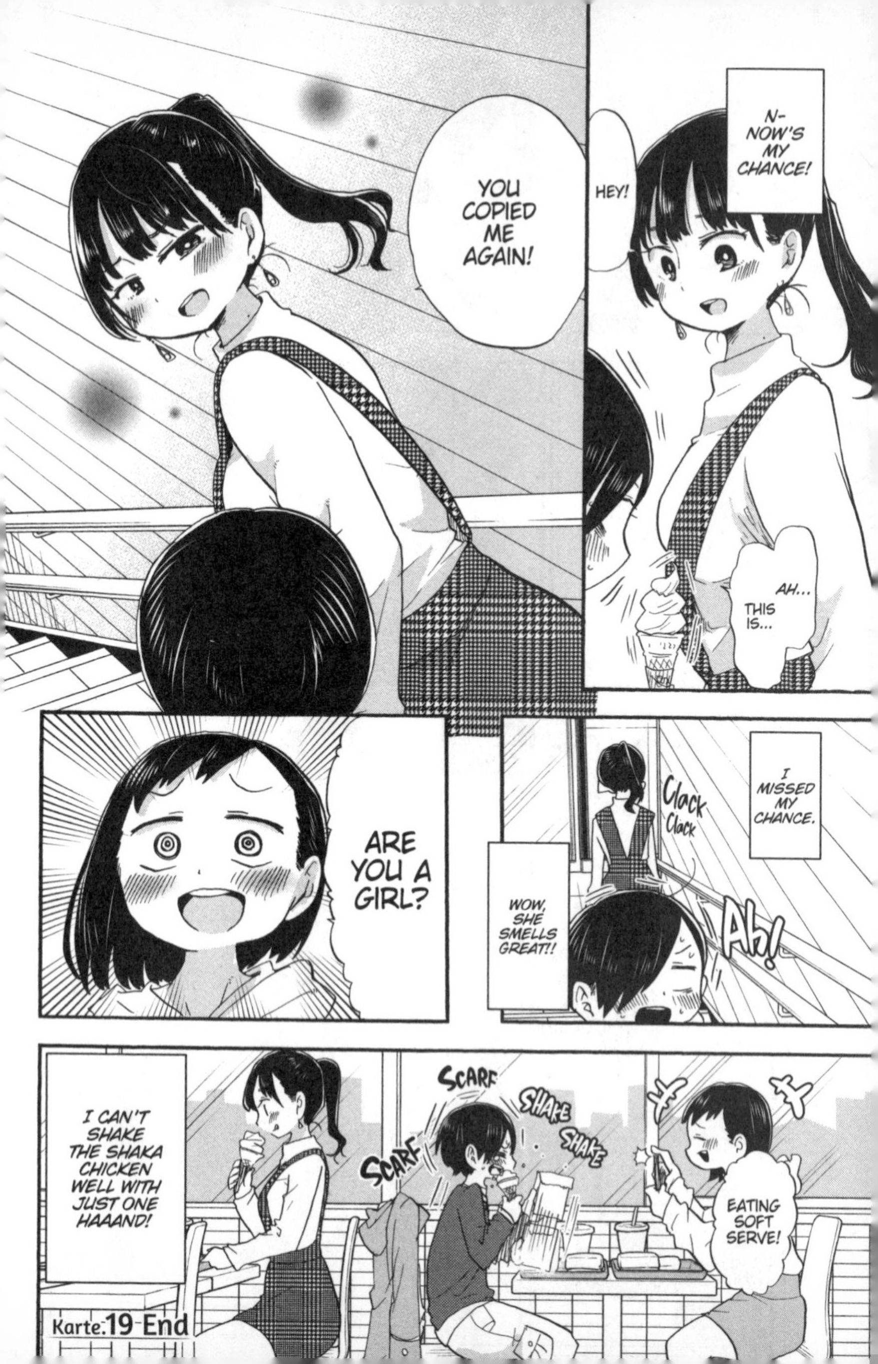
N-NOW'S MY CHANCE!
HEY!
AH... THIS IS...
YOU COPIED ME AGAIN!
I MISSED MY CHANCE.
Clack Clack
Ah!
WOW, SHE SMELLS GREAT!!
ARE YOU A GIRL?
EATING SOFT SERVE!
SHAKE
SHAKE
SCARF
SCARF
I CAN'T SHAKE THE SHAKA CHICKEN WELL WITH JUST ONE HAAAND!
Karte.19-End

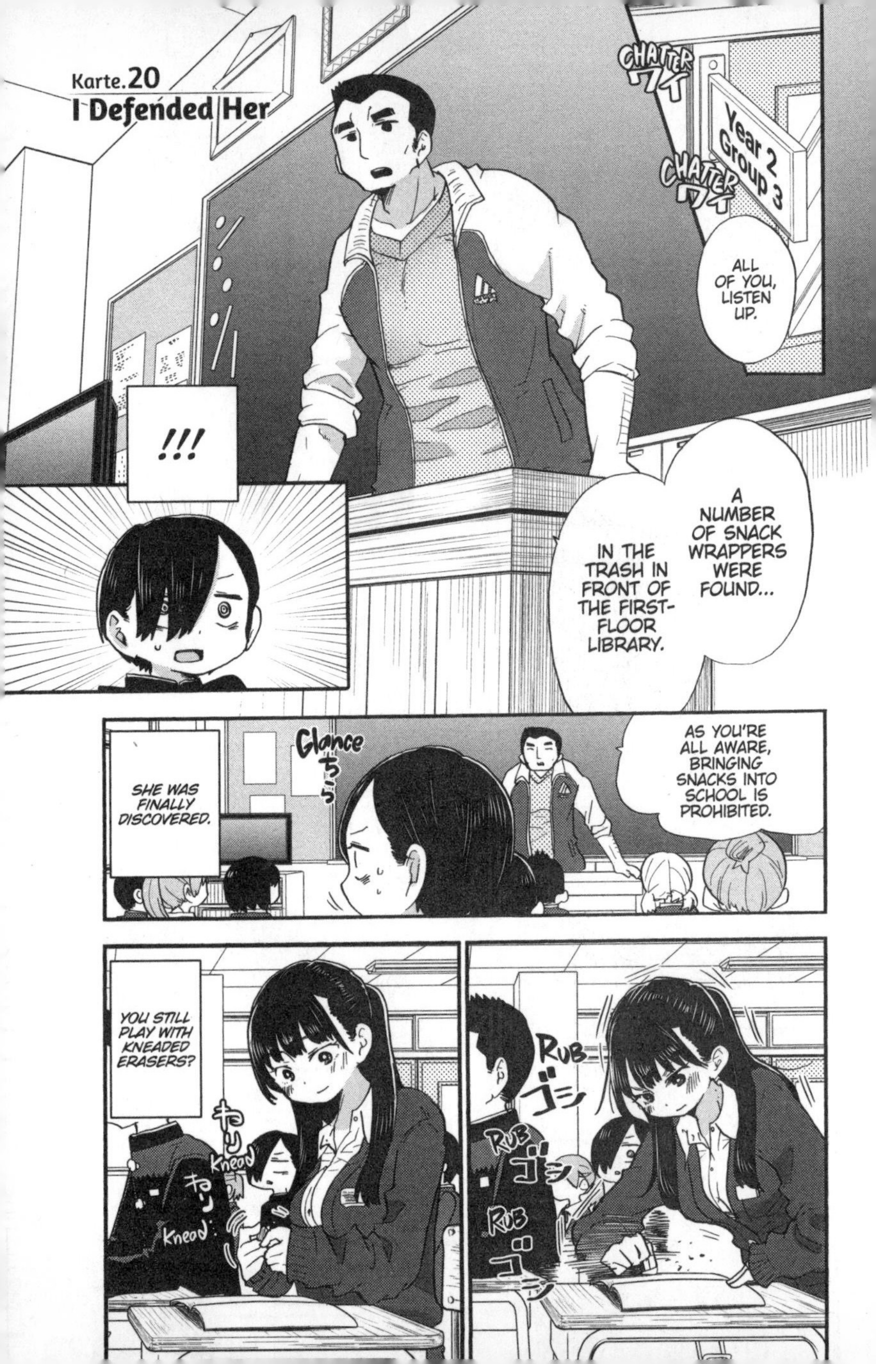
Karte.20
I Defended Her
CHATTER ワイ
Year 2 Group 3
CHATTER ワイ
ALL OF YOU, LISTEN UP.
!!!
A NUMBER OF SNACK WRAPPERS WERE FOUND...
IN THE TRASH IN FRONT OF THE FIRST-FLOOR LIBRARY.
AS YOU'RE ALL AWARE, BRINGING SNACKS INTO SCHOOL IS PROHIBITED.
Glance ちら
SHE WAS FINALLY DISCOVERED.
RUB ゴシ
RUB ゴシ
RUB ゴシ
YOU STILL PLAY WITH KNEADED ERASERS?
キリ Knead
キリ Knead

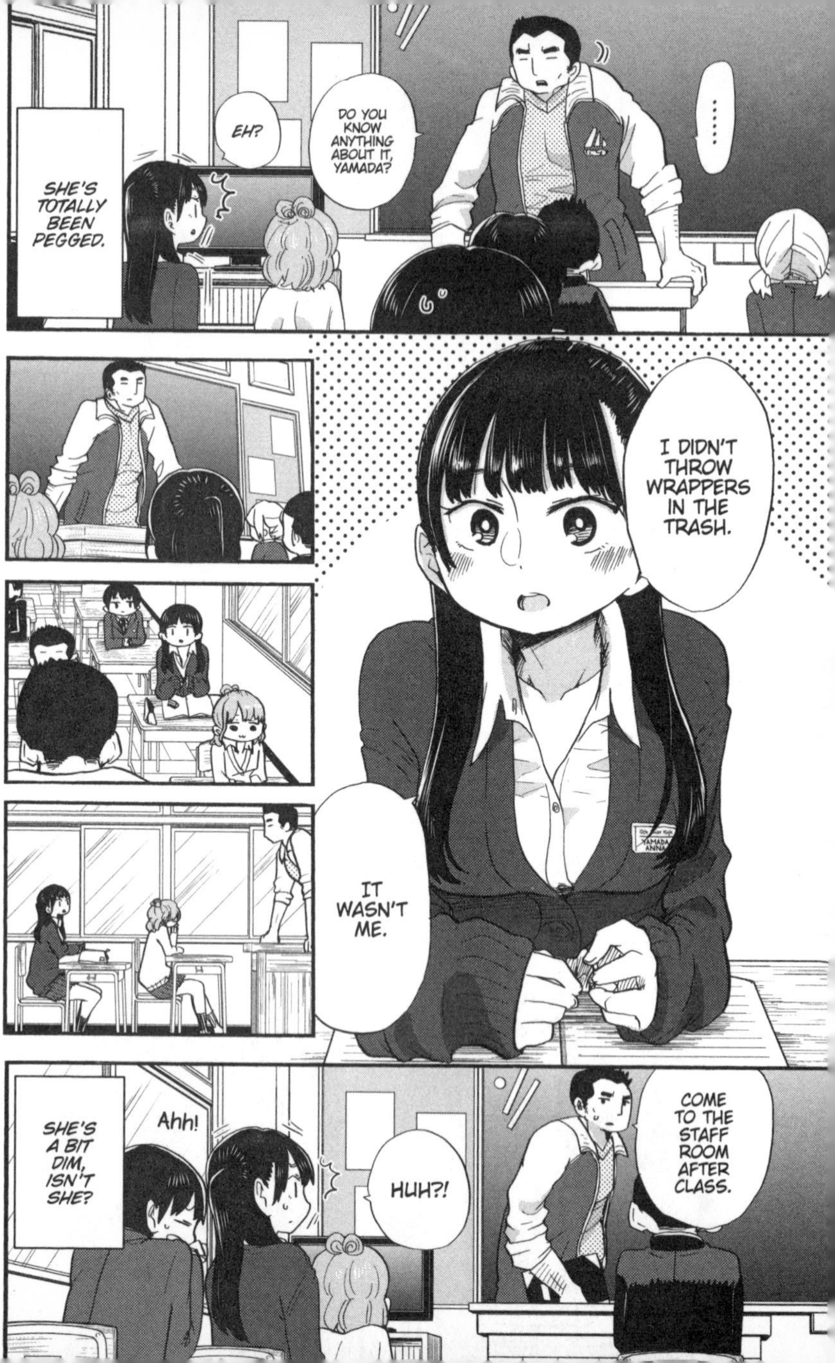
......
DO YOU KNOW ANYTHING ABOUT IT, YAMADA?
EH?
SHE'S TOTALLY BEEN PEGGED.
I DIDN'T THROW WRAPPERS IN THE TRASH.
IT WASN'T ME.
COME TO THE STAFF ROOM AFTER CLASS.
HUH?!
Ahh!
SHE'S A BIT DIM, ISN'T SHE?

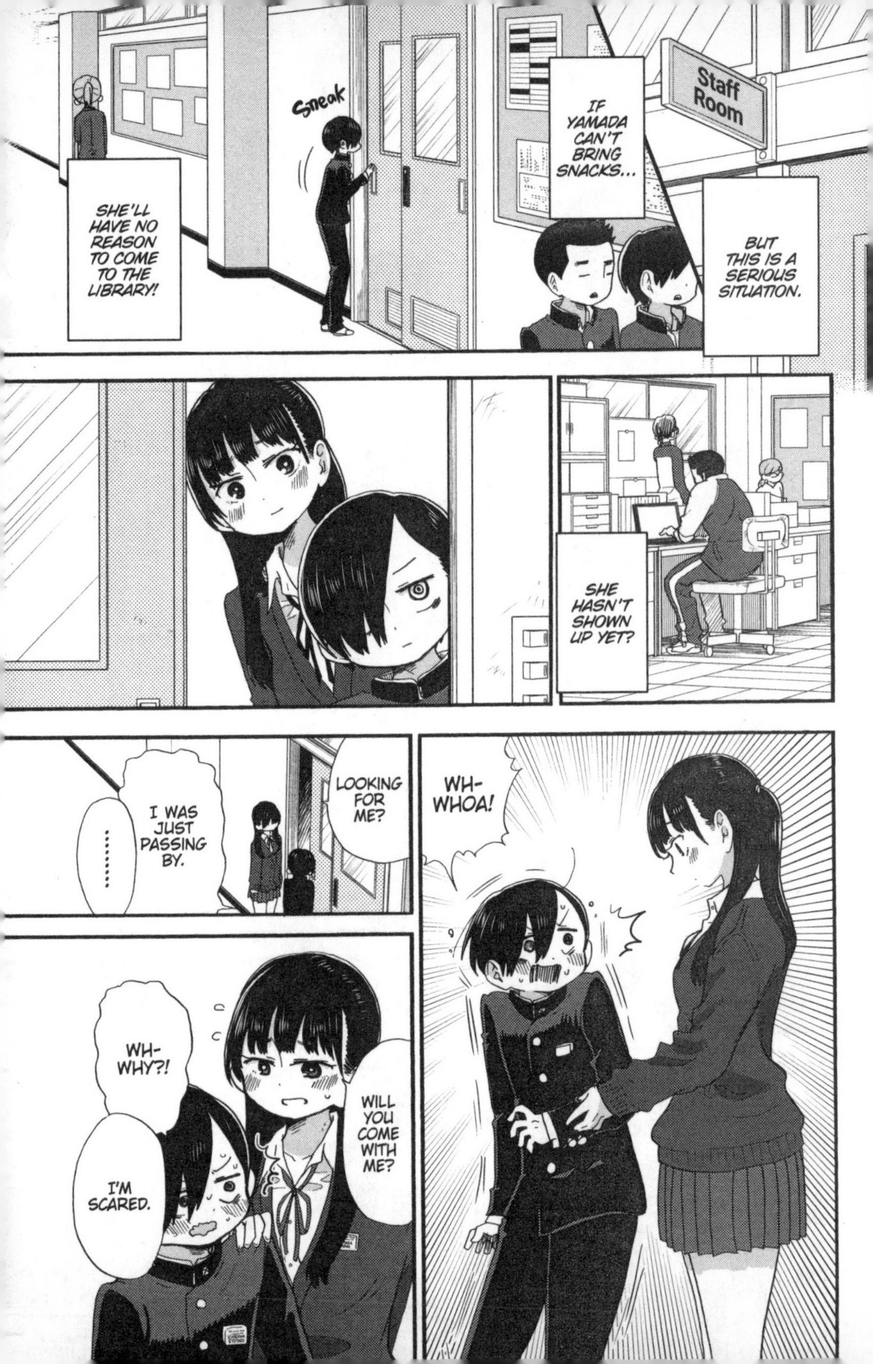
Staff Room
IF YAMADA CAN'T BRING SNACKS...
BUT THIS IS A SERIOUS SITUATION.
Sneak
SHE'LL HAVE NO REASON TO COME TO THE LIBRARY!
SHE HASN'T SHOWN UP YET?
WH- WHOA!
LOOKING FOR ME?
I WAS JUST PASSING BY.
......
WILL YOU COME WITH ME?
WH- WHY?!
I'M SCARED.

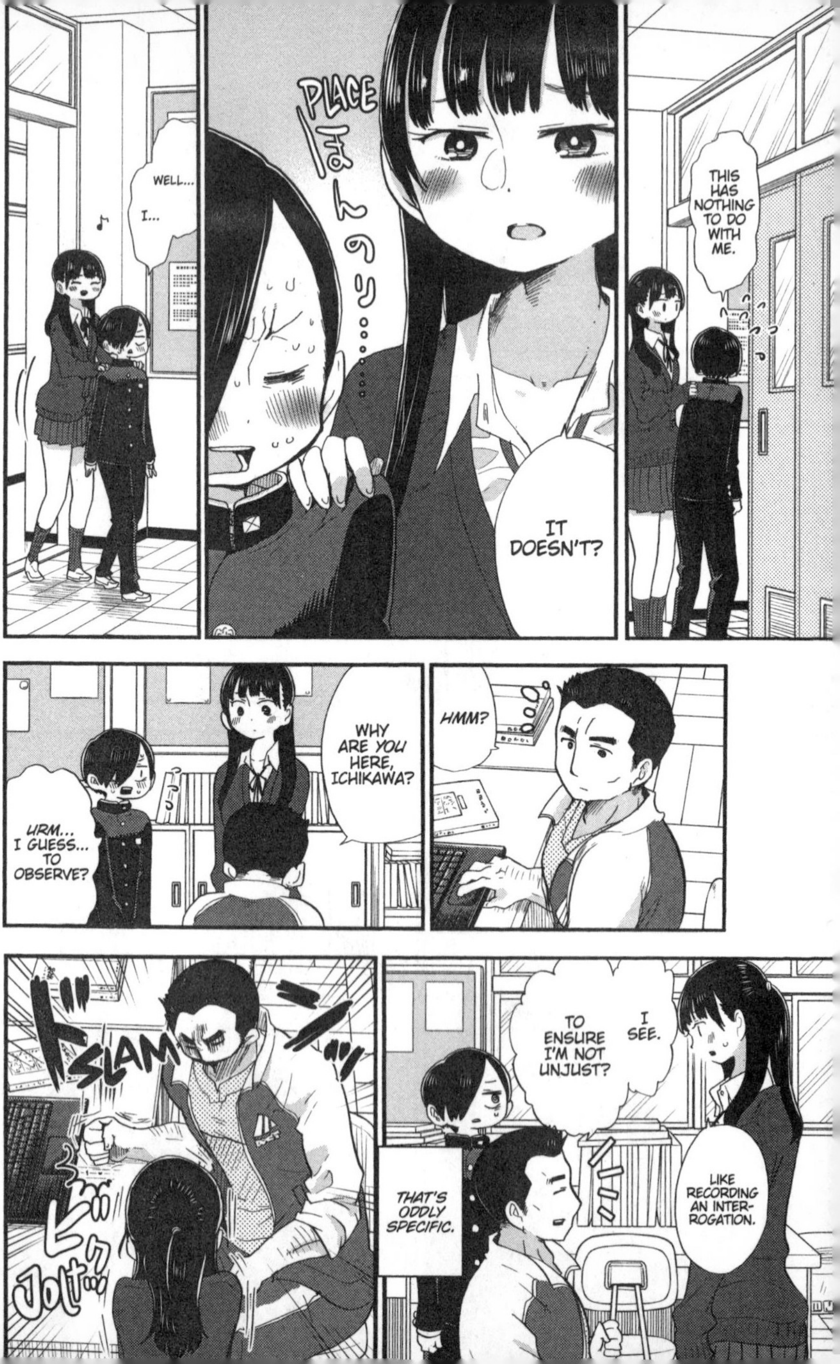
THIS HAS NOTHING TO DO WITH ME.
PLACE
ほんのり……
IT DOESN'T?
WELL... I...
HMM?
WHY ARE YOU HERE, ICHIKAWA?
URM... I GUESS... TO OBSERVE?
I SEE.
TO ENSURE I'M NOT UNJUST?
LIKE RECORDING AN INTER-ROGATION.
THAT'S ODDLY SPECIFIC.
SLAM
JOLT

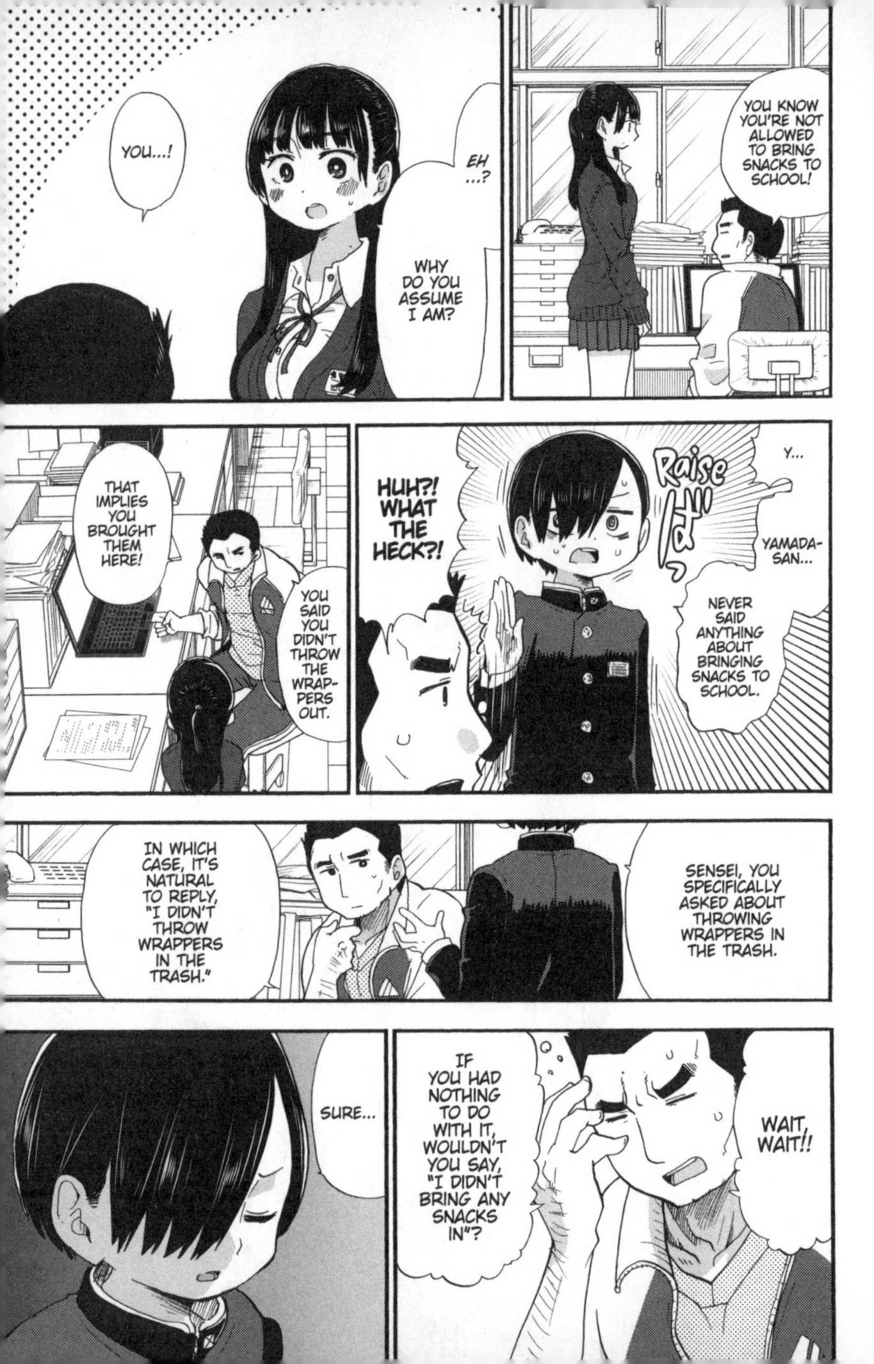
YOU KNOW YOU'RE NOT ALLOWED TO BRING SNACKS TO SCHOOL!
EH ...?
WHY DO YOU ASSUME I AM?
YOU...!
Y...
YAMADA-SAN...
NEVER SAID ANYTHING ABOUT BRINGING SNACKS TO SCHOOL.
Raise
ばっ
HUH?! WHAT THE HECK?!
YOU SAID YOU DIDN'T THROW THE WRAPPERS OUT.
THAT IMPLIES YOU BROUGHT THEM HERE!
SENSEI, YOU SPECIFICALLY ASKED ABOUT THROWING WRAPPERS IN THE TRASH.
IN WHICH CASE, IT'S NATURAL TO REPLY, "I DIDN'T THROW WRAPPERS IN THE TRASH."
WAIT, WAIT!!
IF YOU HAD NOTHING TO DO WITH IT, WOULDN'T YOU SAY, "I DIDN'T BRING ANY SNACKS IN"?
SURE...

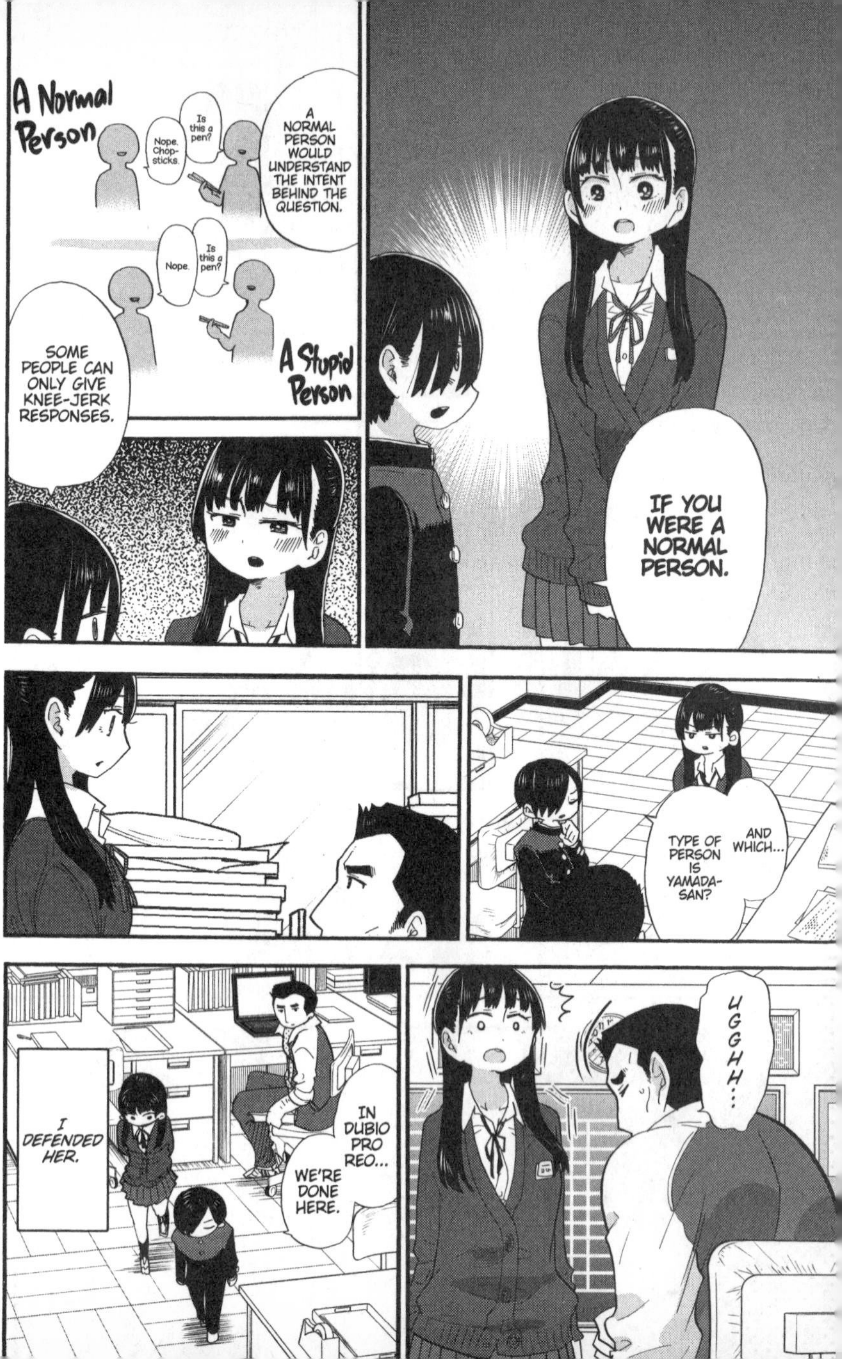
IF YOU WERE A NORMAL PERSON.
A NORMAL PERSON WOULD UNDERSTAND THE INTENT BEHIND THE QUESTION.
A Normal Person
Is this a pen?
Nope. Chop-sticks.
Is this a pen?
Nope.
A Stupid Person
SOME PEOPLE CAN ONLY GIVE KNEE-JERK RESPONSES.
AND WHICH...
TYPE OF PERSON IS YAMADA-SAN?
UGGHH...
IN DUBIO PRO REO...
WE'RE DONE HERE.
I DEFENDED HER.

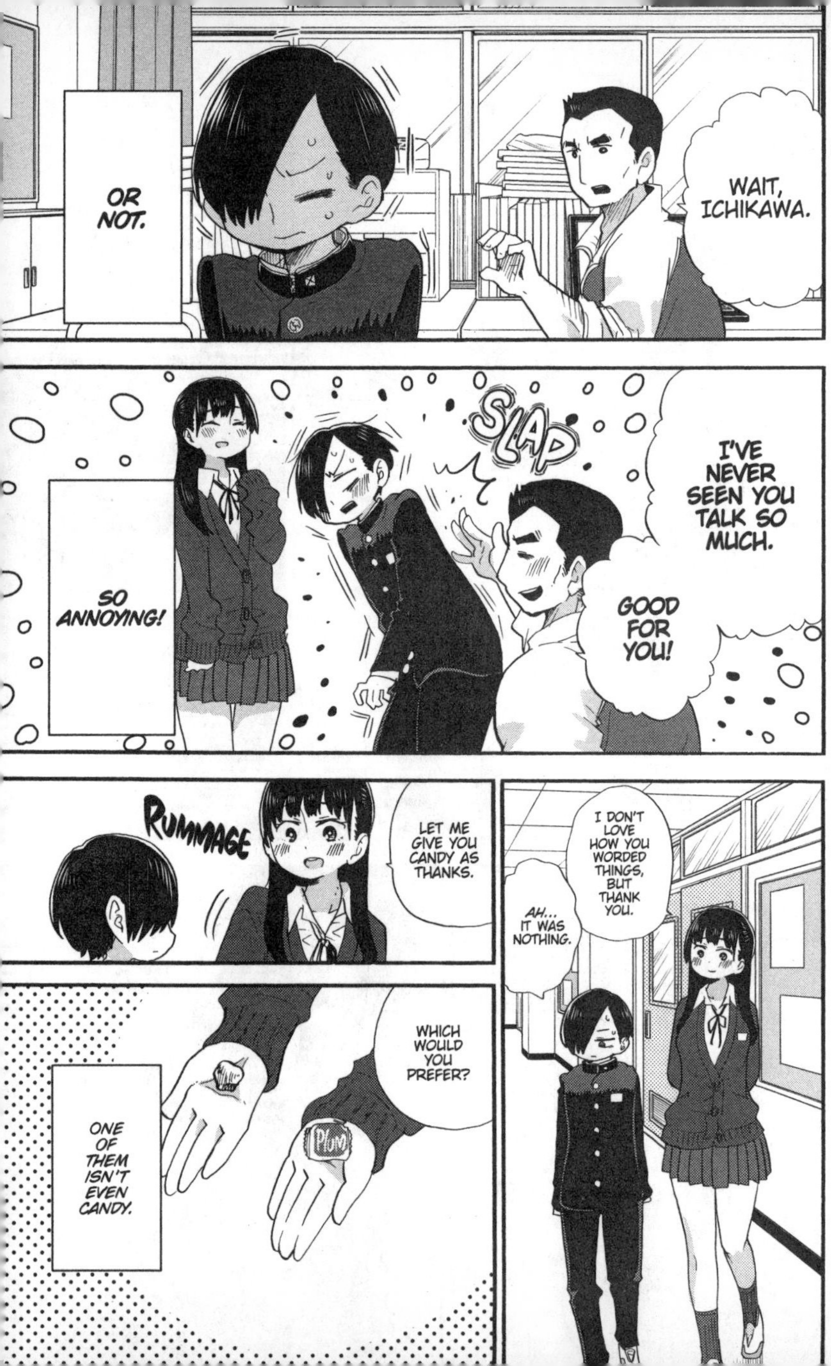
WAIT, ICHIKAWA.
OR NOT.
I'VE NEVER SEEN YOU TALK SO MUCH.
GOOD FOR YOU!
SLAP
SO ANNOYING!
I DON'T LOVE HOW YOU WORDED THINGS, BUT THANK YOU.
AH... IT WAS NOTHING.
LET ME GIVE YOU CANDY AS THANKS.
RUMMAGE
WHICH WOULD YOU PREFER?
PLUM
ONE OF THEM ISN'T EVEN CANDY.

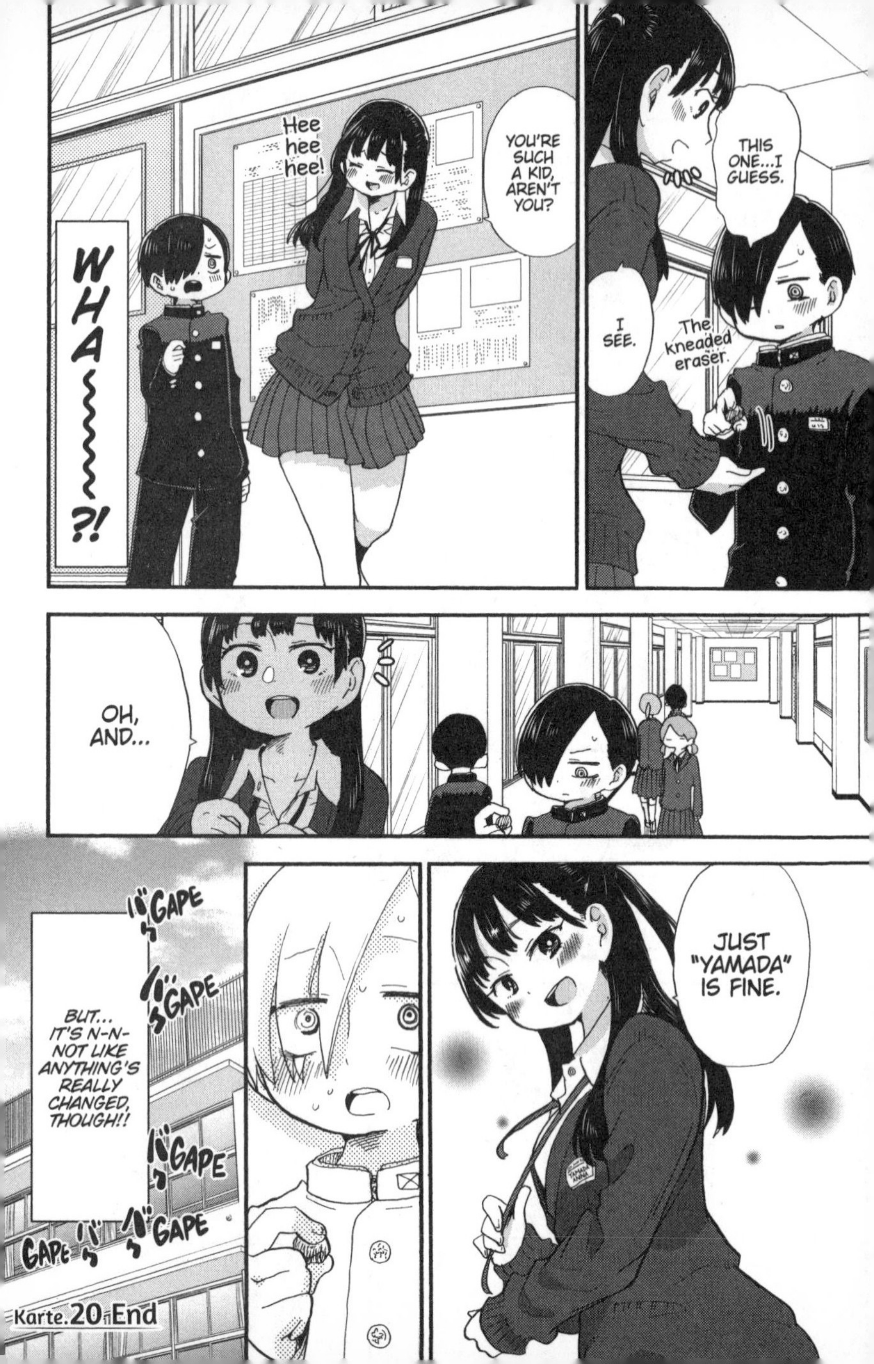
THIS ONE...I GUESS.
The kneaded eraser.
I SEE.
YOU'RE SUCH A KID, AREN'T YOU?
Hee hee hee!
WHA~~~?!
OH, AND...
JUST "YAMADA" IS FINE.
GAPE
GAPE
BUT... IT'S N-N-NOT LIKE ANYTHING'S REALLY CHANGED, THOUGH!!
GAPE
GAPE
GAPE
Karte.20 End

• Excuses •

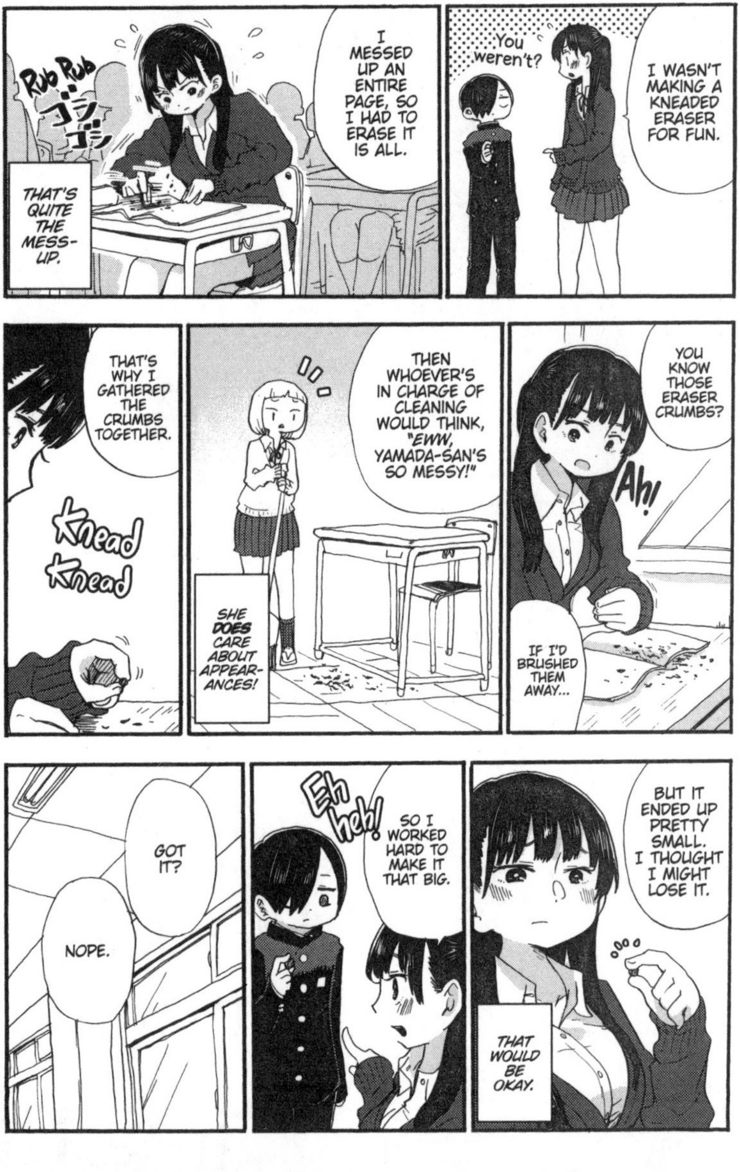
I WASN'T MAKING A KNEADED ERASER FOR FUN.
You weren't?
I MESSED UP AN ENTIRE PAGE, SO I HAD TO ERASE IT IS ALL.
Rub Rub
ゴシゴシ
THAT'S QUITE THE MESS-UP.
YOU KNOW THOSE ERASER CRUMBS?
Ah!
IF I'D BRUSHED THEM AWAY...
THEN WHOEVER'S IN CHARGE OF CLEANING WOULD THINK, "EWW, YAMADA-SAN'S SO MESSY!"
SHE DOES CARE ABOUT APPEARANCES!
THAT'S WHY I GATHERED THE CRUMBS TOGETHER.
Knead Knead
BUT IT ENDED UP PRETTY SMALL. I THOUGHT I MIGHT LOSE IT.
THAT WOULD BE OKAY.
Eh heh!
SO I WORKED HARD TO MAKE IT THAT BIG.
GOT IT?
NOPE.

The
Dangers
in My
Heart

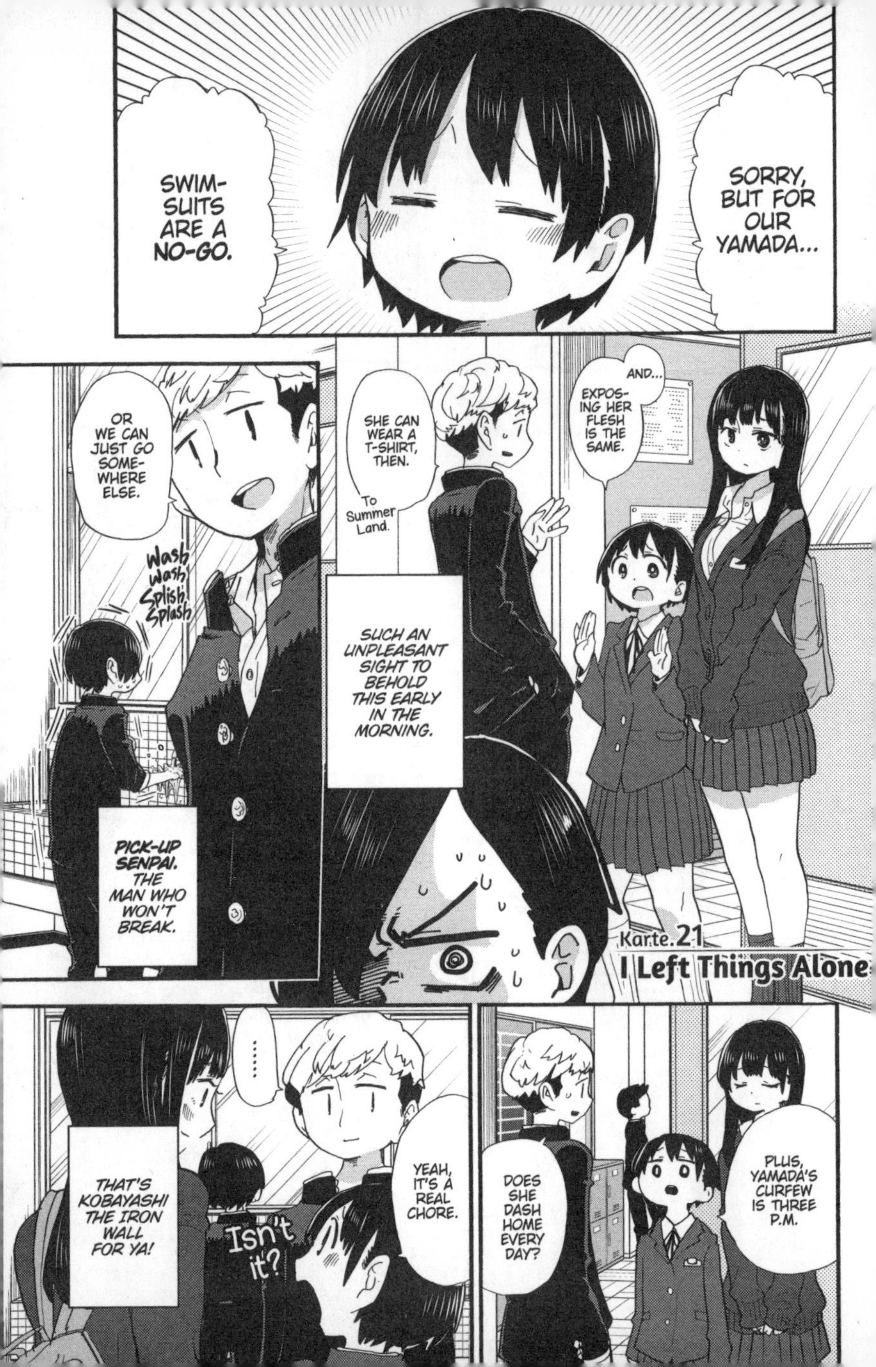
SORRY, BUT FOR OUR YAMADA...
SWIM-SUITS ARE A NO-GO.
AND...
EXPOSING HER FLESH IS THE SAME.
SHE CAN WEAR A T-SHIRT, THEN.
To Summer Land.
SUCH AN UNPLEASANT SIGHT TO BEHOLD THIS EARLY IN THE MORNING.
Karte. 21
I Left Things Alone
OR WE CAN JUST GO SOMEWHERE ELSE.
Wash Wash Splish Splash
PICK-UP SENPAI. THE MAN WHO WON'T BREAK.
PLUS, YAMADA'S CURFEW IS THREE P.M.
DOES SHE DASH HOME EVERY DAY?
YEAH, IT'S A REAL CHORE.
......
Isn't it?
THAT'S KOBAYASHI THE IRON WALL FOR YA!

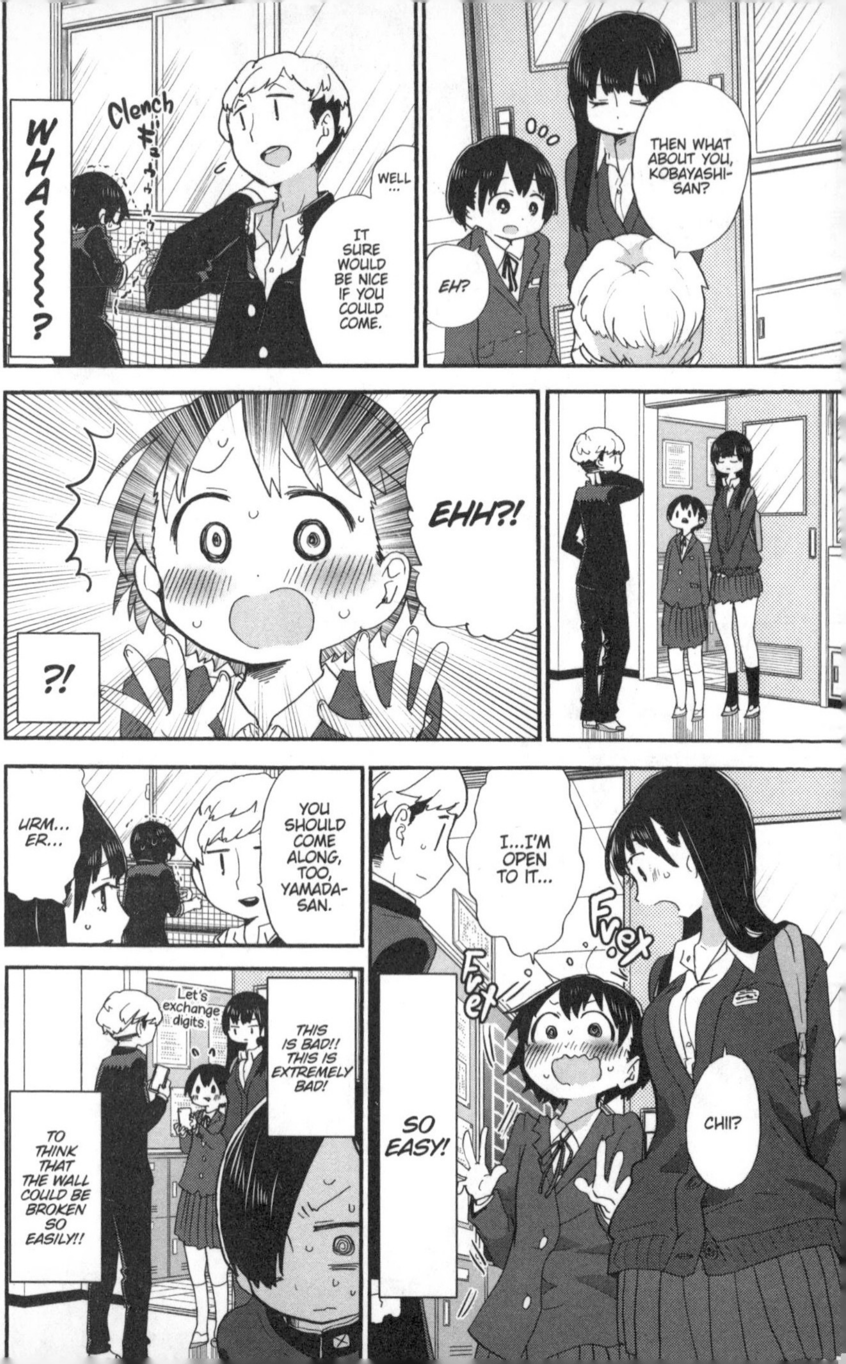
THEN WHAT ABOUT YOU, KOBAYASHI-SAN?
Ooo
EH?
WELL ...
IT SURE WOULD BE NICE IF YOU COULD COME.
Clench
WHA~~~?
EHH?!
?!
I...I'M OPEN TO IT...
Fret
Fret
CHII?
SO EASY!
YOU SHOULD COME ALONG, TOO, YAMADA-SAN.
URM... ER...
THIS IS BAD!! THIS IS EXTREMELY BAD!
Let's exchange digits.
TO THINK THAT THE WALL COULD BE BROKEN SO EASILY!!

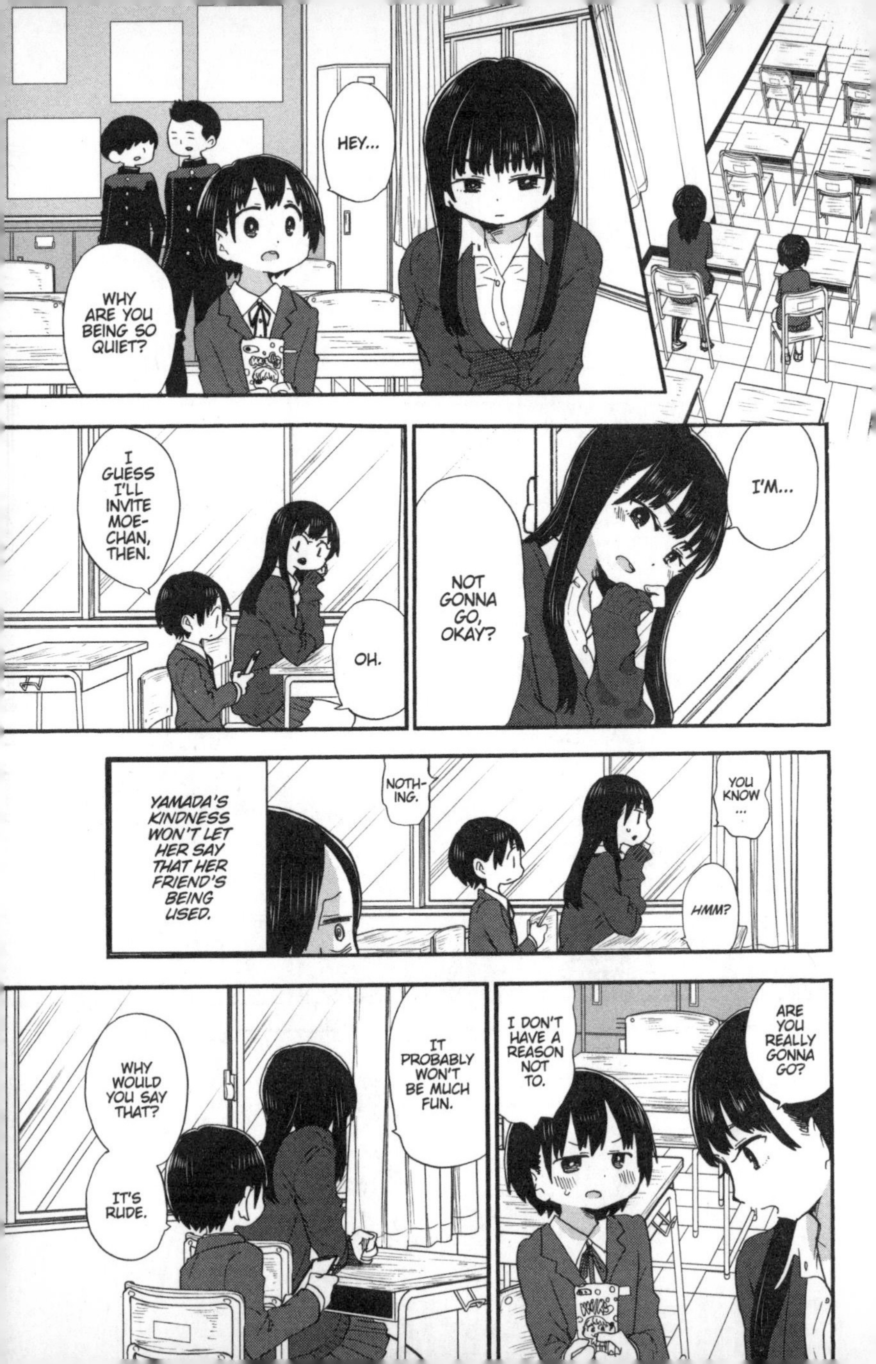
HEY...
WHY ARE YOU BEING SO QUIET?
I'M...
NOT GONNA GO, OKAY?
OH.
I GUESS I'LL INVITE MOE-CHAN, THEN.
YOU KNOW...
HMM?
NOTH-ING.
YAMADA'S KINDNESS WON'T LET HER SAY THAT HER FRIEND'S BEING USED.
ARE YOU REALLY GONNA GO?
I DON'T HAVE A REASON NOT TO.
IT PROBABLY WON'T BE MUCH FUN.
WHY WOULD YOU SAY THAT?
IT'S RUDE.

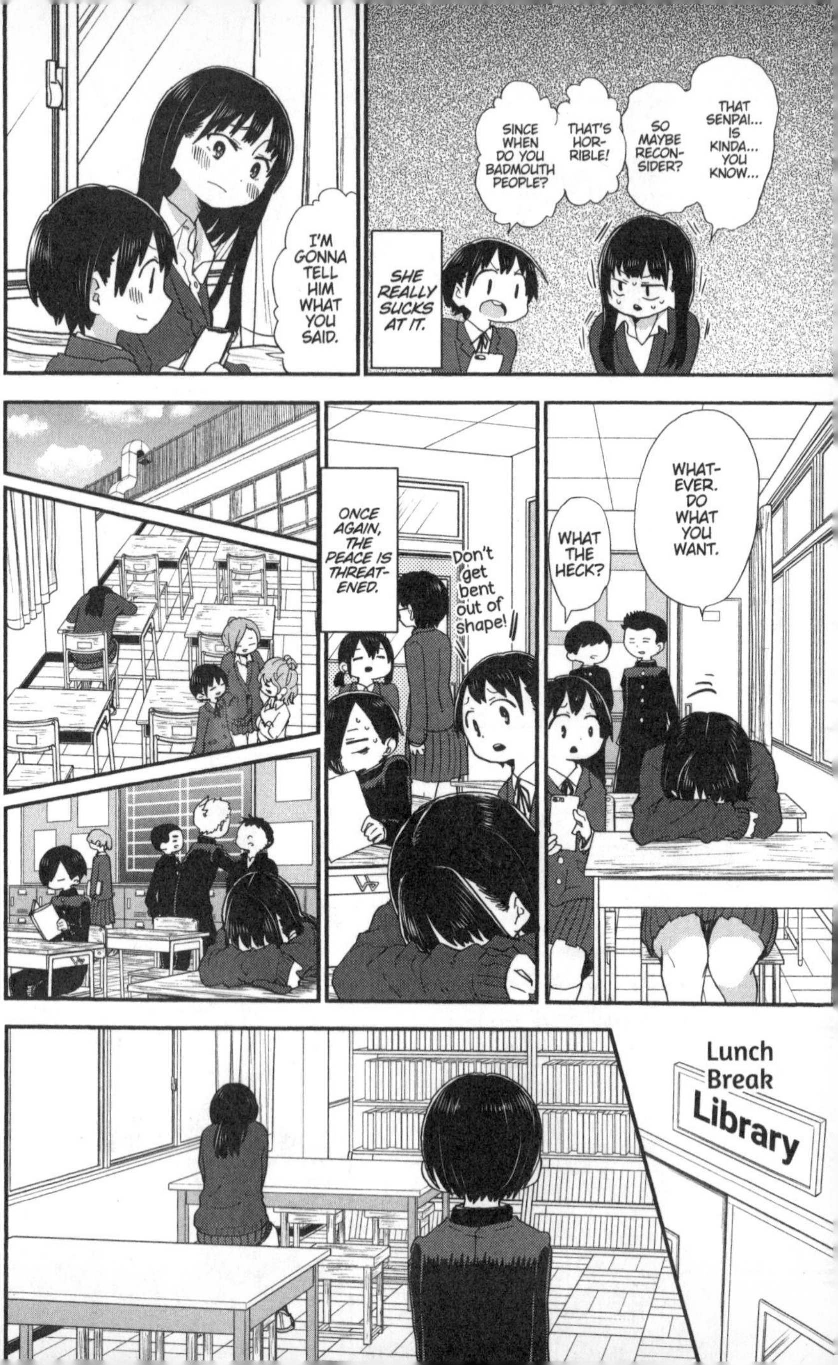
THAT SENPAI... IS KINDA... YOU KNOW...
SO MAYBE RECONSIDER?
THAT'S HORRIBLE!
SINCE WHEN DO YOU BADMOUTH PEOPLE?
SHE REALLY SUCKS AT IT.
I'M GONNA TELL HIM WHAT YOU SAID.
WHATEVER. DO WHAT YOU WANT.
WHAT THE HECK?
Don't get bent out of shape!
ONCE AGAIN, THE PEACE IS THREATENED.
Lunch Break
Library

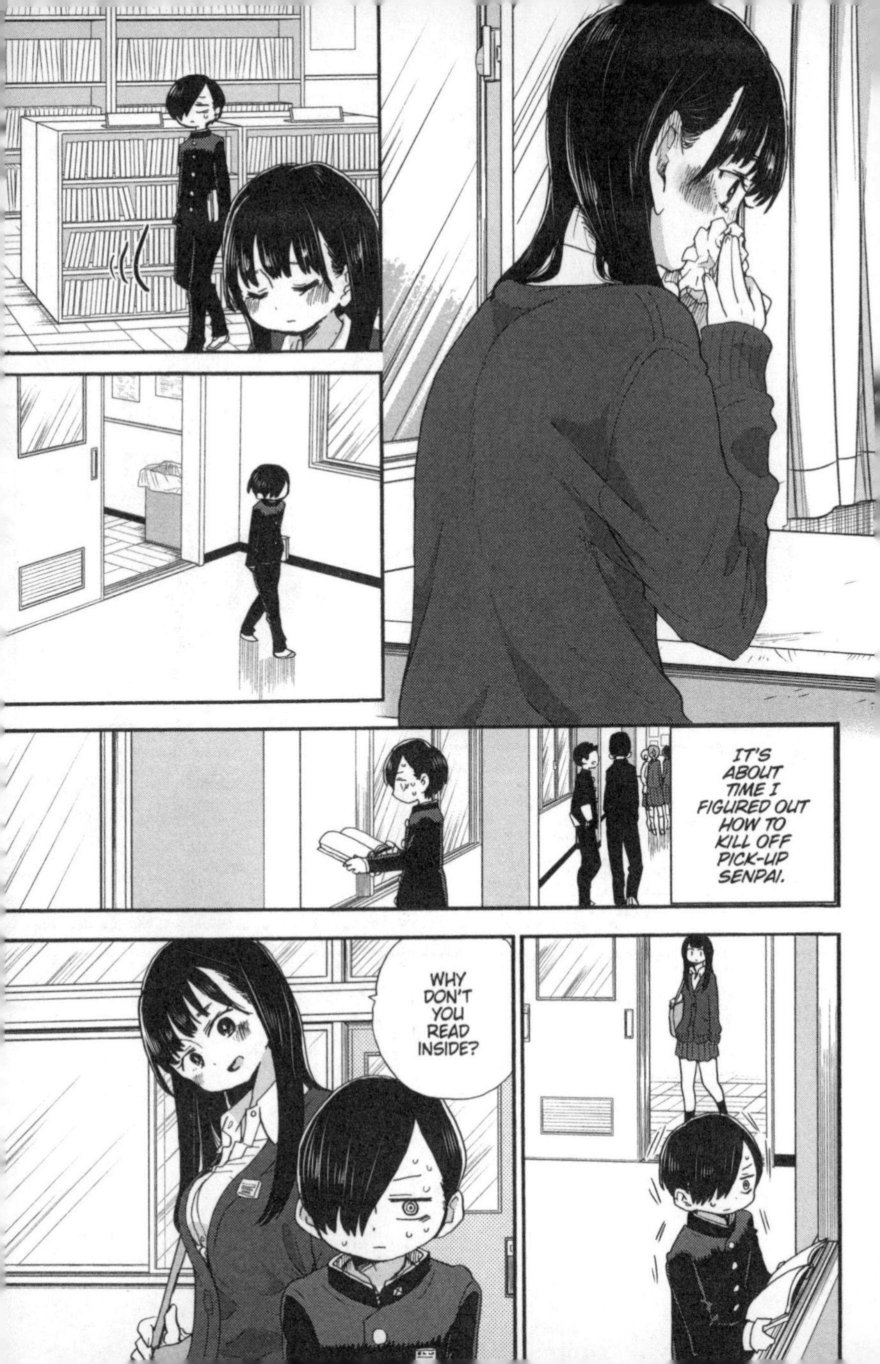
IT'S ABOUT TIME I FIGURED OUT HOW TO KILL OFF PICK-UP SENPAI.
WHY DON'T YOU READ INSIDE?

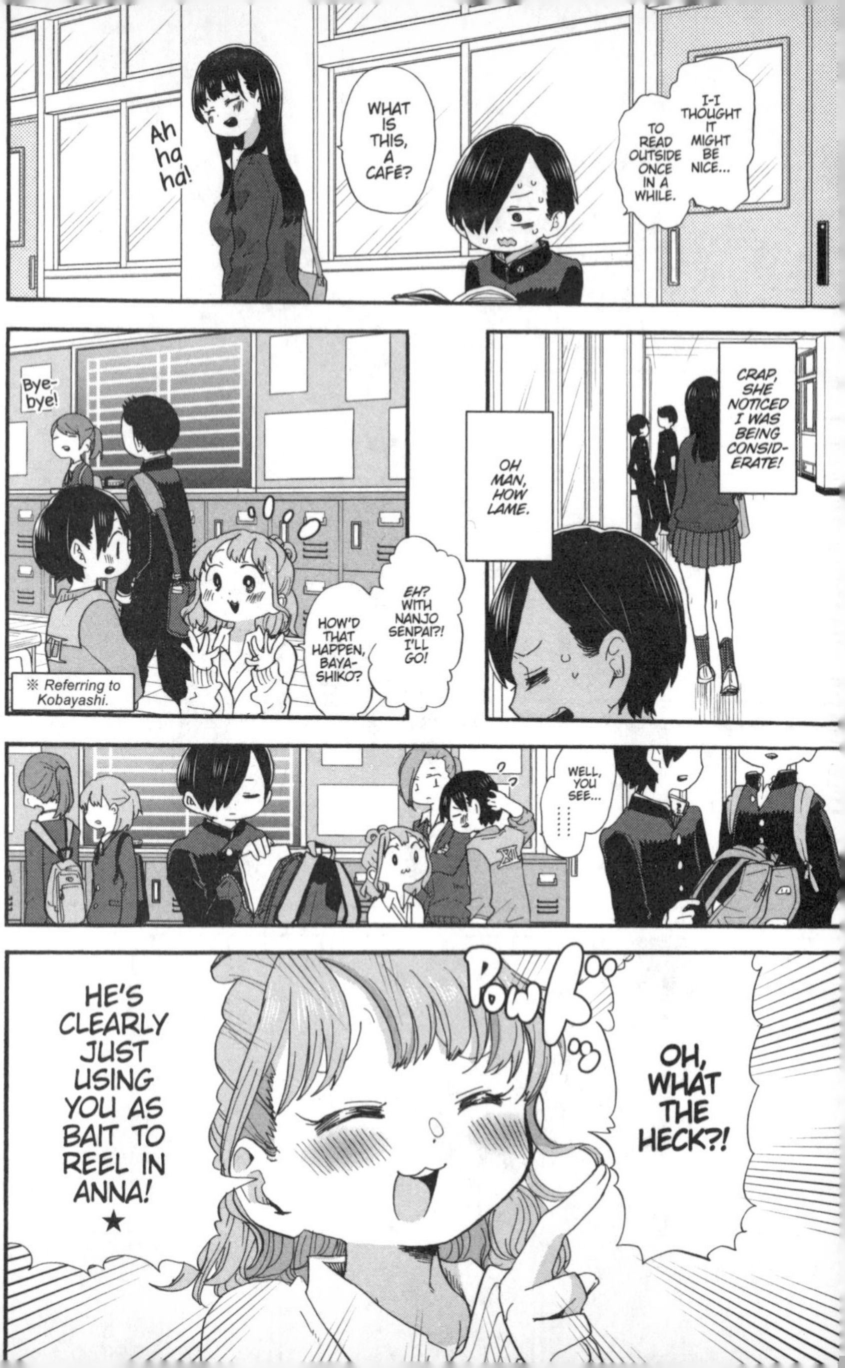
I-I THOUGHT IT MIGHT BE NICE... TO READ OUTSIDE ONCE IN A WHILE.
WHAT IS THIS, A CAFÉ?
Ah ha ha!
CRAP, SHE NOTICED I WAS BEING CONSIDERATE!
OH MAN, HOW LAME.
EH? WITH NANJO SENPAI?! I'LL GO!
HOW'D THAT HAPPEN, BAYASHIKO?
Bye-bye!
※ Referring to Kobayashi.
WELL, YOU SEE... ......
OH, WHAT THE HECK?!
Powk...
HE'S CLEARLY JUST USING YOU AS BAIT TO REEL IN ANNA! ★

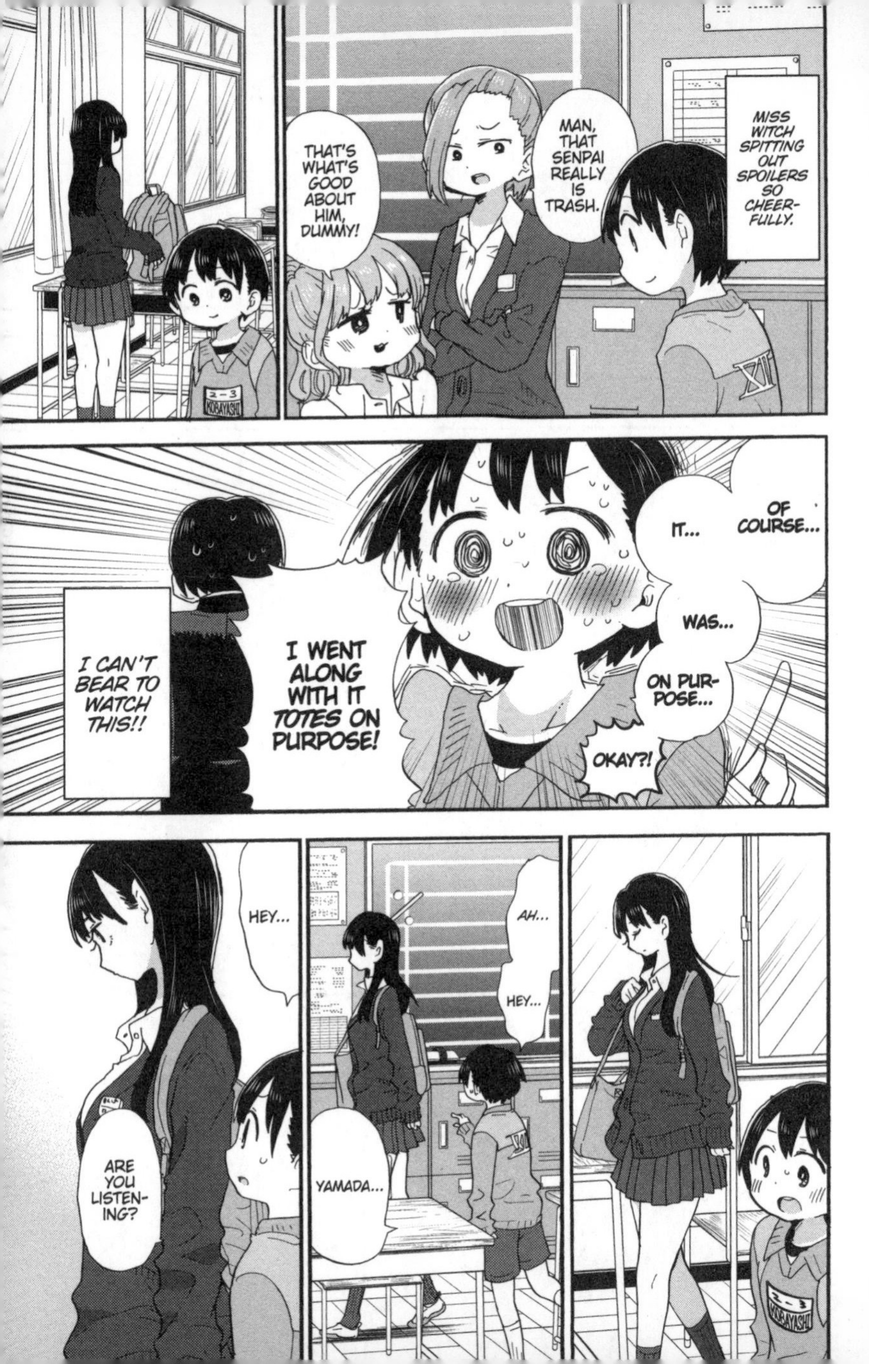
MISS WITCH SPITTING OUT SPOILERS SO CHEERFULLY.
MAN, THAT SENPAI REALLY IS TRASH.
THAT'S WHAT'S GOOD ABOUT HIM, DUMMY!
OF COURSE...
IT...
WAS...
ON PURPOSE...
OKAY?!
I WENT ALONG WITH IT *TOTES* ON PURPOSE!
I CAN'T BEAR TO WATCH THIS!!
AH...
HEY...
YAMADA...
HEY...
ARE YOU LISTENING?

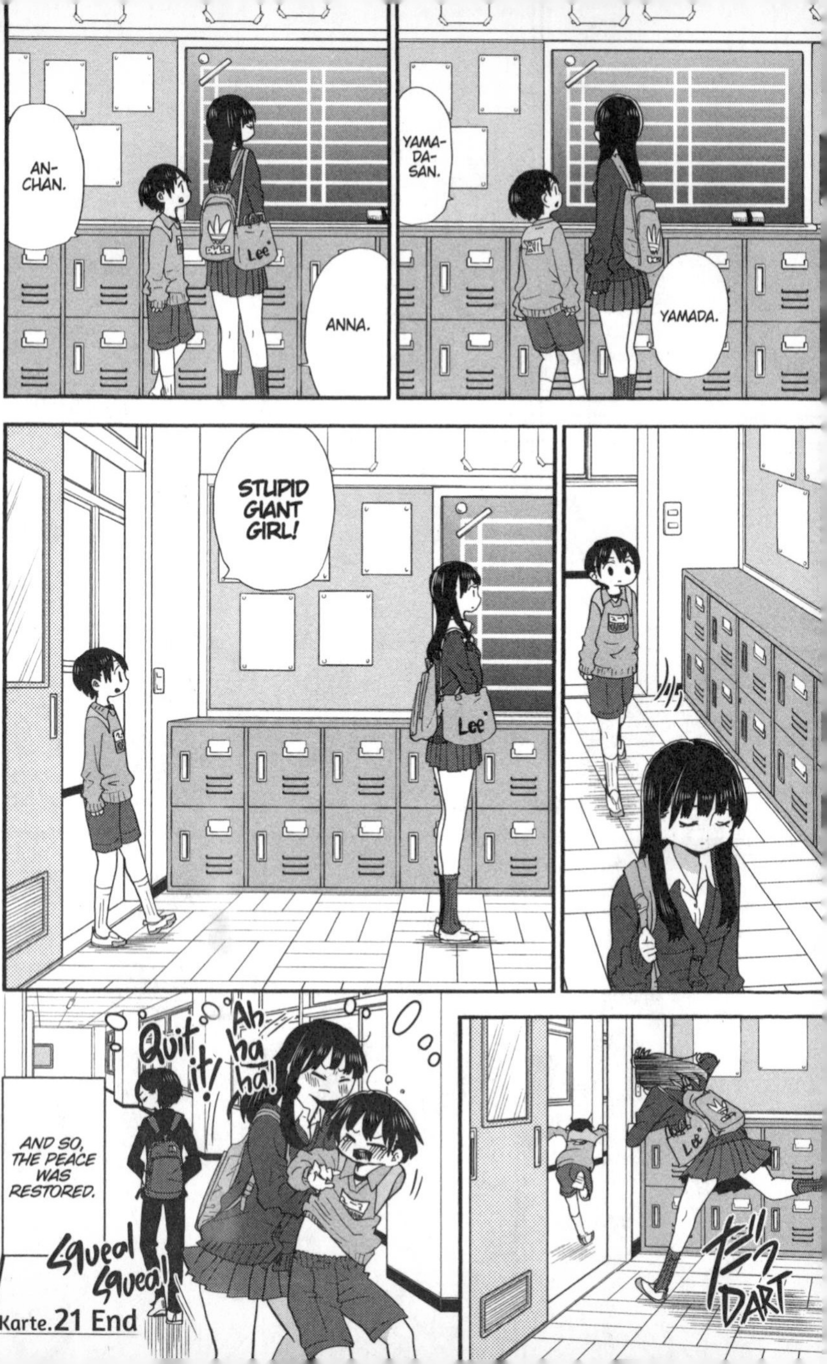
YAMADA-SAN.
YAMADA.
AN-CHAN.
ANNA.
STUPID GIANT GIRL!
DART
Ah ha ha!
Quit it!
AND SO, THE PEACE WAS RESTORED.
Squeal squeal
Karte.21 End

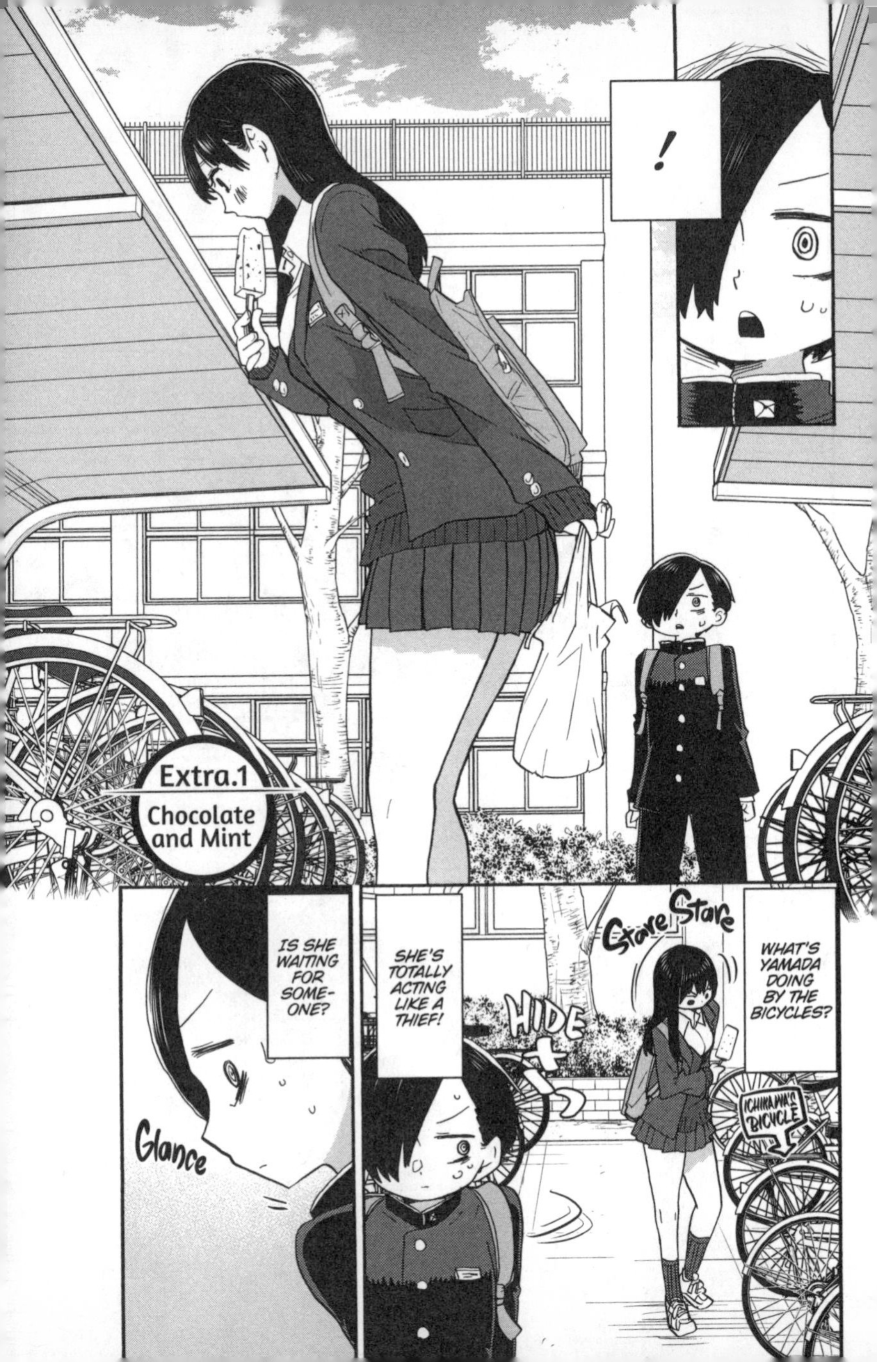
!
Extra.1
Chocolate and Mint
WHAT'S YAMADA DOING BY THE BICYCLES?
Stare Stare
ICHIKAWA'S BICYCLE
HIDE
SHE'S TOTALLY ACTING LIKE A THIEF!
IS SHE WAITING FOR SOME-ONE?
Glance

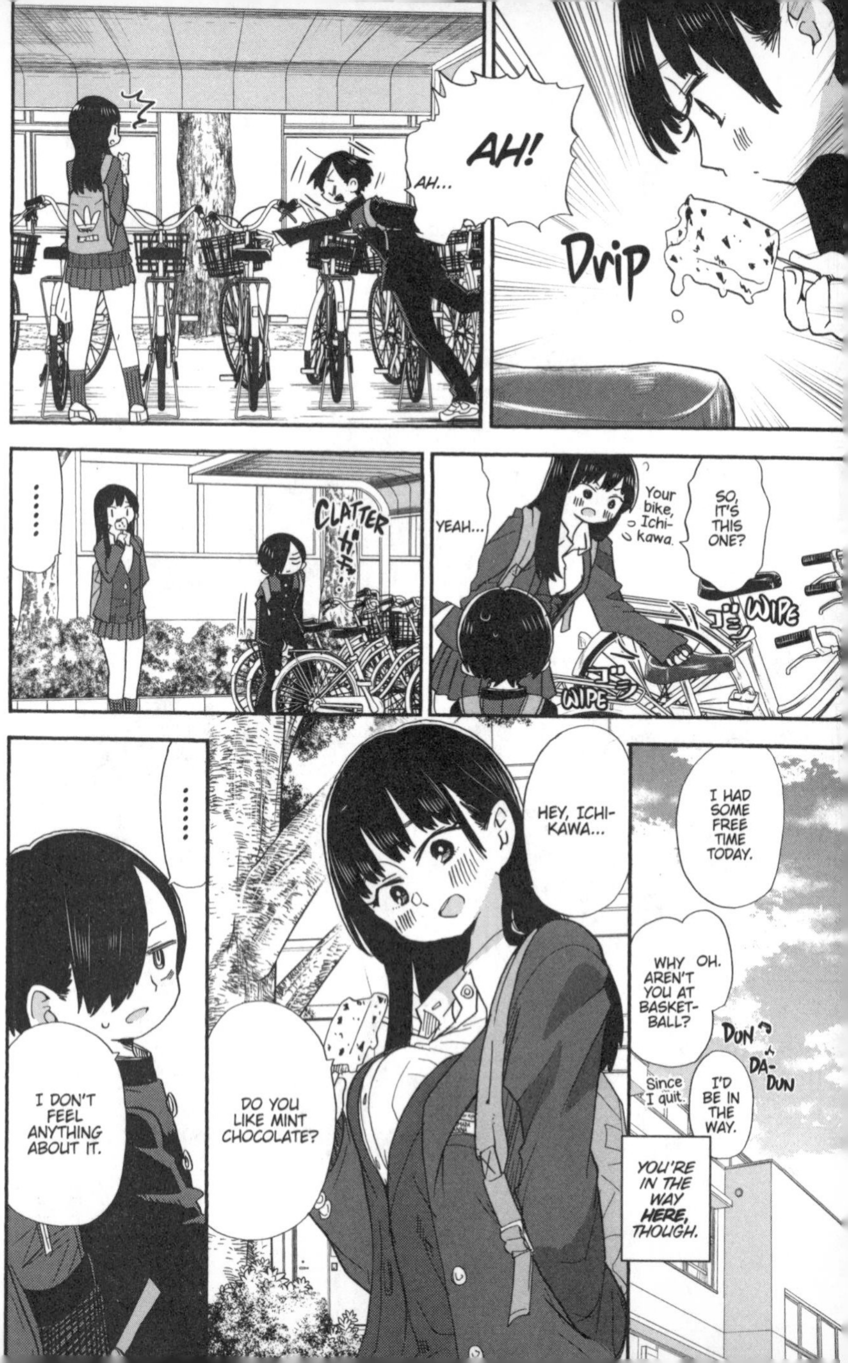
AH!
Drip
AH...
SO, IT'S THIS ONE?
Your bike, Ichikawa.
YEAH...
WIPE
WIPE
......
CLATTER
I HAD SOME FREE TIME TODAY.
OH.
WHY AREN'T YOU AT BASKETBALL?
I'D BE IN THE WAY.
Since I quit.
DUN DA-DUN
YOU'RE IN THE WAY HERE, THOUGH.
HEY, ICHIKAWA...
DO YOU LIKE MINT CHOCOLATE?
......
I DON'T FEEL ANYTHING ABOUT IT.

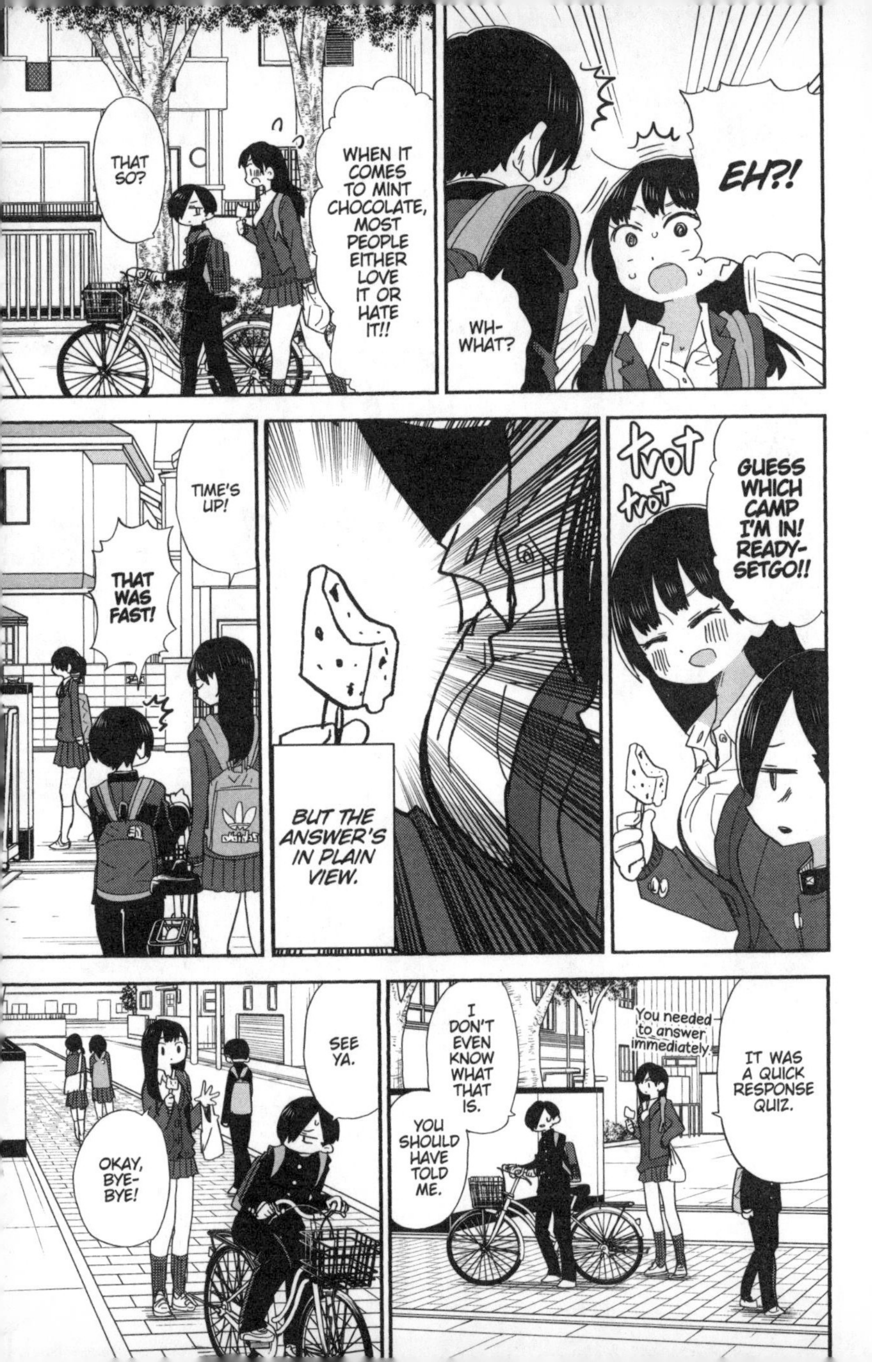
EH?!
WH-WHAT?
WHEN IT COMES TO MINT CHOCOLATE, MOST PEOPLE EITHER LOVE IT OR HATE IT!!
THAT SO?
trot trot
GUESS WHICH CAMP I'M IN! READY-SETGO!!
BUT THE ANSWER'S IN PLAIN VIEW.
TIME'S UP!
THAT WAS FAST!
IT WAS A QUICK RESPONSE QUIZ.
You needed to answer immediately.
I DON'T EVEN KNOW WHAT THAT IS.
YOU SHOULD HAVE TOLD ME.
SEE YA.
OKAY, BYE-BYE!

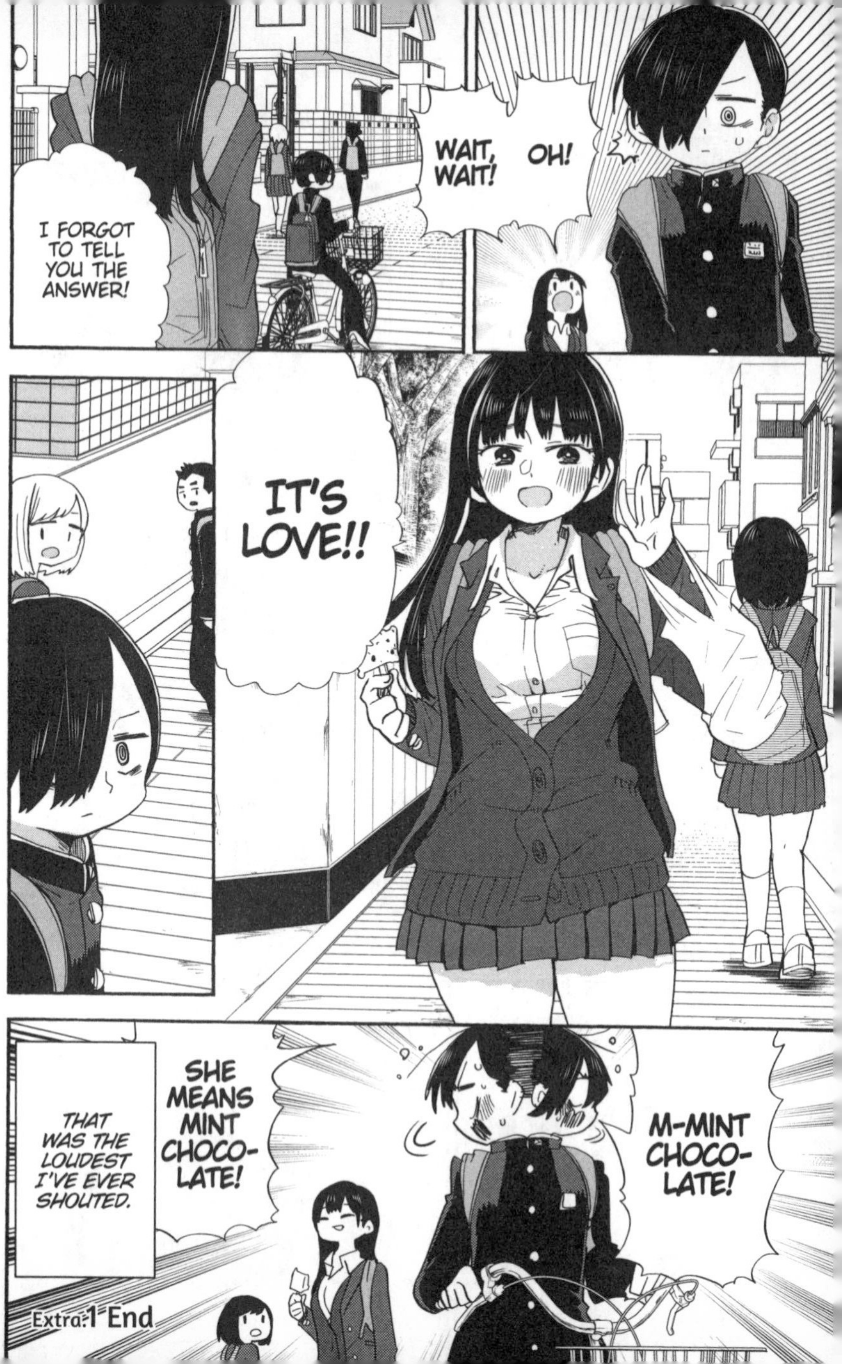
OH!
WAIT, WAIT!
I FORGOT TO TELL YOU THE ANSWER!
IT'S LOVE!!
M-MINT CHOCO-LATE!
SHE MEANS MINT CHOCO-LATE!
THAT WAS THE LOUDEST I'VE EVER SHOUTED.
Extra:1 End

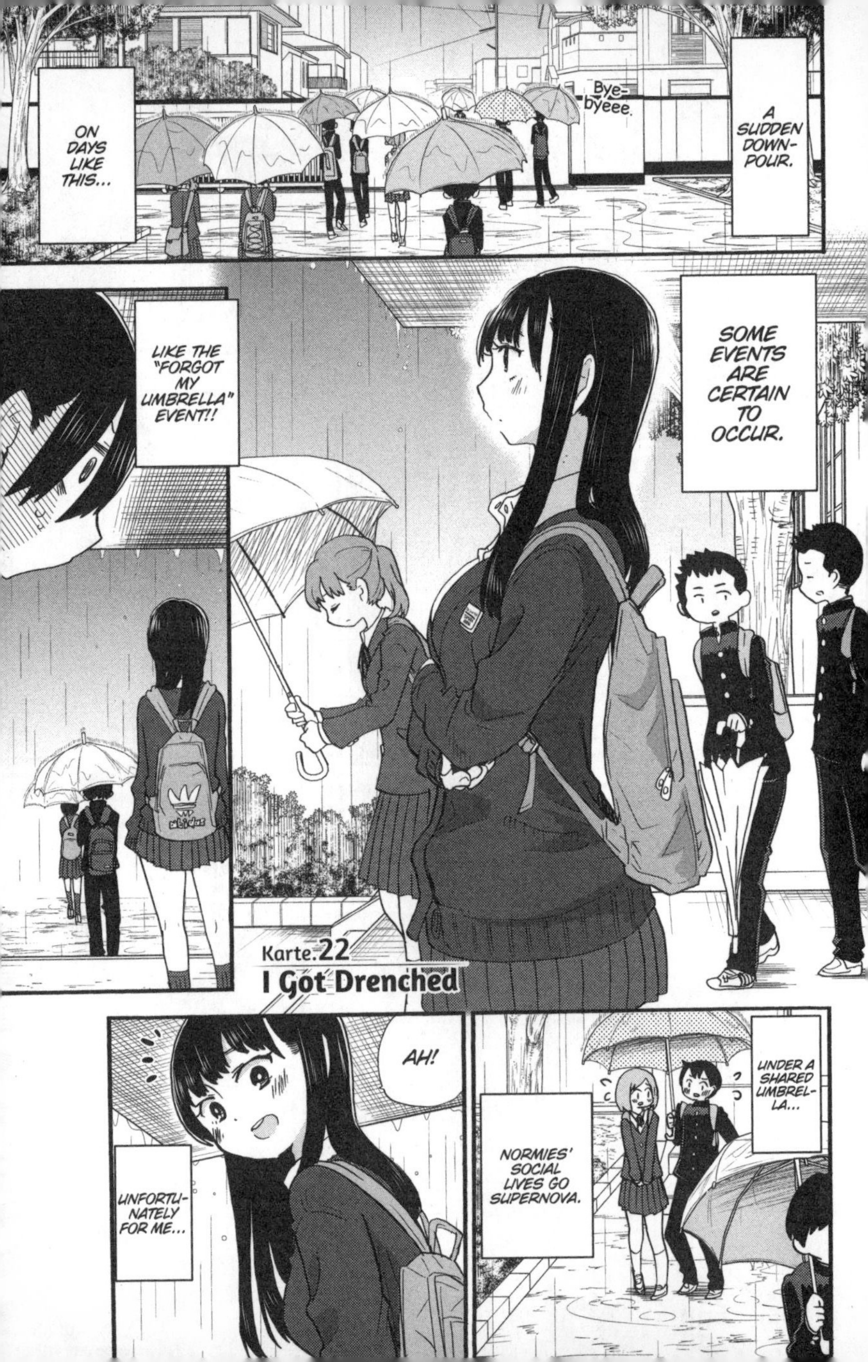
A SUDDEN DOWNPOUR.
Bye-byeee.
ON DAYS LIKE THIS...
SOME EVENTS ARE CERTAIN TO OCCUR.
Karte.22
I Got Drenched
LIKE THE "FORGOT MY UMBRELLA" EVENT!!
UNDER A SHARED UMBRELLA...
NORMIES' SOCIAL LIVES GO SUPERNOVA.
AH!
UNFORTUNATELY FOR ME...

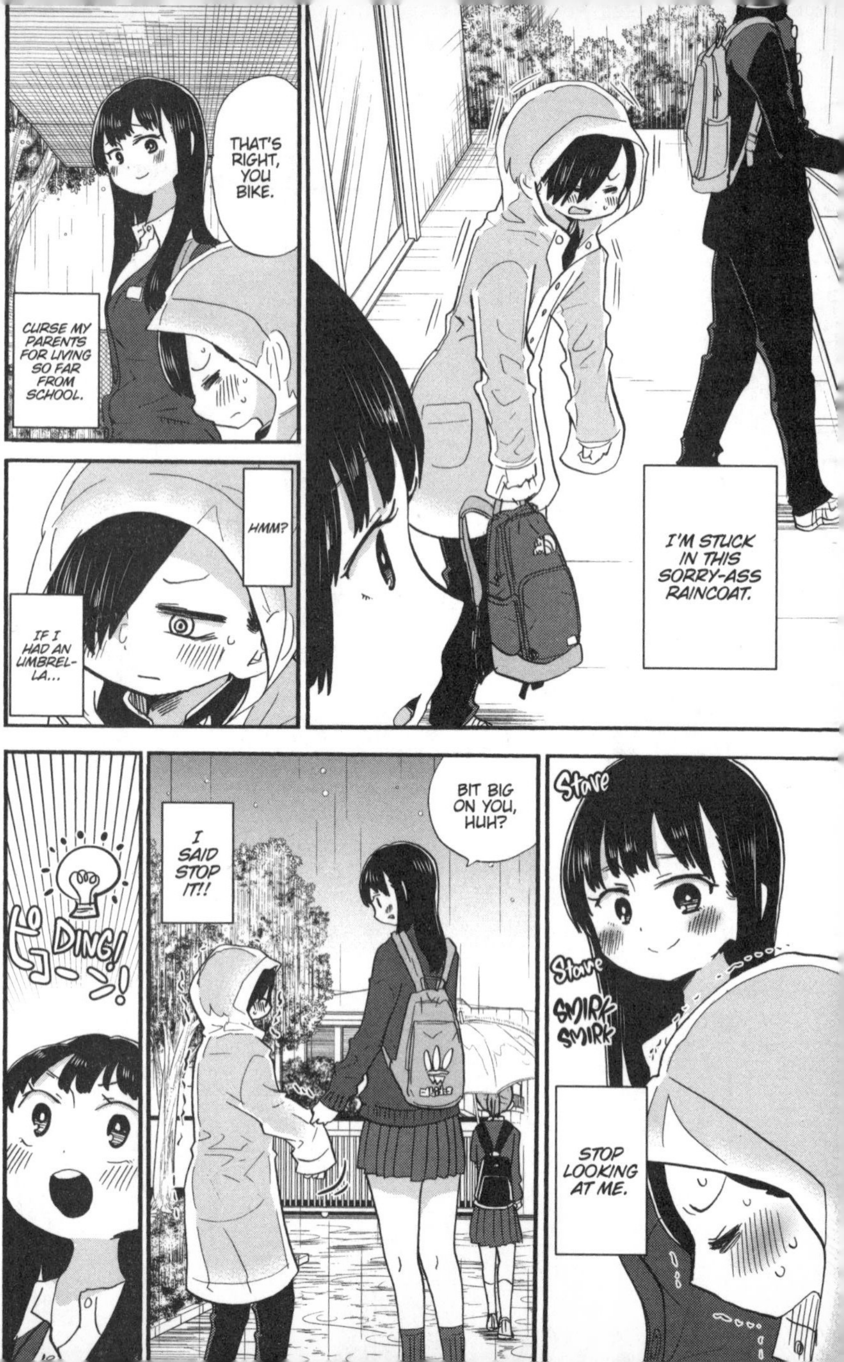
I'M STUCK IN THIS SORRY-ASS RAINCOAT.
THAT'S RIGHT, YOU BIKE.
CURSE MY PARENTS FOR LIVING SO FAR FROM SCHOOL.
HMM?
IF I HAD AN UMBREL-LA...
Stare
Stare
SMIRK SMIRK
STOP LOOKING AT ME.
BIT BIG ON YOU, HUH?
I SAID STOP IT!!
DING!
ピコーン!

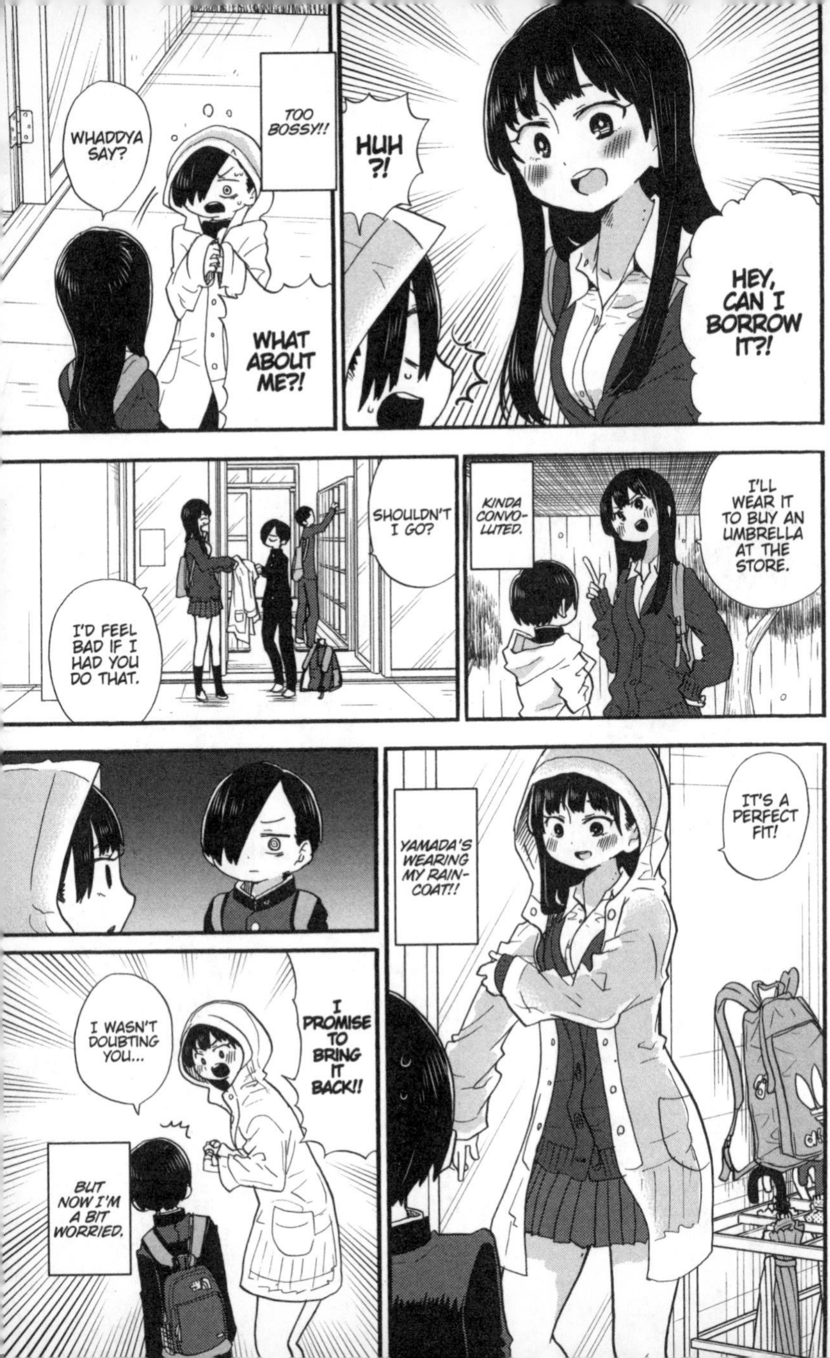
HEY, CAN I BORROW IT?!
HUH ?!
TOO BOSSY!!
WHADDYA SAY?
WHAT ABOUT ME?!
I'LL WEAR IT TO BUY AN UMBRELLA AT THE STORE.
KINDA CONVOLUTED.
SHOULDN'T I GO?
I'D FEEL BAD IF I HAD YOU DO THAT.
IT'S A PERFECT FIT!
YAMADA'S WEARING MY RAIN-COAT!!
I PROMISE TO BRING IT BACK!!
I WASN'T DOUBTING YOU...
BUT NOW I'M A BIT WORRIED.

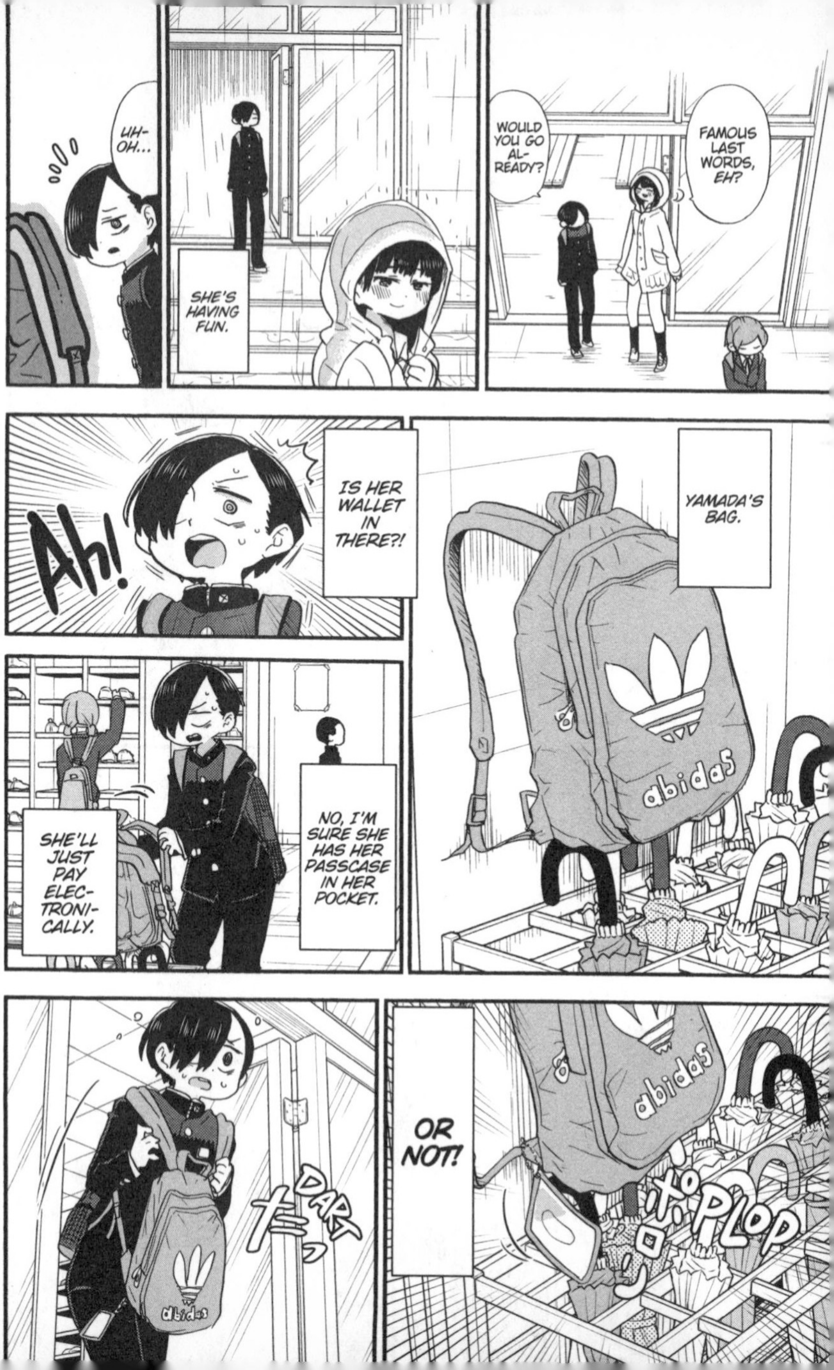
FAMOUS LAST WORDS, EH?
WOULD YOU GO AL-READY?
SHE'S HAVING FUN.
UH-OH...
YAMADA'S BAG.
abidas
IS HER WALLET IN THERE?!
Ah!
NO, I'M SURE SHE HAS HER PASSCASE IN HER POCKET.
SHE'LL JUST PAY ELEC-TRONI-CALLY.
OR NOT!
abidas
PLOP
DART
abidas

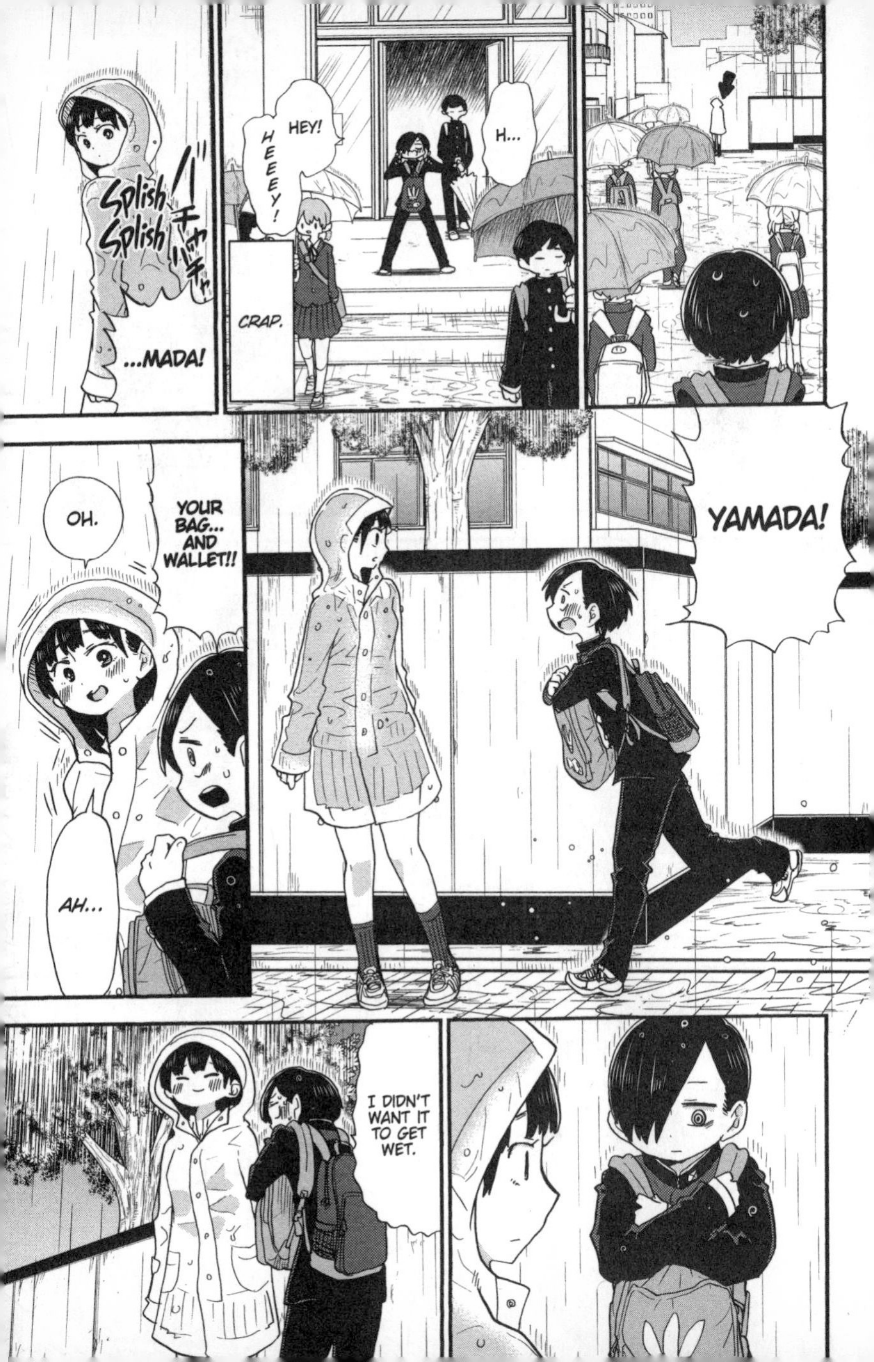
H...
HEY!
HEEEEY!
CRAP.
Splish Splish
...MADA!
YAMADA!
YOUR BAG... AND WALLET!!
OH.
AH...
...
I DIDN'T WANT IT TO GET WET.

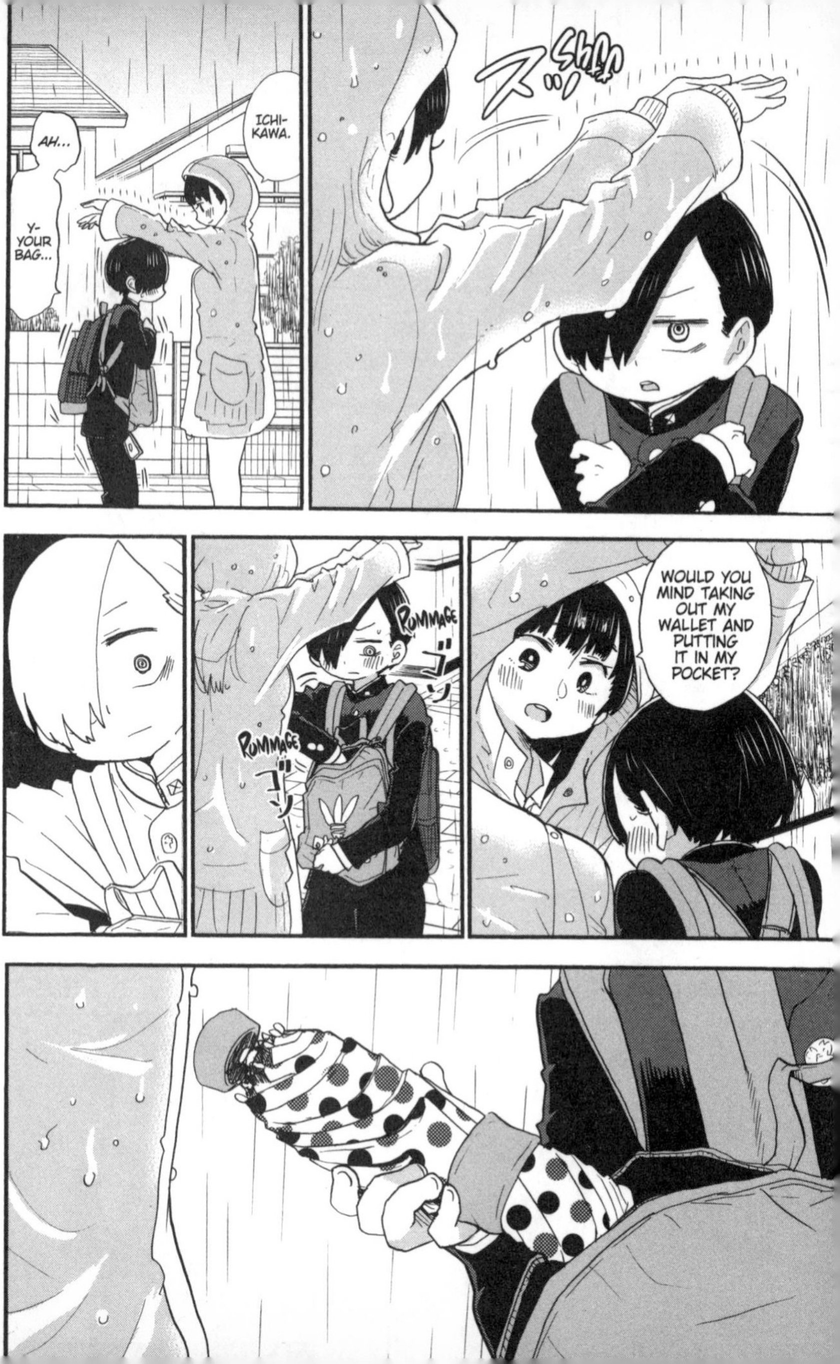
スッ
ICHI-KAWA.
AH...
Y-YOUR BAG...
WOULD YOU MIND TAKING OUT MY WALLET AND PUTTING IT IN MY POCKET?
RUMMAGE
ゴソ
RUMMAGE
ゴソ

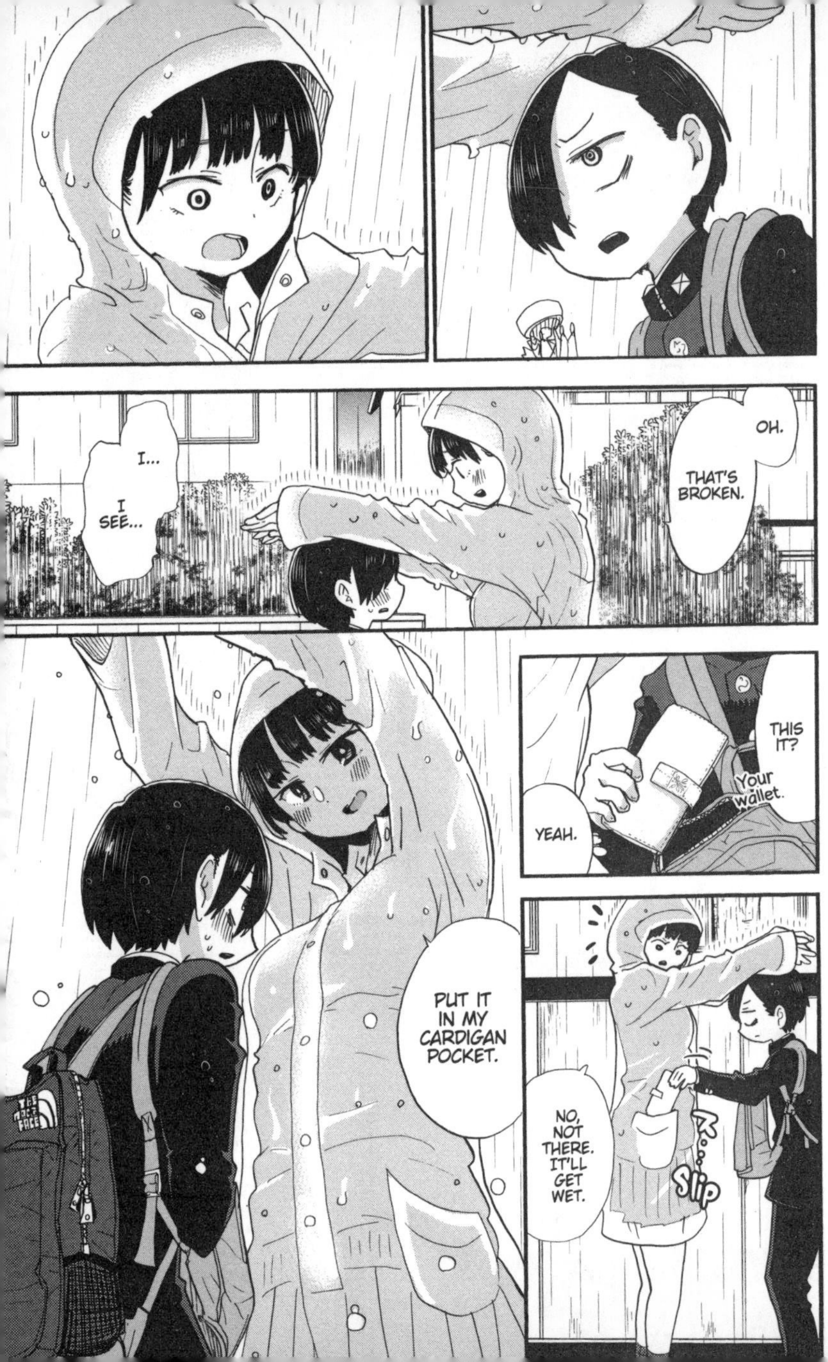
OH.
THAT'S BROKEN.
I...
I SEE...
THIS IT?
Your wallet.
YEAH.
NO, NOT THERE. IT'LL GET WET.
Slip
PUT IT IN MY CARDIGAN POCKET.

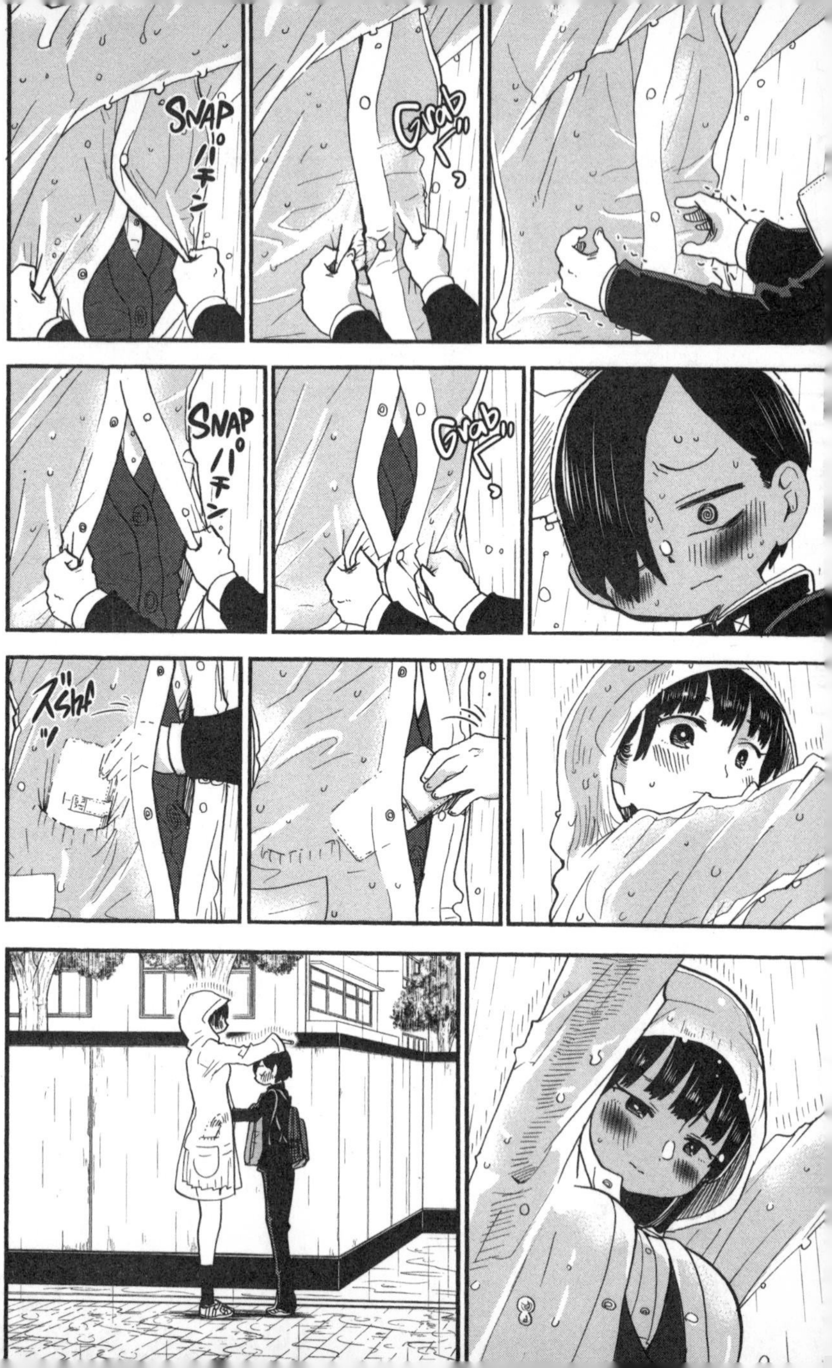
Grab
ぐっ
SNAP
パチン
Grab
ぐっ
SNAP
パチン
ズShf
ッ

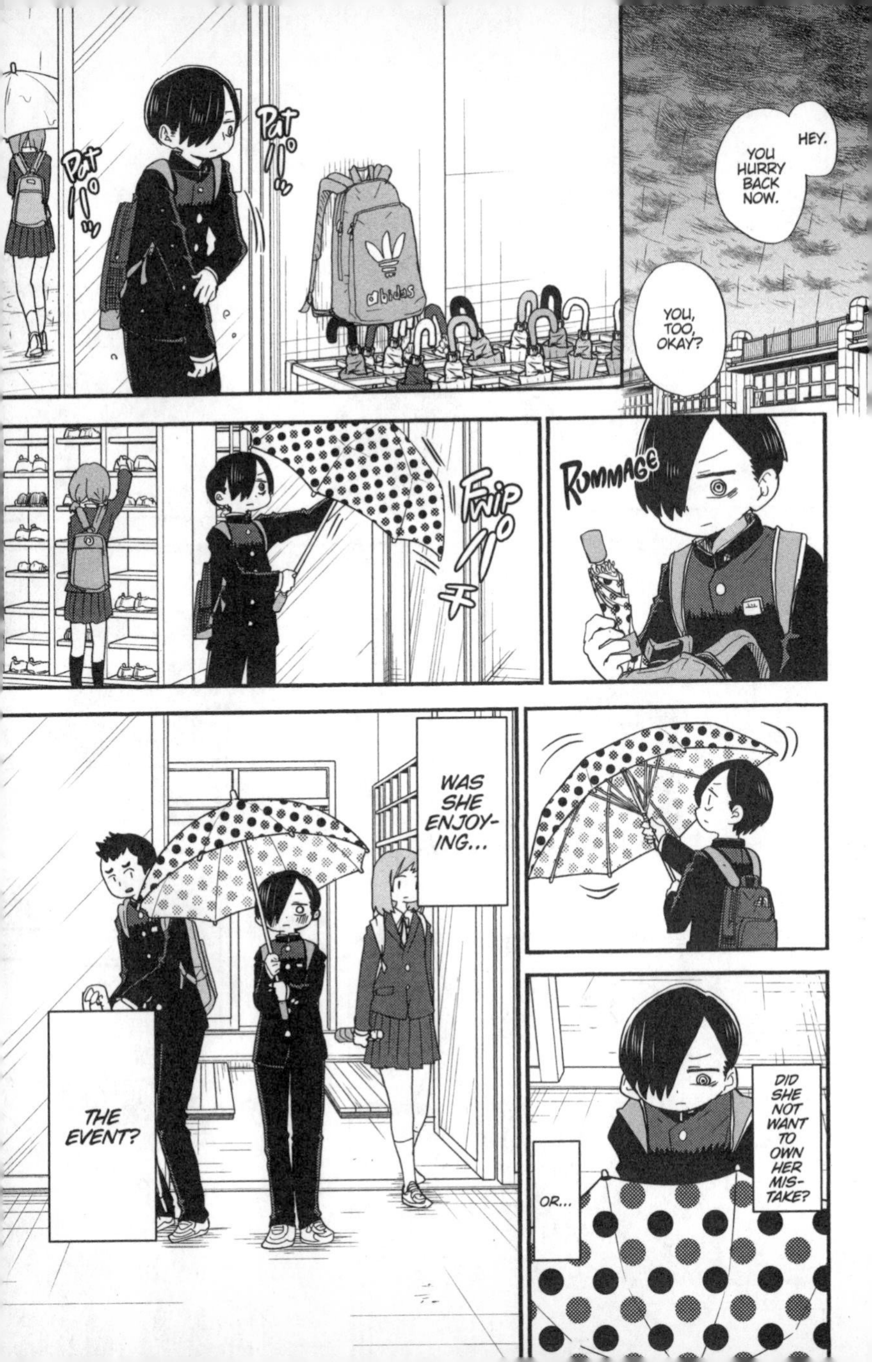
HEY.
YOU HURRY BACK NOW.
YOU, TOO, OKAY?
Pat
Pat
RUMMAGE
Fwip
DID SHE NOT WANT TO OWN HER MIS-TAKE?
OR...
WAS SHE ENJOY-ING...
THE EVENT?

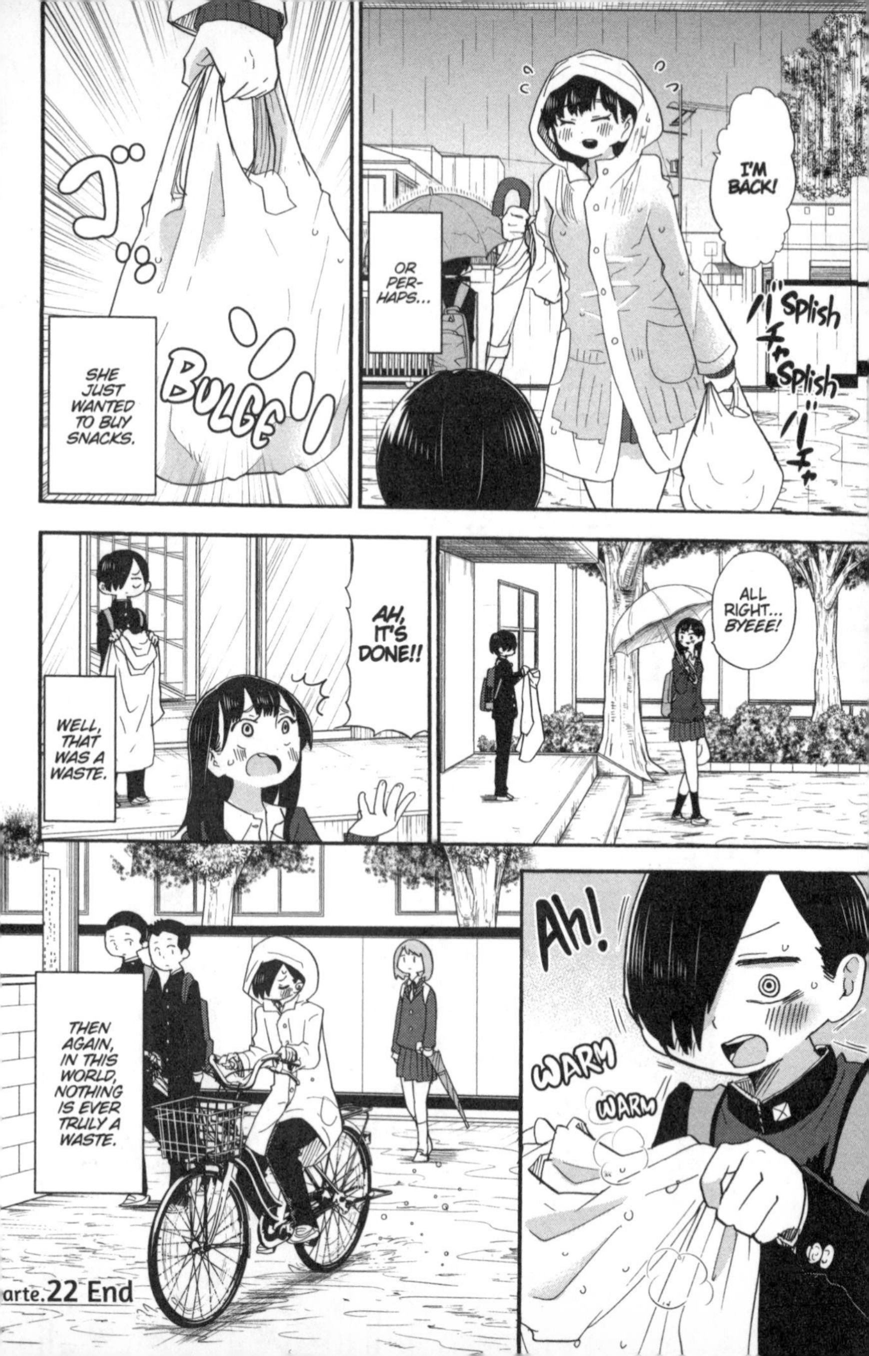
I'M BACK!
OR PER-HAPS...
Splish
パチャ
Splish
パチャ
BULGE
SHE JUST WANTED TO BUY SNACKS.
ALL RIGHT... BYEEE!
AH, IT'S DONE!!
WELL, THAT WAS A WASTE.
Ah!
WARM
WARM
THEN AGAIN, IN THIS WORLD, NOTHING IS EVER TRULY A WASTE.
arte.22 End

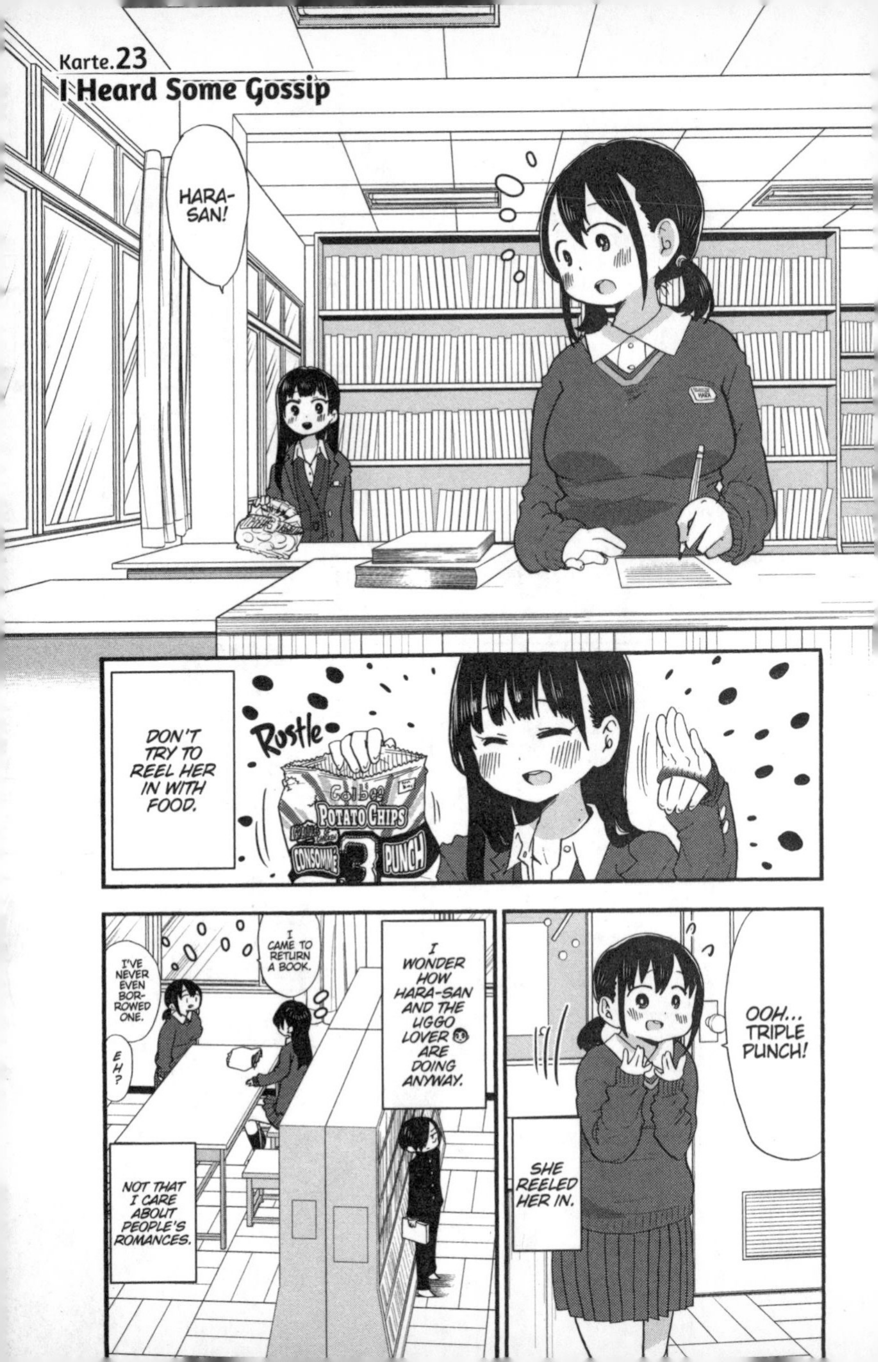
Karte.23
I Heard Some Gossip
HARA-SAN!
Rustle
DON'T TRY TO REEL HER IN WITH FOOD.
POTATO CHIPS
CONSOMME
3
PUNCH
OOH... TRIPLE PUNCH!
SHE REELED HER IN.
I WONDER HOW HARA-SAN AND THE UGGO LOVER ARE DOING ANYWAY.
I CAME TO RETURN A BOOK.
I'VE NEVER EVEN BORROWED ONE.
EH?
NOT THAT I CARE ABOUT PEOPLE'S ROMANCES.

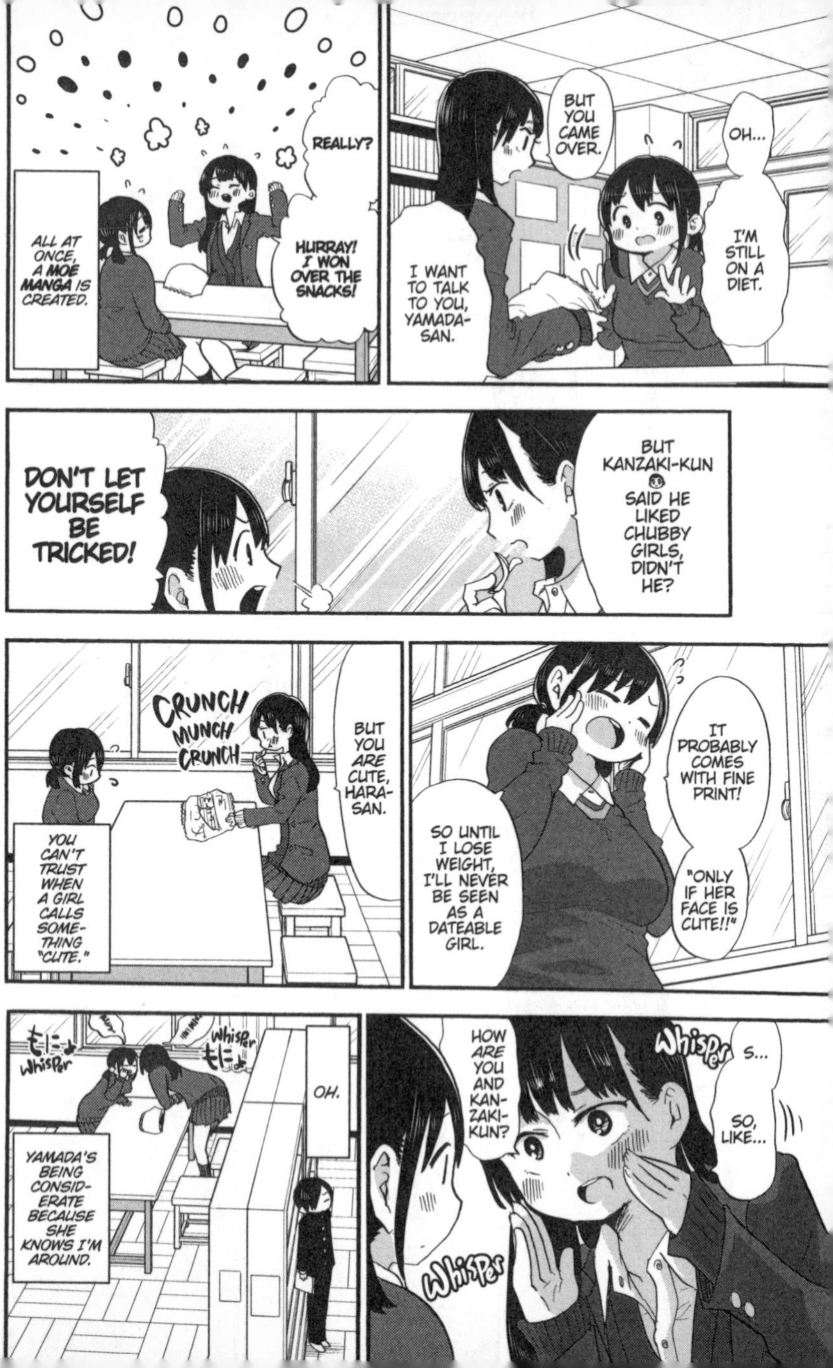
OH...
I'M STILL ON A DIET.
BUT YOU CAME OVER.
I WANT TO TALK TO YOU, YAMADA-SAN.
REALLY?
HURRAY! I WON OVER THE SNACKS!
ALL AT ONCE, A MOE MANGA IS CREATED.
BUT KANZAKI-KUN SAID HE LIKED CHUBBY GIRLS, DIDN'T HE?
DON'T LET YOURSELF BE TRICKED!
IT PROBABLY COMES WITH FINE PRINT!
"ONLY IF HER FACE IS CUTE!!"
SO UNTIL I LOSE WEIGHT, I'LL NEVER BE SEEN AS A DATEABLE GIRL.
BUT YOU ARE CUTE, HARA-SAN.
CRUNCH MUNCH CRUNCH
YOU CAN'T TRUST WHEN A GIRL CALLS SOME-THING "CUTE."
Whisper
S...
SO, LIKE...
HOW ARE YOU AND KAN-ZAKI-KUN?
Whisper
OH.
Whisper もにょ
もにょ Whisper
YAMADA'S BEING CONSID-ERATE BECAUSE SHE KNOWS I'M AROUND.

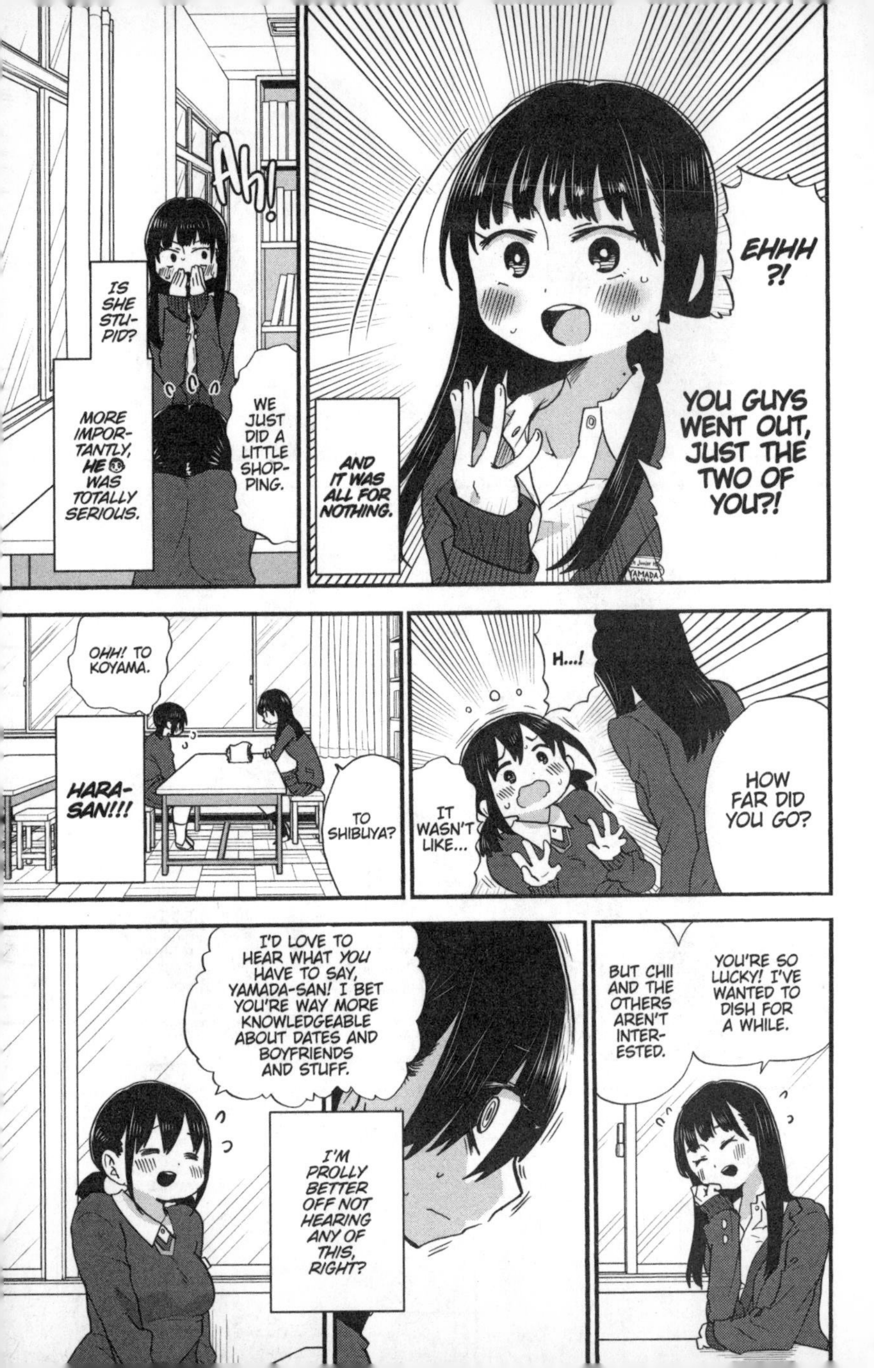
EHHH ?!
YOU GUYS WENT OUT, JUST THE TWO OF YOU?!
AND IT WAS ALL FOR NOTHING.
Ah!
IS SHE STUPID?
WE JUST DID A LITTLE SHOPPING.
MORE IMPORTANTLY, HE ☺ WAS TOTALLY SERIOUS.
HOW FAR DID YOU GO?
H...!
IT WASN'T LIKE...
TO SHIBUYA?
OHH! TO KOYAMA.
HARA-SAN!!!
YOU'RE SO LUCKY! I'VE WANTED TO DISH FOR A WHILE.
BUT CHII AND THE OTHERS AREN'T INTERESTED.
I'D LOVE TO HEAR WHAT YOU HAVE TO SAY, YAMADA-SAN! I BET YOU'RE WAY MORE KNOWLEDGEABLE ABOUT DATES AND BOYFRIENDS AND STUFF.
I'M PROLLY BETTER OFF NOT HEARING ANY OF THIS, RIGHT?

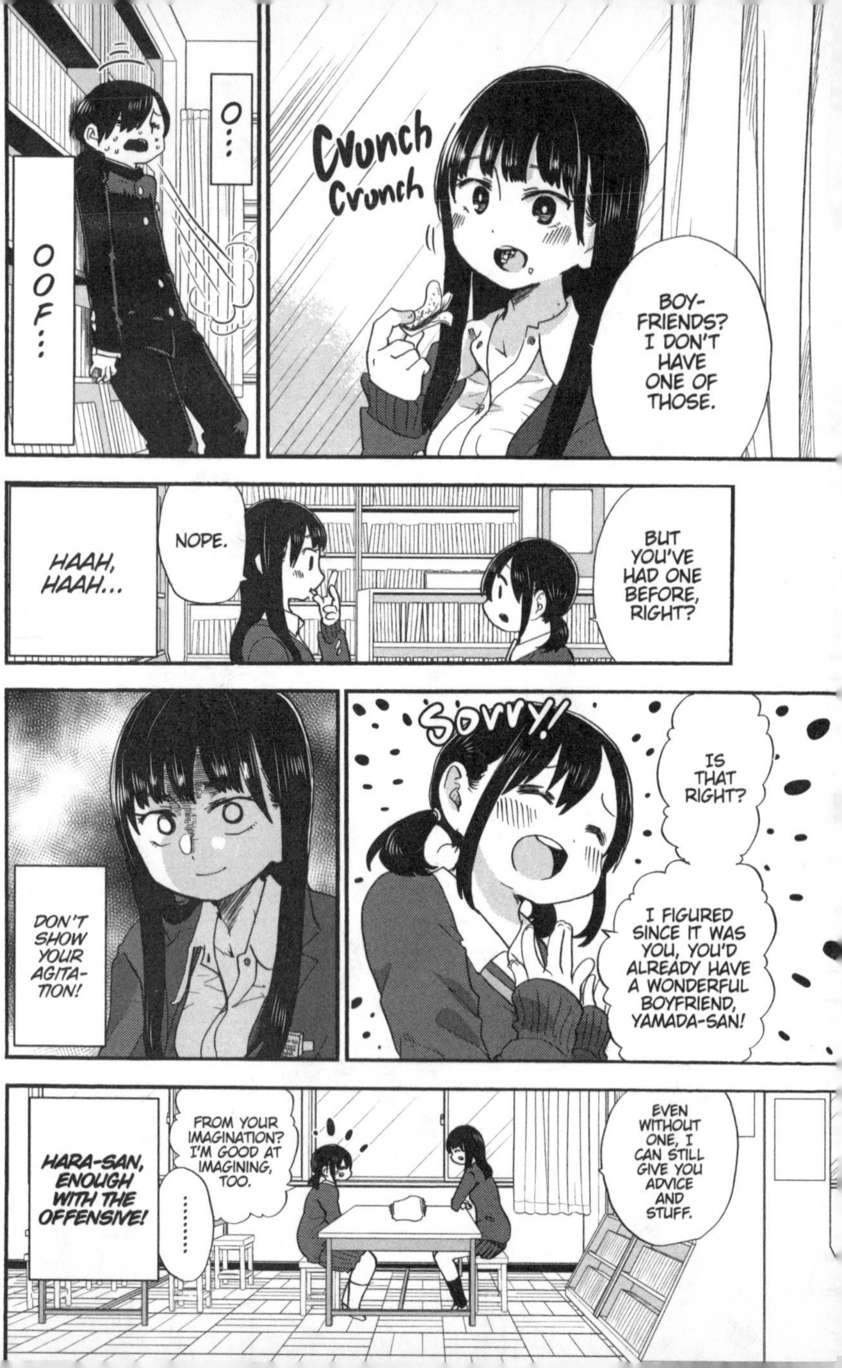
Crunch Crunch
BOY-FRIENDS? I DON'T HAVE ONE OF THOSE.
O...
OOF...
BUT YOU'VE HAD ONE BEFORE, RIGHT?
NOPE.
HAAH, HAAH...
Sorry!
IS THAT RIGHT?
I FIGURED SINCE IT WAS YOU, YOU'D ALREADY HAVE A WONDERFUL BOYFRIEND, YAMADA-SAN!
DON'T SHOW YOUR AGITA-TION!
EVEN WITHOUT ONE, I CAN STILL GIVE YOU ADVICE AND STUFF.
FROM YOUR IMAGINATION? I'M GOOD AT IMAGINING, TOO.
......
HARA-SAN, ENOUGH WITH THE OFFENSIVE!

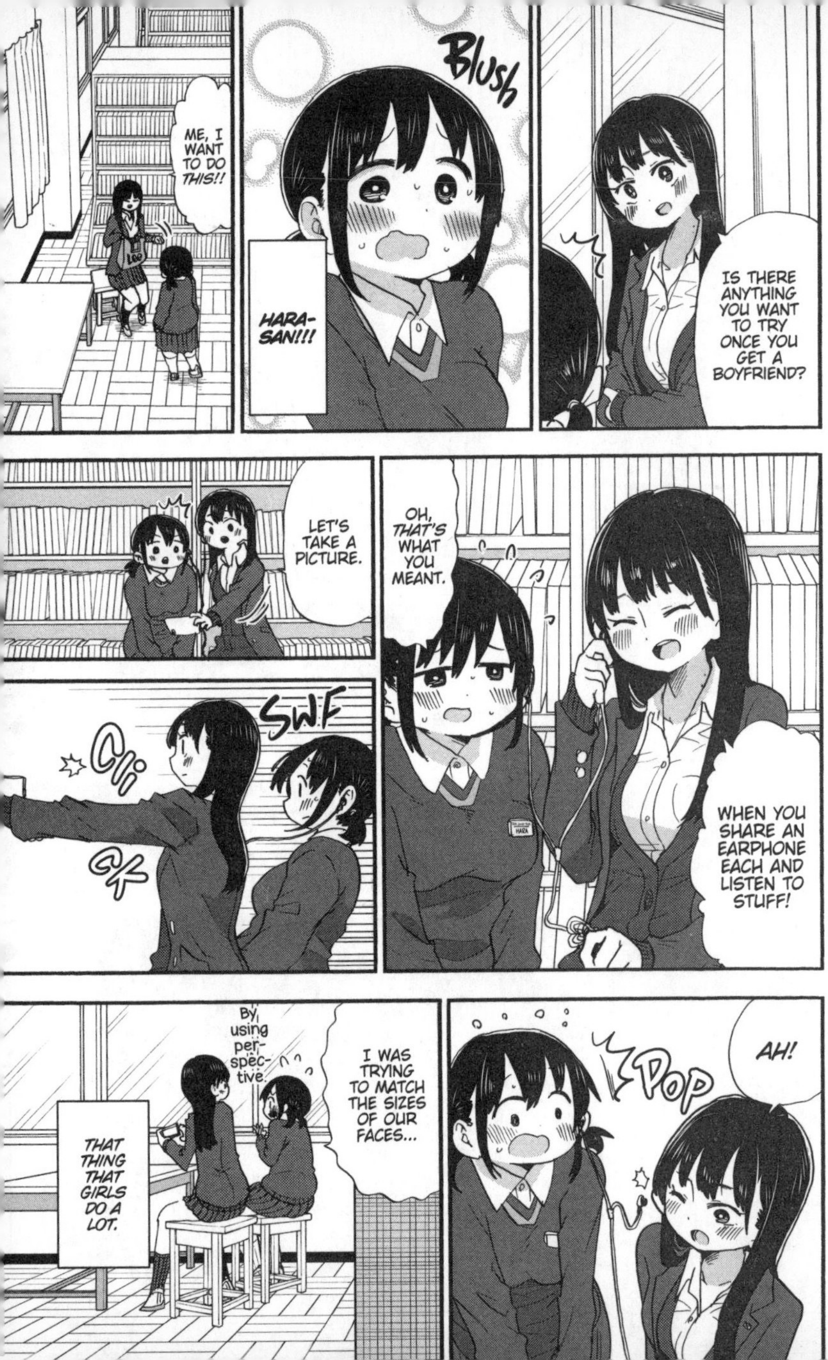
IS THERE ANYTHING YOU WANT TO TRY ONCE YOU GET A BOYFRIEND?
Blush
HARA-SAN!!!
ME, I WANT TO DO THIS!!
WHEN YOU SHARE AN EARPHONE EACH AND LISTEN TO STUFF!
OH, THAT'S WHAT YOU MEANT.
LET'S TAKE A PICTURE.
SWF
Click
AH!
Pop
I WAS TRYING TO MATCH THE SIZES OF OUR FACES...
By using per-spec-tive.
THAT THING THAT GIRLS DO A LOT.

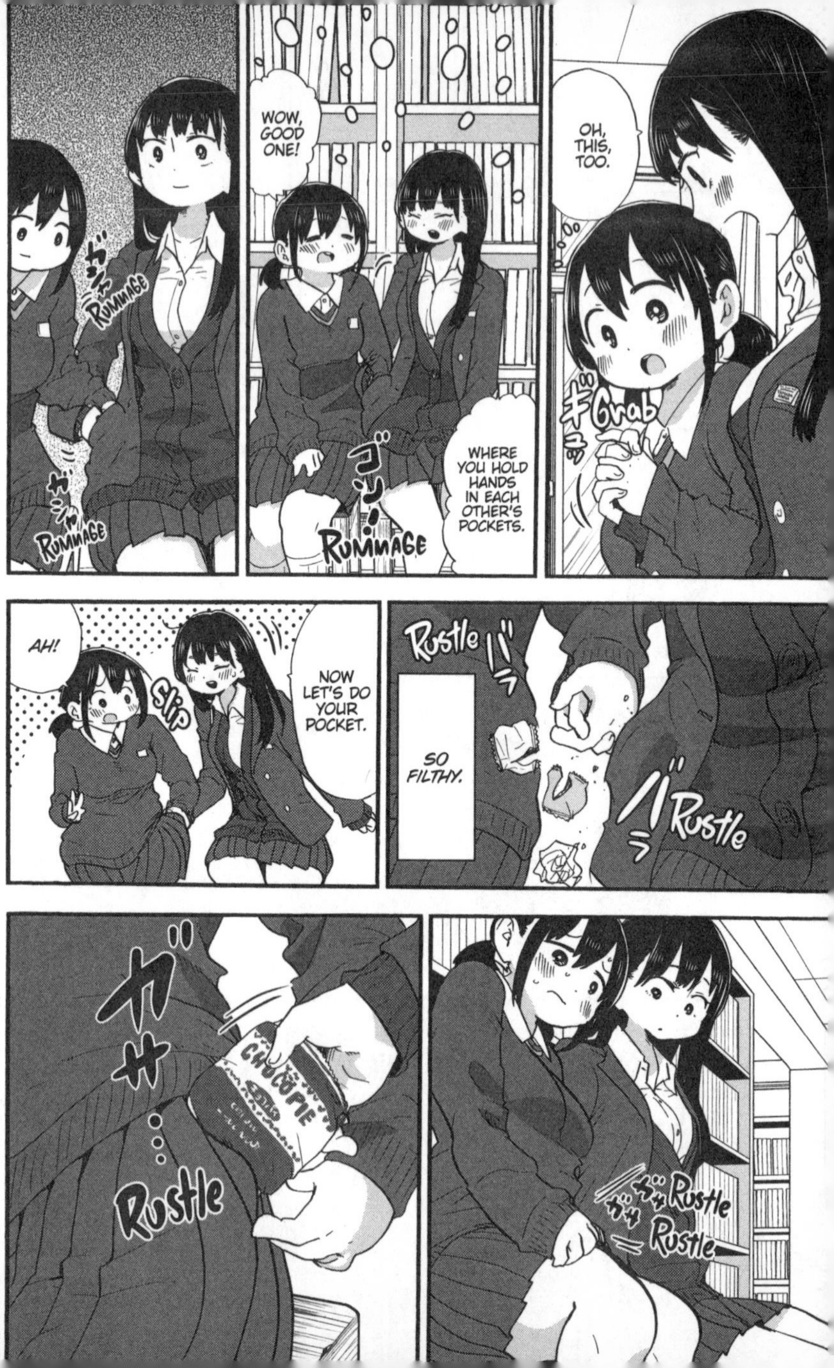
OH, THIS, TOO.
Grab
WOW, GOOD ONE!
WHERE YOU HOLD HANDS IN EACH OTHER'S POCKETS.
RUMMAGE
RUMMAGE
RUMMAGE
Rustle
SO FILTHY.
Rustle
NOW LET'S DO YOUR POCKET.
Slip
AH!
Rustle
Rustle
CHOCOPIE
...
Rustle

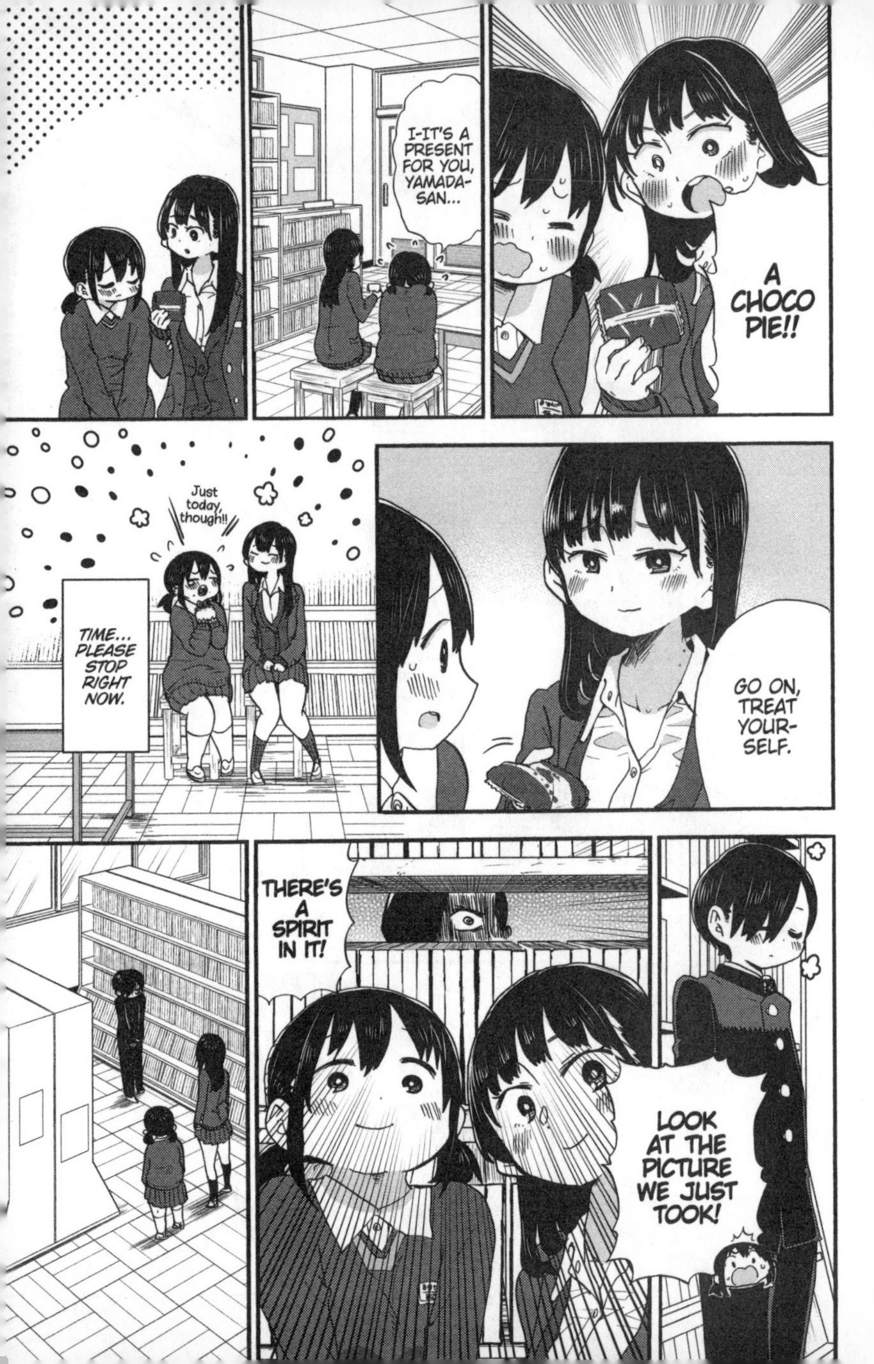
A CHOCO PIE!!
I-IT'S A PRESENT FOR YOU, YAMADA-SAN...
GO ON, TREAT YOURSELF.
Just today, though!!
TIME... PLEASE STOP RIGHT NOW.
LOOK AT THE PICTURE WE JUST TOOK!
THERE'S A SPIRIT IN IT!

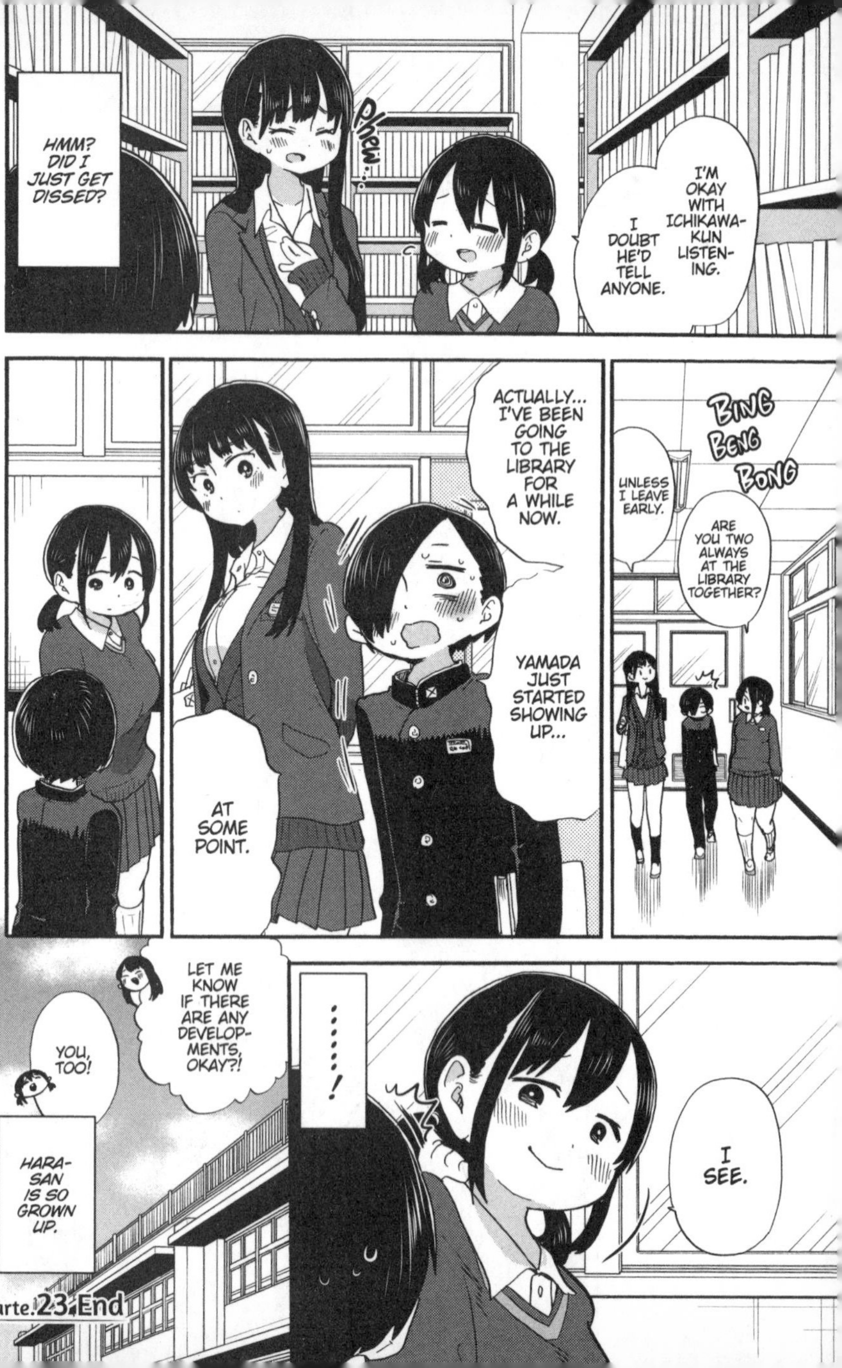
I'M OKAY WITH ICHIKAWA-KUN LISTEN-ING.
I DOUBT HE'D TELL ANYONE.
Phew...
HMM? DID I JUST GET DISSED?
BING BENG BONG
ARE YOU TWO ALWAYS AT THE LIBRARY TOGETHER?
UNLESS I LEAVE EARLY.
ACTUALLY... I'VE BEEN GOING TO THE LIBRARY FOR A WHILE NOW.
YAMADA JUST STARTED SHOWING UP...
AT SOME POINT.
I SEE.
......!
LET ME KNOW IF THERE ARE ANY DEVELOP-MENTS, OKAY?!
YOU, TOO!
HARA-SAN IS SO GROWN UP.
Karte. 23 End

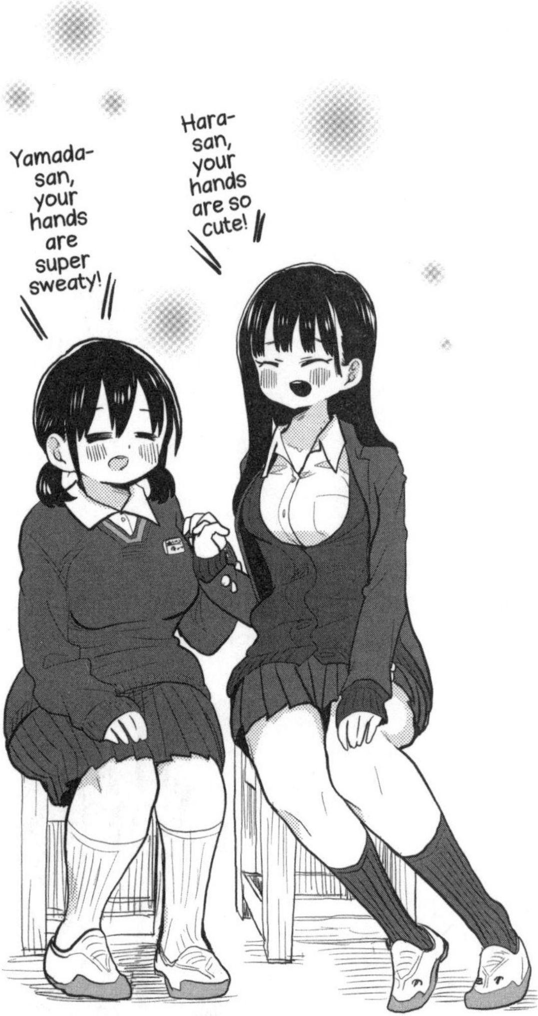
Hara-san, your hands are so cute!
Yamada-san, your hands are super sweaty!

The
Dangers
in My
Heart

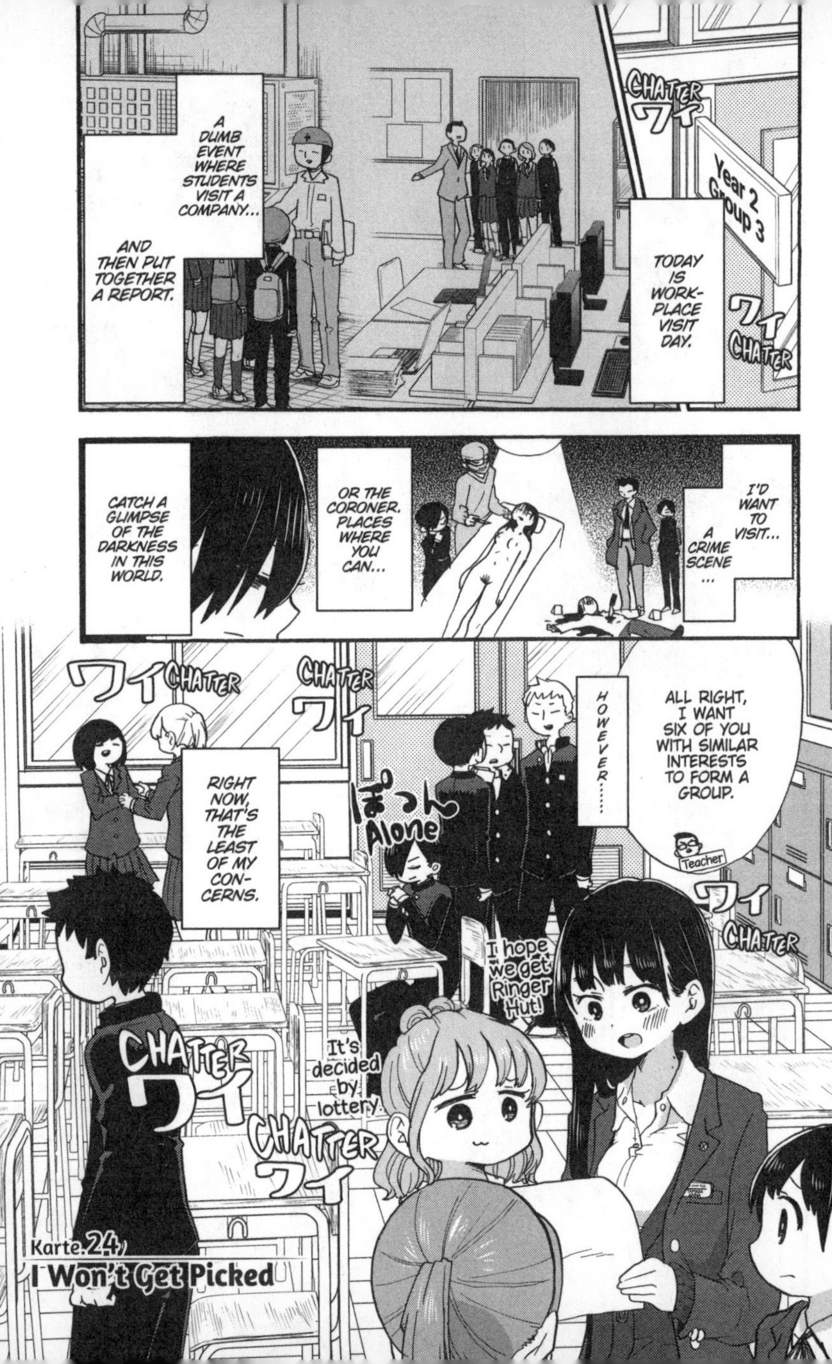
CHATTER ワイ
Year 2 Group 3
TODAY IS WORK-PLACE VISIT DAY.
ワイ CHATTER
A DUMB EVENT WHERE STUDENTS VISIT A COMPANY...
AND THEN PUT TOGETHER A REPORT.
I'D WANT TO VISIT...
A CRIME SCENE ...
OR THE CORONER. PLACES WHERE YOU CAN...
CATCH A GLIMPSE OF THE DARKNESS IN THIS WORLD.
ALL RIGHT, I WANT SIX OF YOU WITH SIMILAR INTERESTS TO FORM A GROUP.
Teacher
HOWEVER......
ワイ CHATTER
CHATTER ワイ
ワイ CHATTER
RIGHT NOW, THAT'S THE LEAST OF MY CONCERNS.
ぽつん Alone
I hope we get Ringer Hut!
It's decided by lottery.
CHATTER ワイ
CHATTER ワイ
Karte.24
I Won't Get Picked

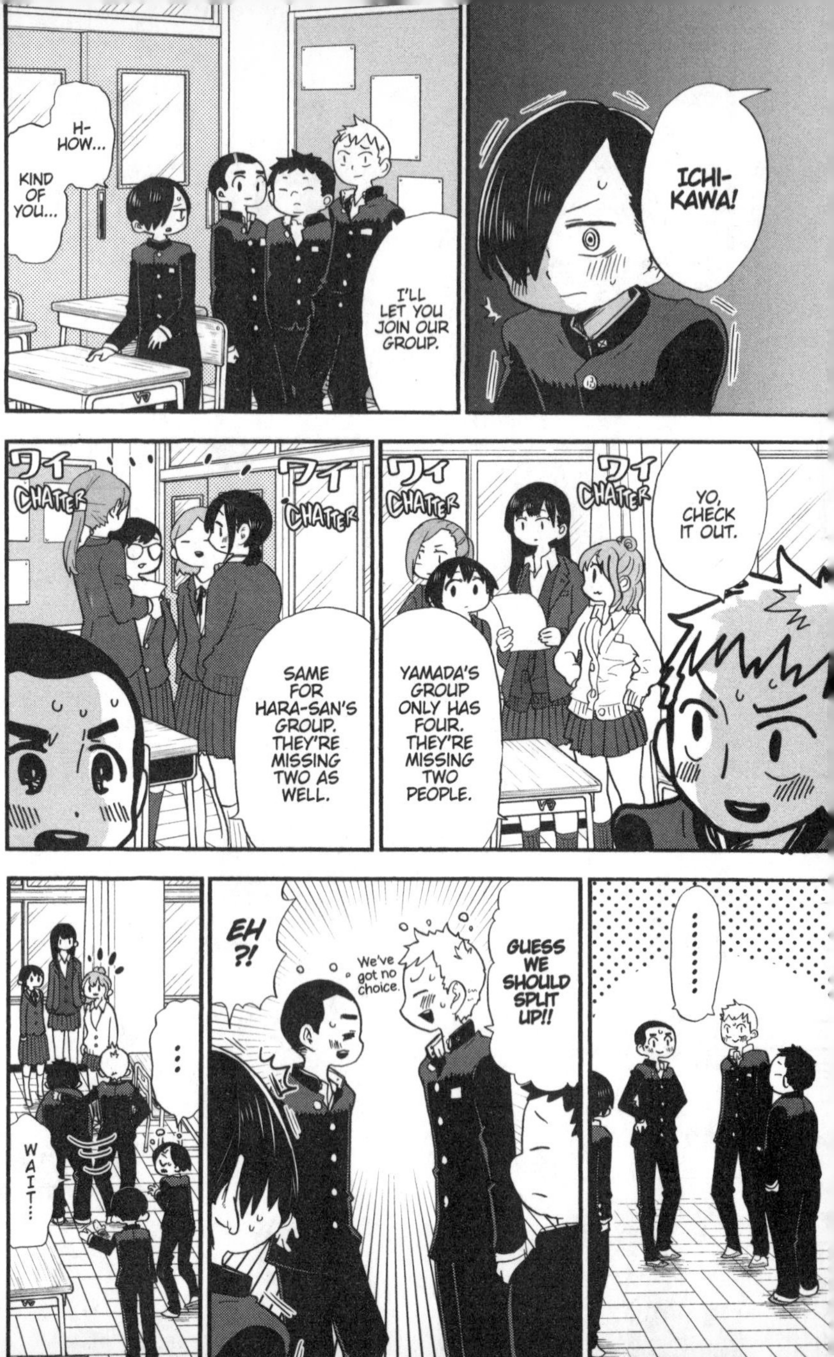
ICHI-KAWA!
I'LL LET YOU JOIN OUR GROUP.
H- HOW... KIND OF YOU...
YO, CHECK IT OUT.
ワイ CHATTER
ワィ CHATTER
YAMADA'S GROUP ONLY HAS FOUR. THEY'RE MISSING TWO PEOPLE.
ワイ CHATTER
ワイ CHATTER
SAME FOR HARA-SAN'S GROUP. THEY'RE MISSING TWO AS WELL.
....
GUESS WE SHOULD SPLIT UP!!
We've got no choice.
EH ?!
...
WAIT...

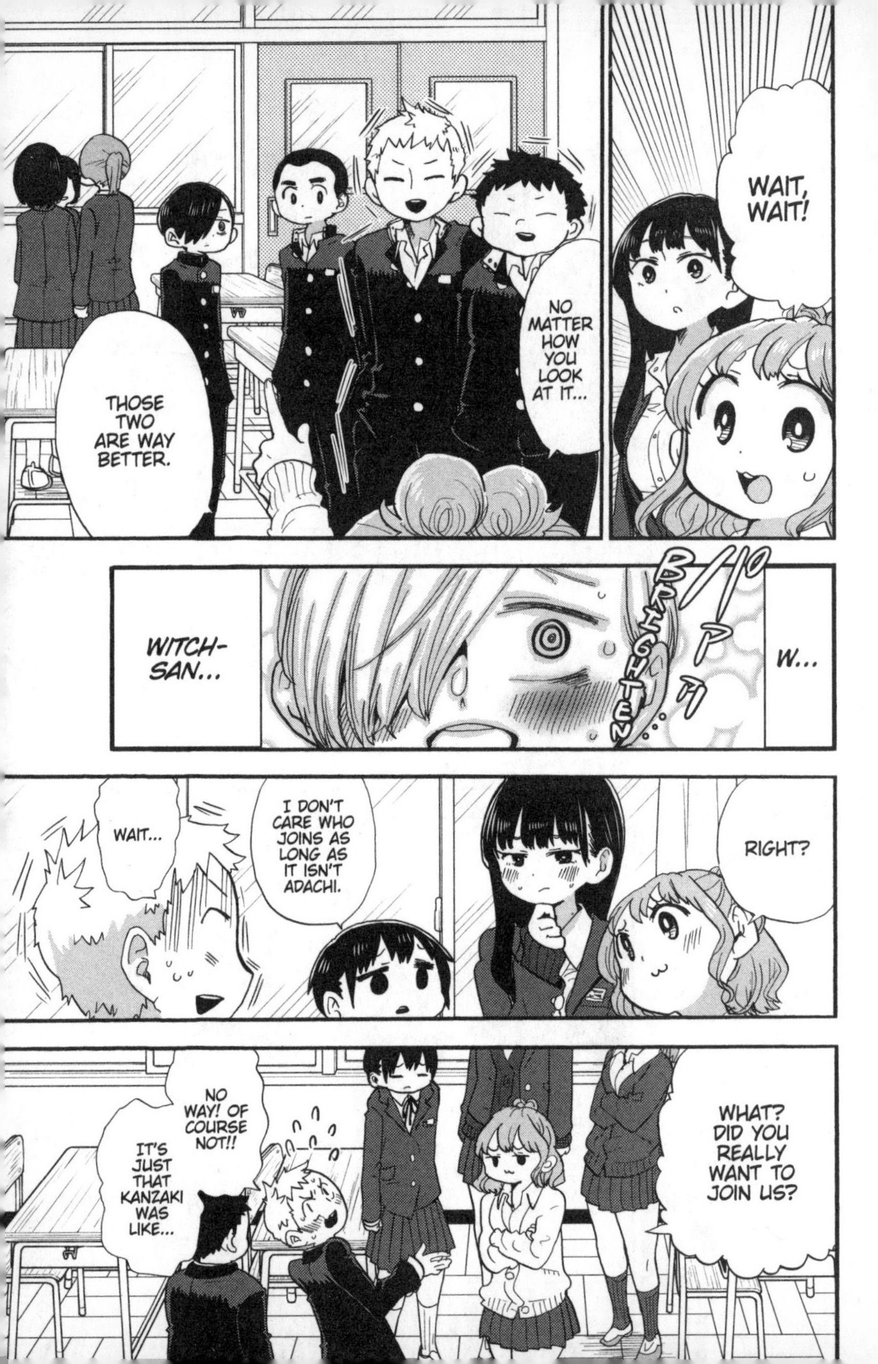
WAIT, WAIT!
NO MATTER HOW YOU LOOK AT IT...
THOSE TWO ARE WAY BETTER.
W...
BRIGHTEN
WITCH-SAN...
RIGHT?
I DON'T CARE WHO JOINS AS LONG AS IT ISN'T ADACHI.
WAIT...
WHAT? DID YOU REALLY WANT TO JOIN US?
NO WAY! OF COURSE NOT!!
IT'S JUST THAT KANZAKI WAS LIKE...

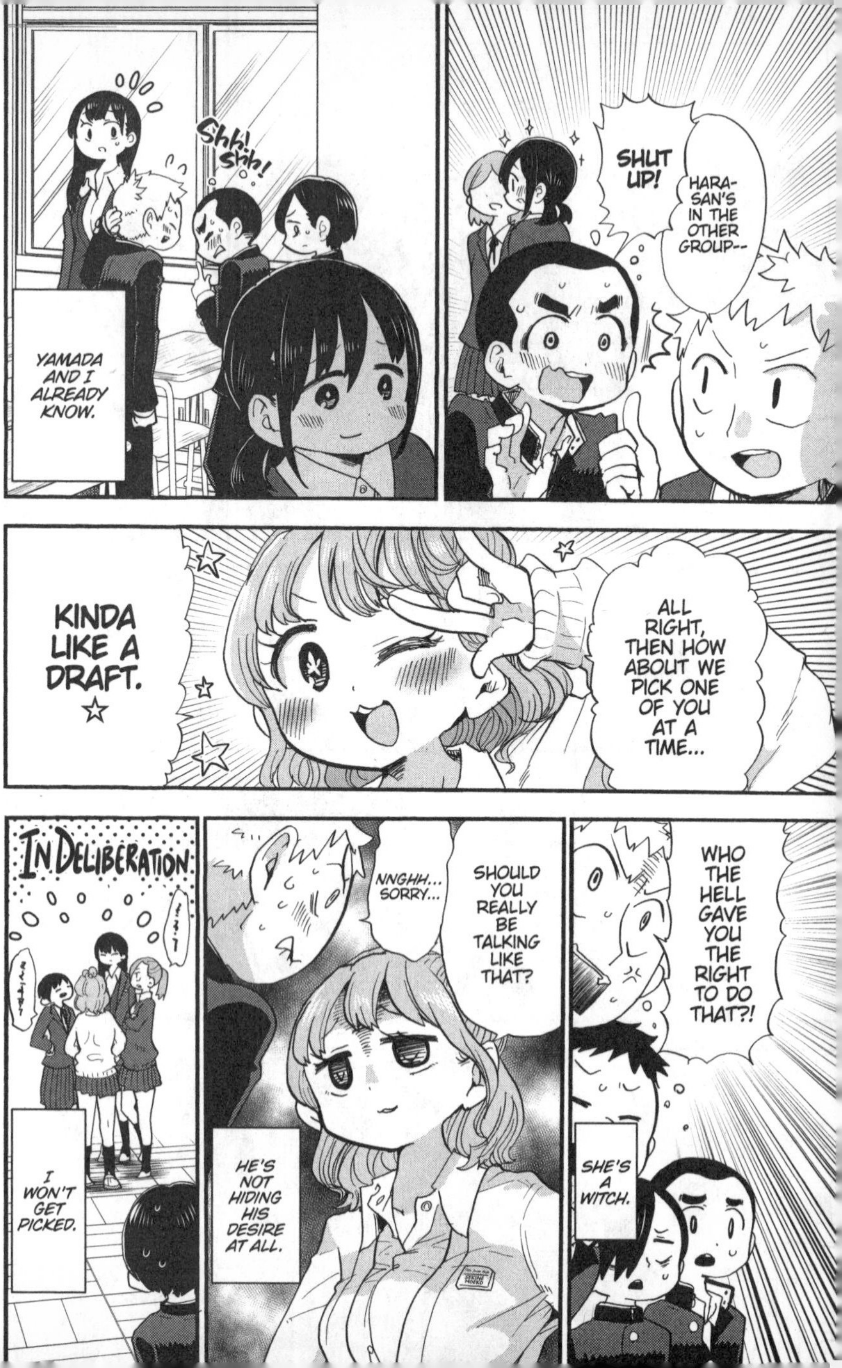
HARA-SAN'S IN THE OTHER GROUP--
SHUT UP!
Shh! Shh!
YAMADA AND I ALREADY KNOW.
ALL RIGHT, THEN HOW ABOUT WE PICK ONE OF YOU AT A TIME...
KINDA LIKE A DRAFT. ☆
WHO THE HELL GAVE YOU THE RIGHT TO DO THAT?!
SHE'S A WITCH.
SHOULD YOU REALLY BE TALKING LIKE THAT?
NNGHH... SORRY...
HE'S NOT HIDING HIS DESIRE AT ALL.
IN DELIBERATION
I WON'T GET PICKED.

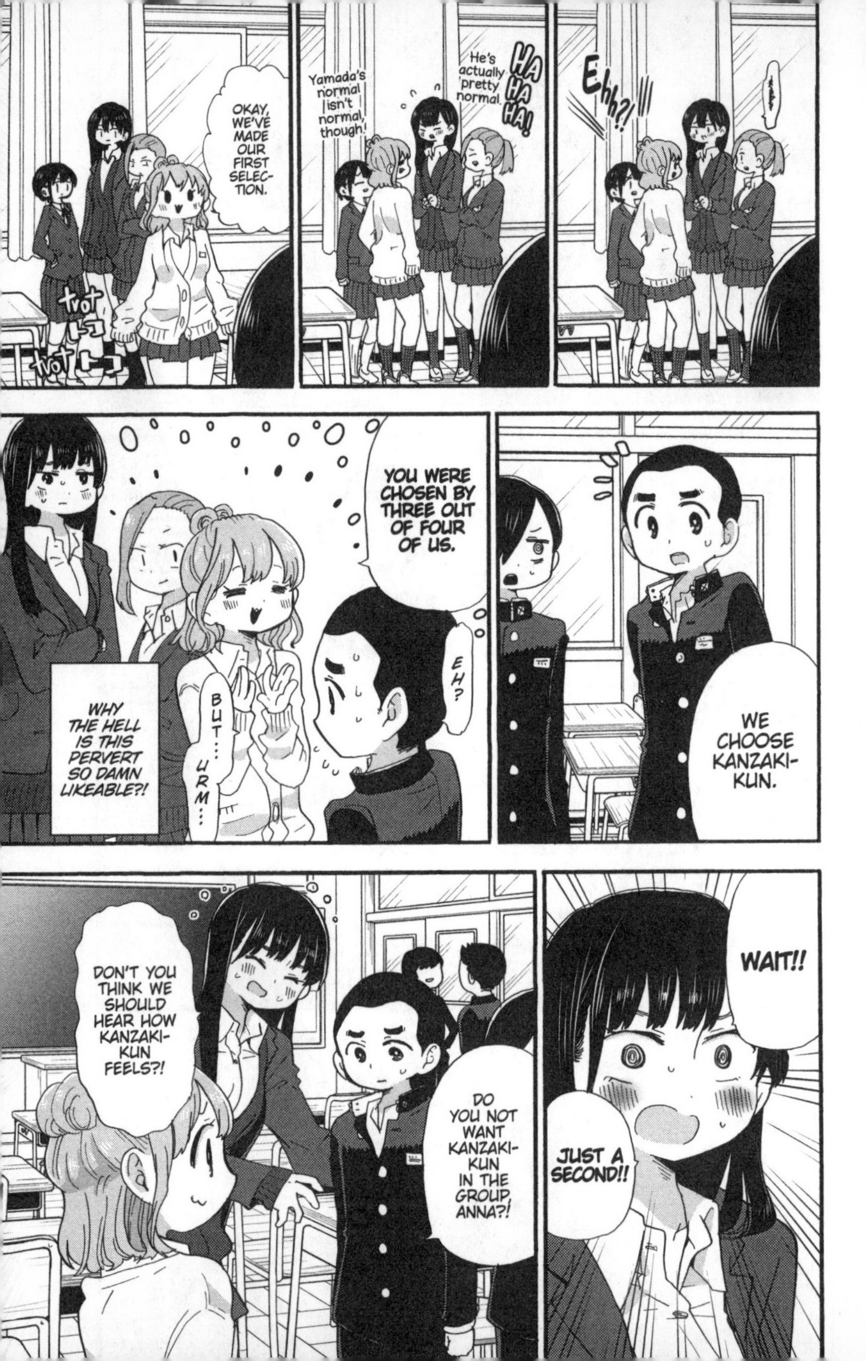
Ehh?!
HA HA HA!
He's actually pretty normal.
Yamada's normal isn't normal, though!
OKAY, WE'VE MADE OUR FIRST SELECTION.
trot トコ
trot トコ
WE CHOOSE KANZAKI-KUN.
YOU WERE CHOSEN BY THREE OUT OF FOUR OF US.
EH?
BUT... URM...
WHY THE HELL IS THIS PERVERT SO DAMN LIKEABLE?!
WAIT!!
JUST A SECOND!!
DO YOU NOT WANT KANZAKI-KUN IN THE GROUP, ANNA?!
DON'T YOU THINK WE SHOULD HEAR HOW KANZAKI-KUN FEELS?!

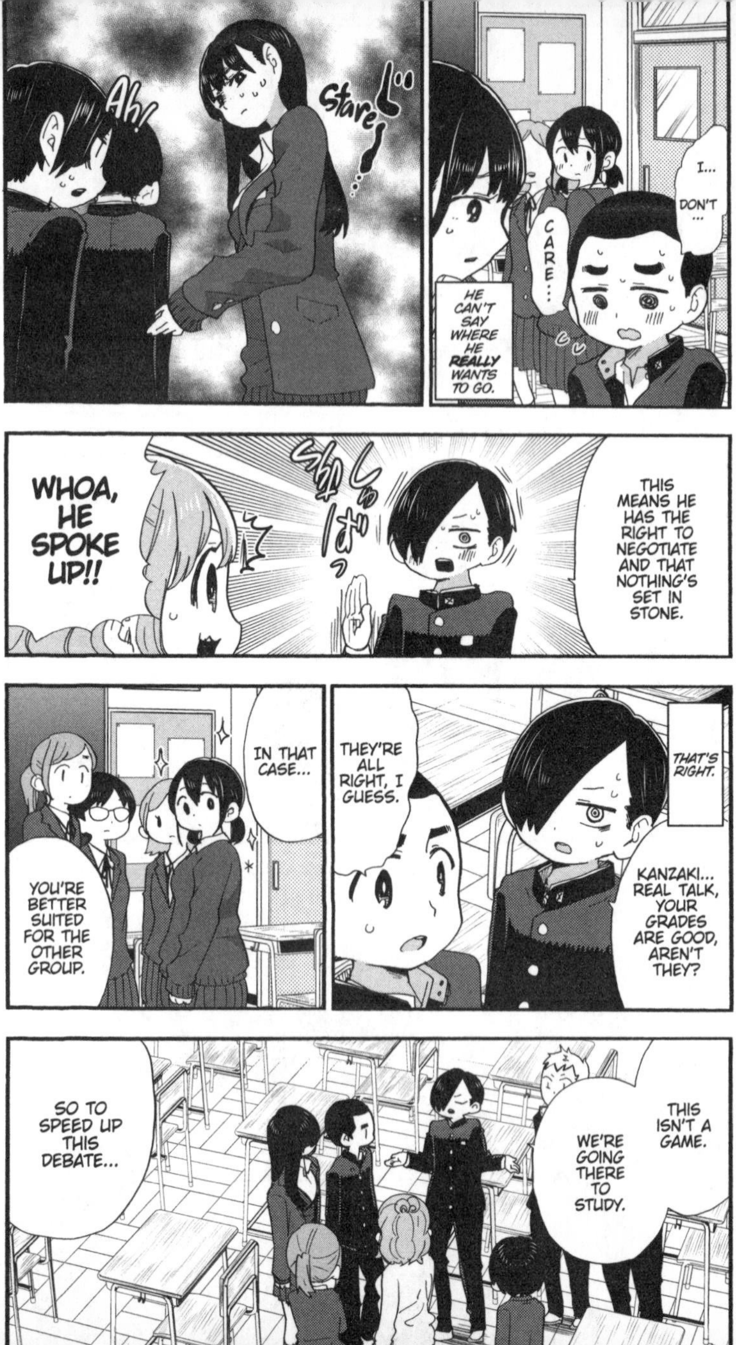
I... DON'T ...
CARE...
HE CAN'T SAY WHERE HE REALLY WANTS TO GO.
Stare
Ah!
THIS MEANS HE HAS THE RIGHT TO NEGOTIATE AND THAT NOTHING'S SET IN STONE.
WHOA, HE SPOKE UP!!
THAT'S RIGHT.
KANZAKI... REAL TALK, YOUR GRADES ARE GOOD, AREN'T THEY?
THEY'RE ALL RIGHT, I GUESS.
IN THAT CASE...
YOU'RE BETTER SUITED FOR THE OTHER GROUP.
THIS ISN'T A GAME.
WE'RE GOING THERE TO STUDY.
SO TO SPEED UP THIS DEBATE...

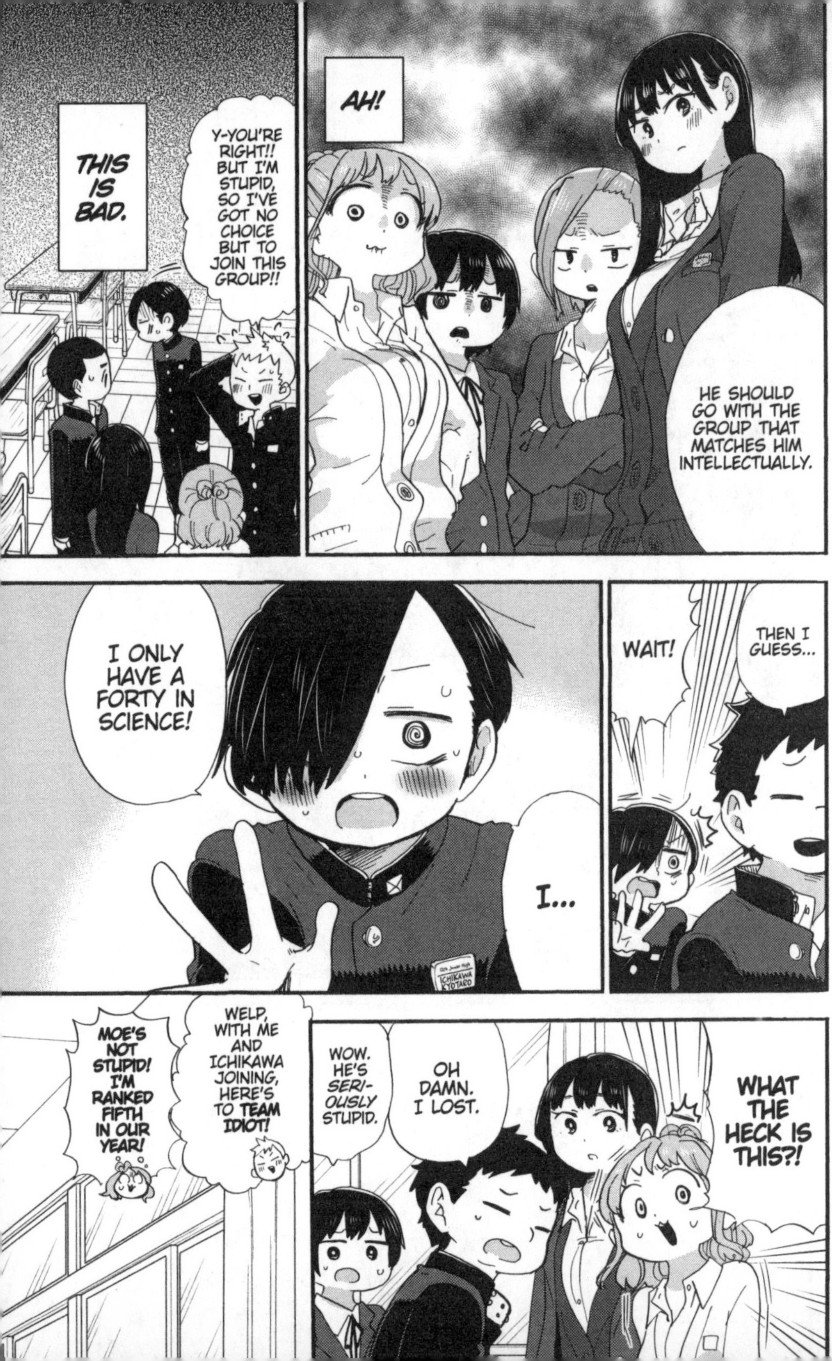
HE SHOULD GO WITH THE GROUP THAT MATCHES HIM INTELLECTUALLY.
AH!
Y-YOU'RE RIGHT!! BUT I'M STUPID, SO I'VE GOT NO CHOICE BUT TO JOIN THIS GROUP!!
THIS IS BAD.
THEN I GUESS...
WAIT!
I...
I ONLY HAVE A FORTY IN SCIENCE!
ICHIKAWA KYOTARO
WHAT THE HECK IS THIS?!
OH DAMN. I LOST.
WOW. HE'S SERI-OUSLY STUPID.
WELP, WITH ME AND ICHIKAWA JOINING, HERE'S TO TEAM IDIOT!
MOE'S NOT STUPID! I'M RANKED FIFTH IN OUR YEAR!

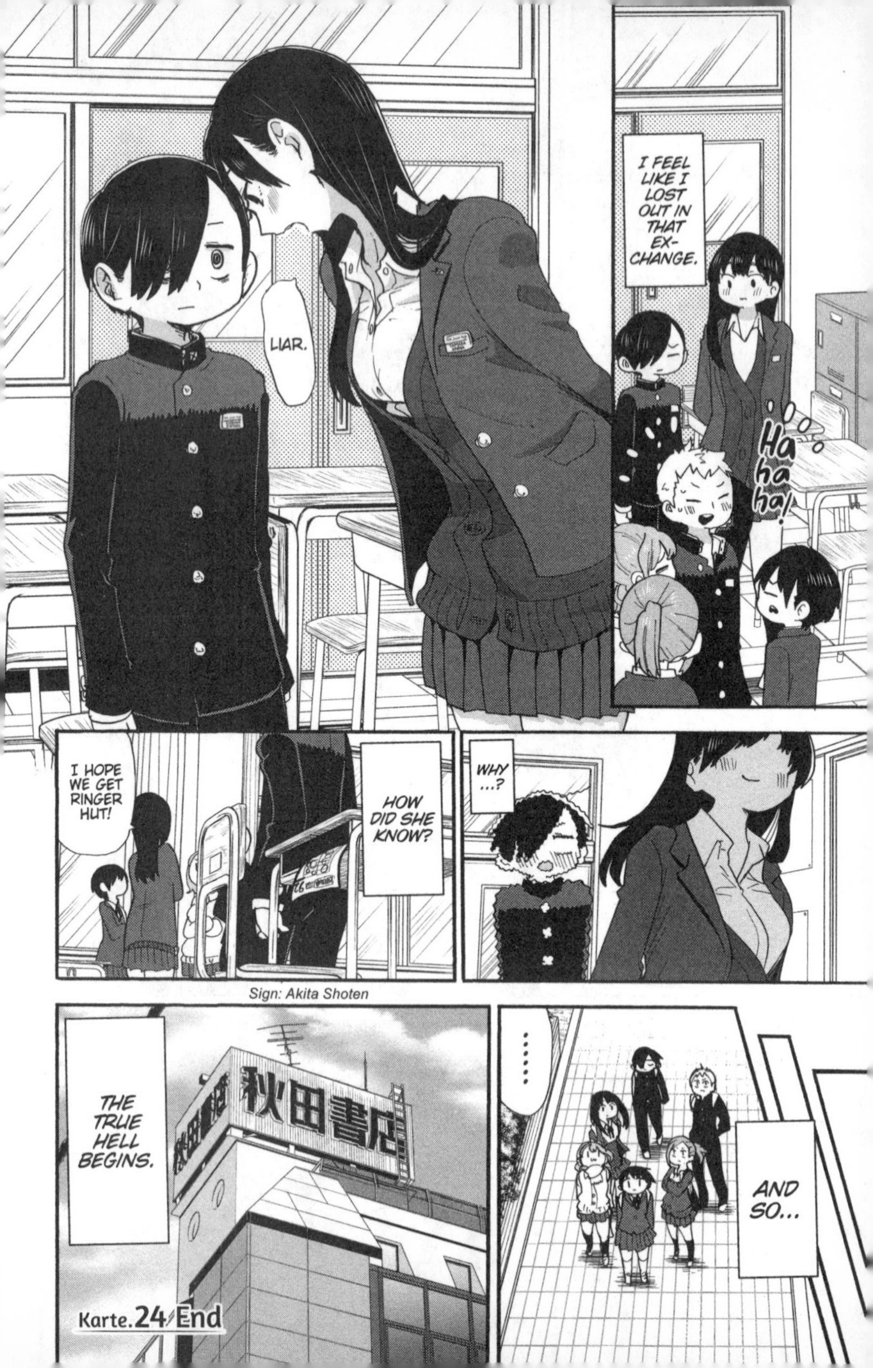
I FEEL LIKE I LOST OUT IN THAT EX-CHANGE.
Ha ha ha!
LIAR.
WHY ...?
HOW DID SHE KNOW?
I HOPE WE GET RINGER HUT!
Sign: Akita Shoten
......
AND SO...
THE TRUE HELL BEGINS.
秋田書店
Karte.24 End

Team Chubster

YAY! WE GOT RINGER HUT!
YAY!
WE MIGHT EVEN GET TO SAMPLE STUFF!
RIGHT?
PIIINCH

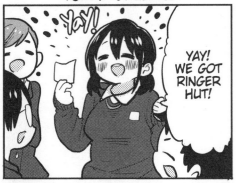

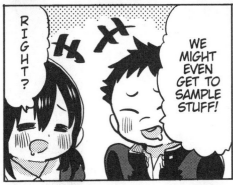

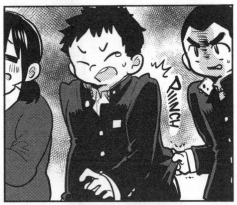

The
Dangers
in My
Heart

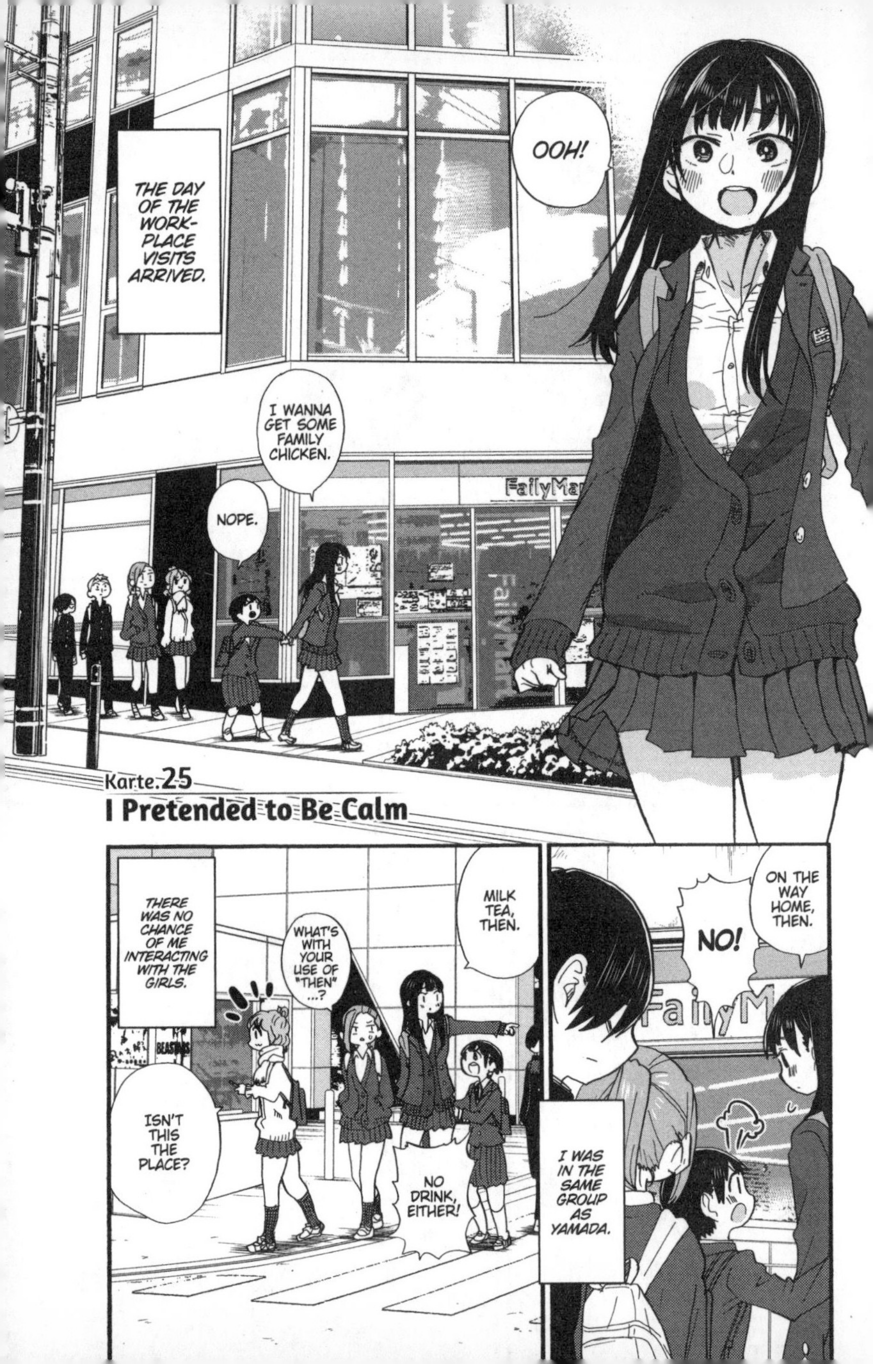
OOH!
THE DAY OF THE WORK-PLACE VISITS ARRIVED.
I WANNA GET SOME FAMILY CHICKEN.
NOPE.
Karte. 25
I Pretended to Be Calm
ON THE WAY HOME, THEN.
NO!
I WAS IN THE SAME GROUP AS YAMADA.
MILK TEA, THEN.
WHAT'S WITH YOUR USE OF "THEN" ...?
THERE WAS NO CHANCE OF ME INTERACTING WITH THE GIRLS.
NO DRINK, EITHER!
ISN'T THIS THE PLACE?

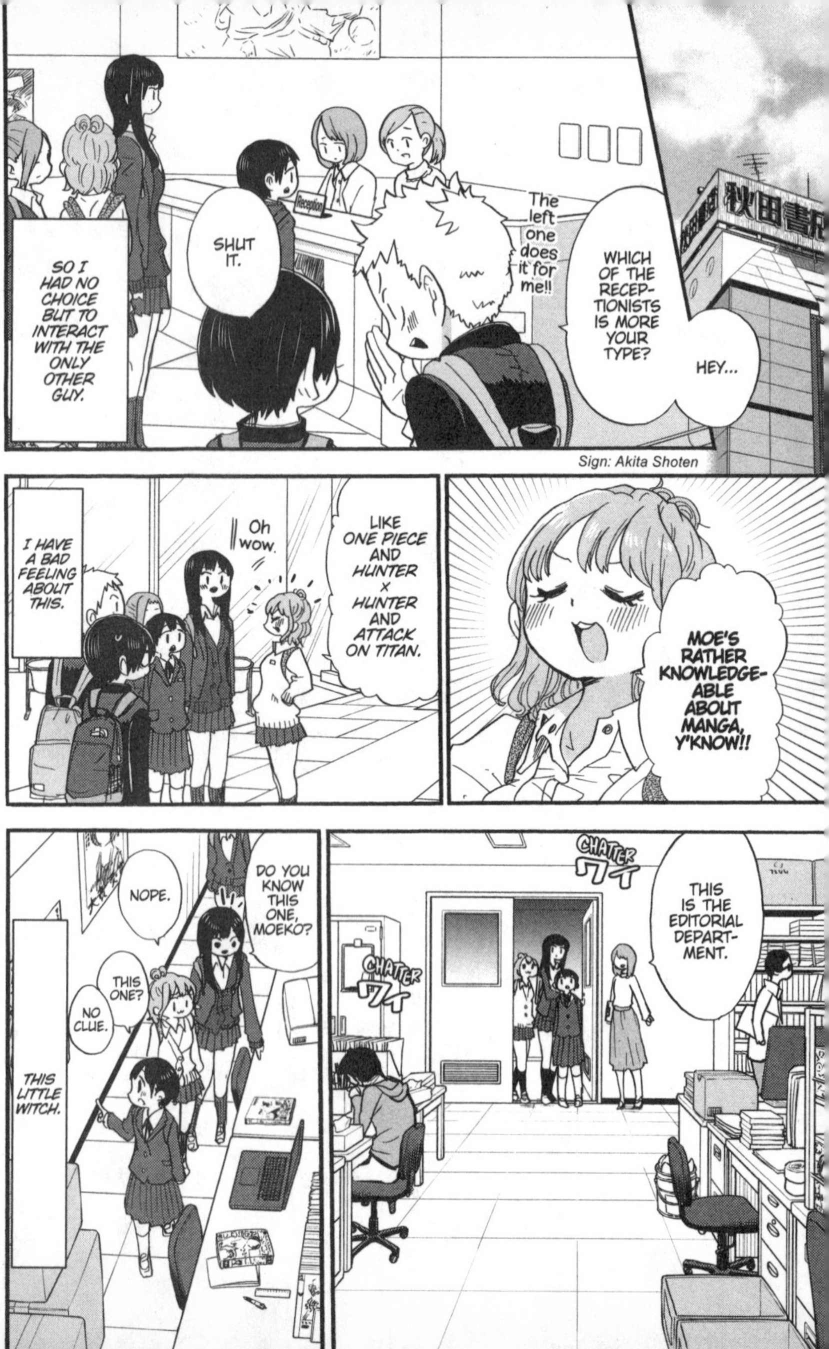
HEY...
WHICH OF THE RECEPTIONISTS IS MORE YOUR TYPE?
The left one does it for me!!
SHUT IT.
Reception
SO I HAD NO CHOICE BUT TO INTERACT WITH THE ONLY OTHER GUY.
Sign: Akita Shoten
MOE'S RATHER KNOWLEDGEABLE ABOUT MANGA, Y'KNOW!!
LIKE ONE PIECE AND HUNTER x HUNTER AND ATTACK ON TITAN.
Oh wow.
I HAVE A BAD FEELING ABOUT THIS.
THIS IS THE EDITORIAL DEPARTMENT.
CHATTER ワイ
CHATTER ワイ
DO YOU KNOW THIS ONE, MOEKO?
NOPE.
THIS ONE?
NO CLUE.
THIS LITTLE WITCH.

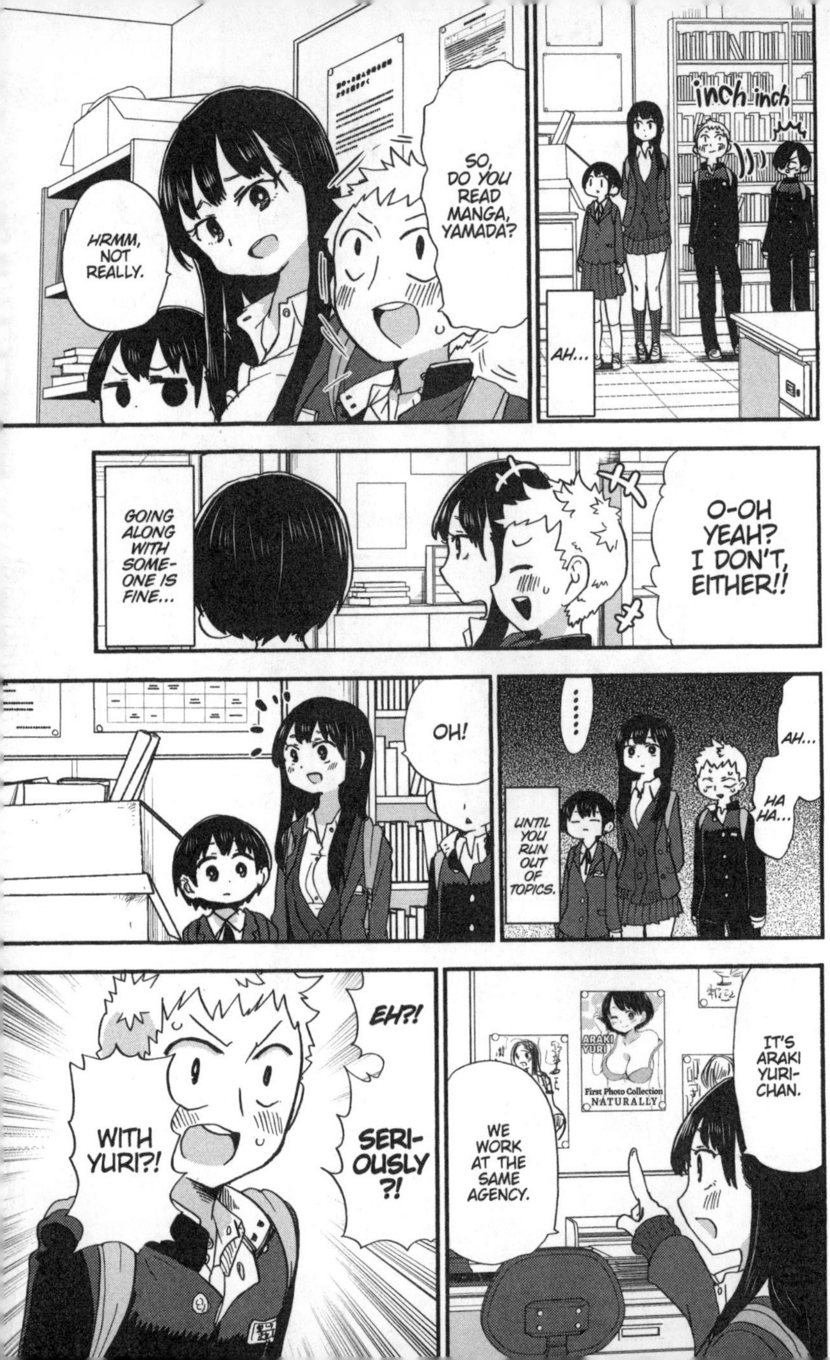
inch inch
AH...
SO, DO YOU READ MANGA, YAMADA?
HRMM, NOT REALLY.
O-OH YEAH? I DON'T, EITHER!!
GOING ALONG WITH SOME-ONE IS FINE...
AH... HA HA...
......
UNTIL YOU RUN OUT OF TOPICS.
OH!
IT'S ARAKI YURI-CHAN.
ARAKI YURI
First Photo Collection
NATURALLY
WE WORK AT THE SAME AGENCY.
EH?!
SERI-OUSLY?!
WITH YURI?!

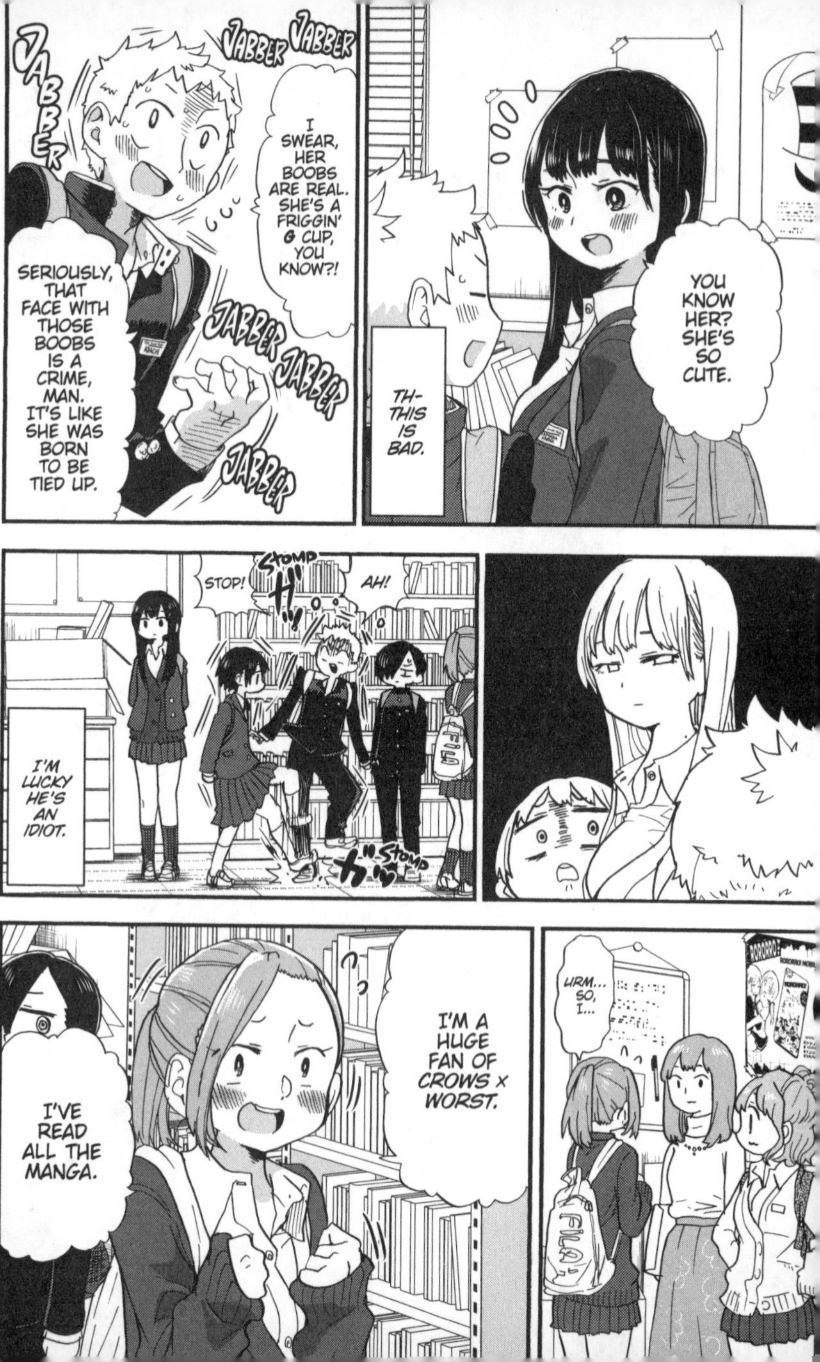
YOU KNOW HER? SHE'S SO CUTE.
TH-THIS IS BAD.
JABBER JABBER
I SWEAR, HER BOOBS ARE REAL. SHE'S A FRIGGIN' G CUP, YOU KNOW?!
JABBER
SERIOUSLY, THAT FACE WITH THOSE BOOBS IS A CRIME, MAN. IT'S LIKE SHE WAS BORN TO BE TIED UP.
JABBER JABBER
JABBER
AH!
STOMP
STOP!
STOMP
I'M LUCKY HE'S AN IDIOT.
URM... SO, I...
I'M A HUGE FAN OF CROWS x WORST.
I'VE READ ALL THE MANGA.

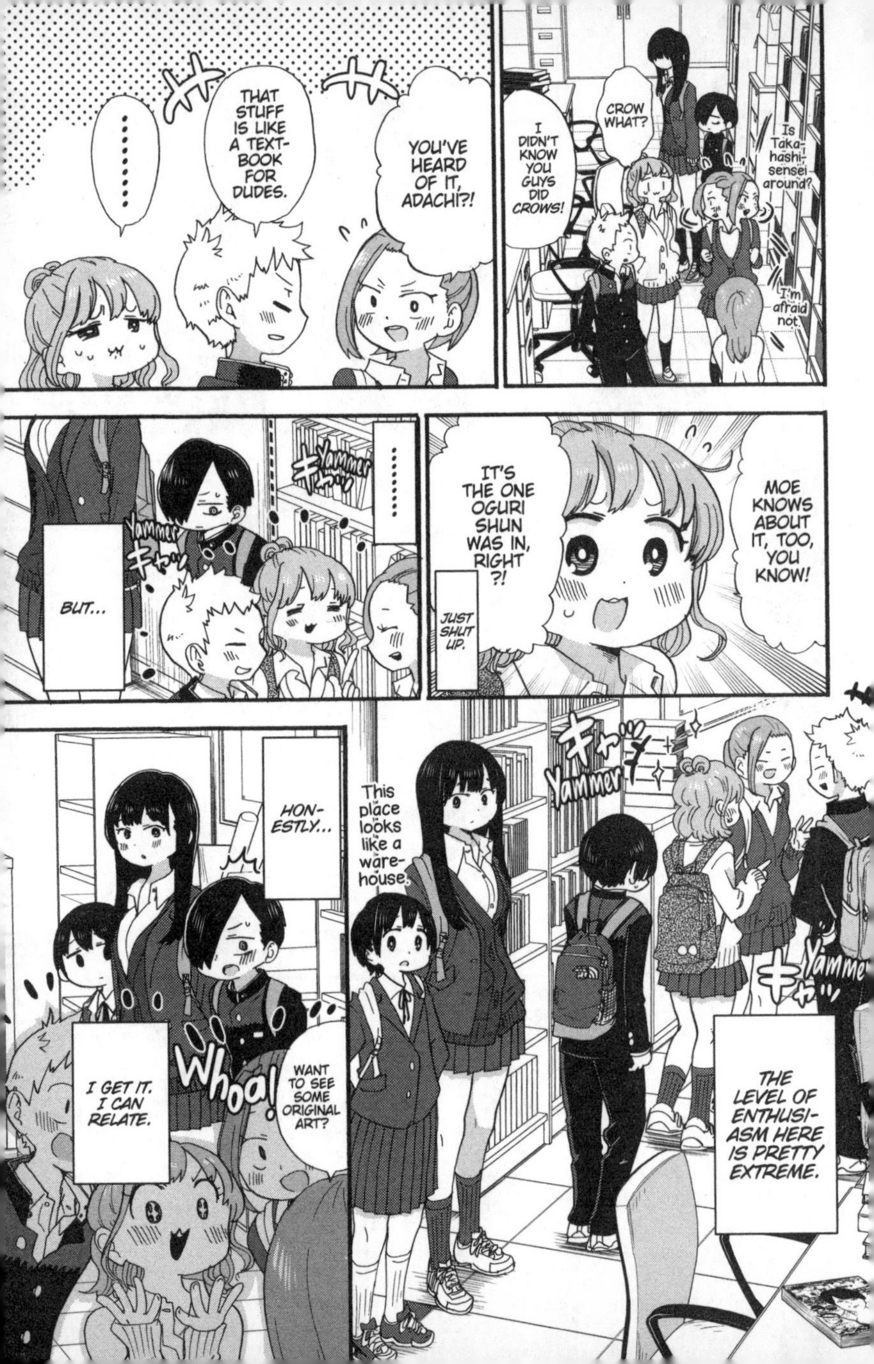
Is Takahashi-sensei around?
CROW WHAT?
I DIDN'T KNOW YOU GUYS DID CROWS!
I'm afraid not.
YOU'VE HEARD OF IT, ADACHI?!
THAT STUFF IS LIKE A TEXT-BOOK FOR DUDES.
....
MOE KNOWS ABOUT IT, TOO, YOU KNOW!
IT'S THE ONE OGURI SHUN WAS IN, RIGHT?!
JUST SHUT UP.
....
Yammer
Yammer
BUT...
Yammer
This place looks like a ware-house.
Yammer
THE LEVEL OF ENTHUSI-ASM HERE IS PRETTY EXTREME.
HON-ESTLY...
Whoa!
WANT TO SEE SOME ORIGINAL ART?
I GET IT. I CAN RELATE.

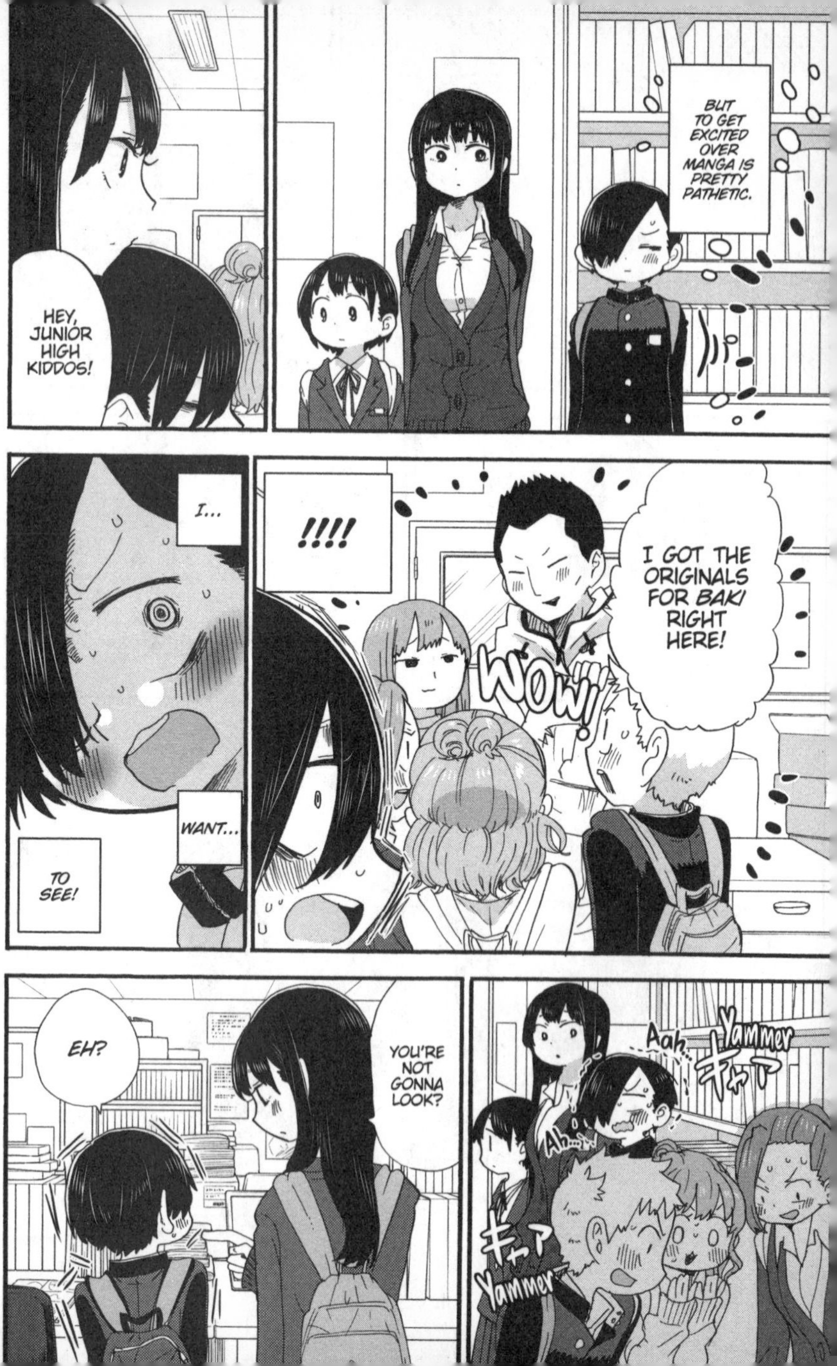
BUT TO GET EXCITED OVER MANGA IS PRETTY PATHETIC.
HEY, JUNIOR HIGH KIDDOS!
I GOT THE ORIGINALS FOR *BAKI* RIGHT HERE!
WOW!
!!!!
I...
WANT...
TO SEE!
Yammer
キャア
Aah...
Ah...
キャア
Yammer
YOU'RE NOT GONNA LOOK?
EH?

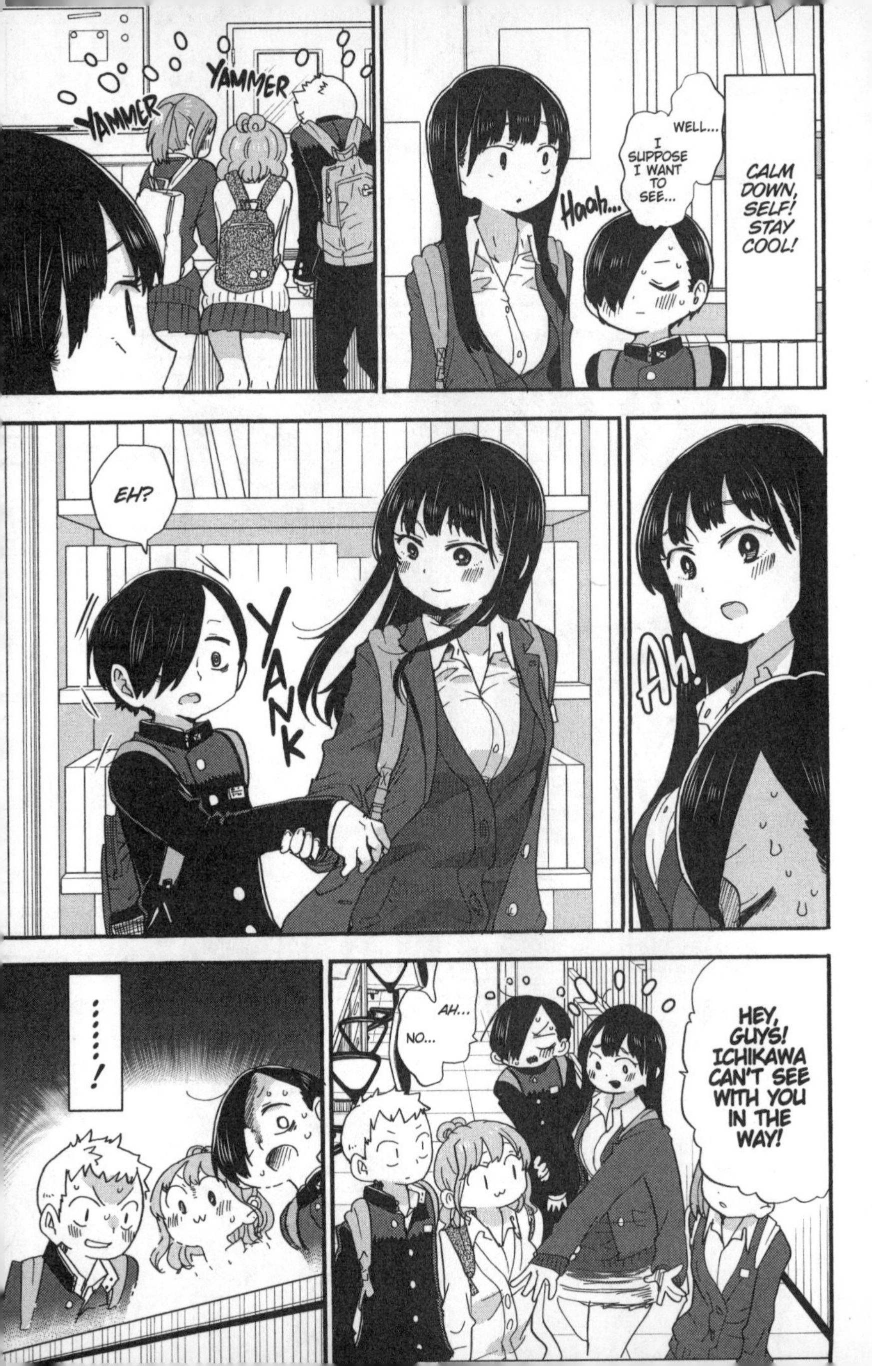
CALM DOWN, SELF! STAY COOL!
WELL... I SUPPOSE I WANT TO SEE...
Haah...
YAMMER
YAMMER
AH!
EH?
YANK
HEY, GUYS! ICHIKAWA CAN'T SEE WITH YOU IN THE WAY!
AH... NO...
......!

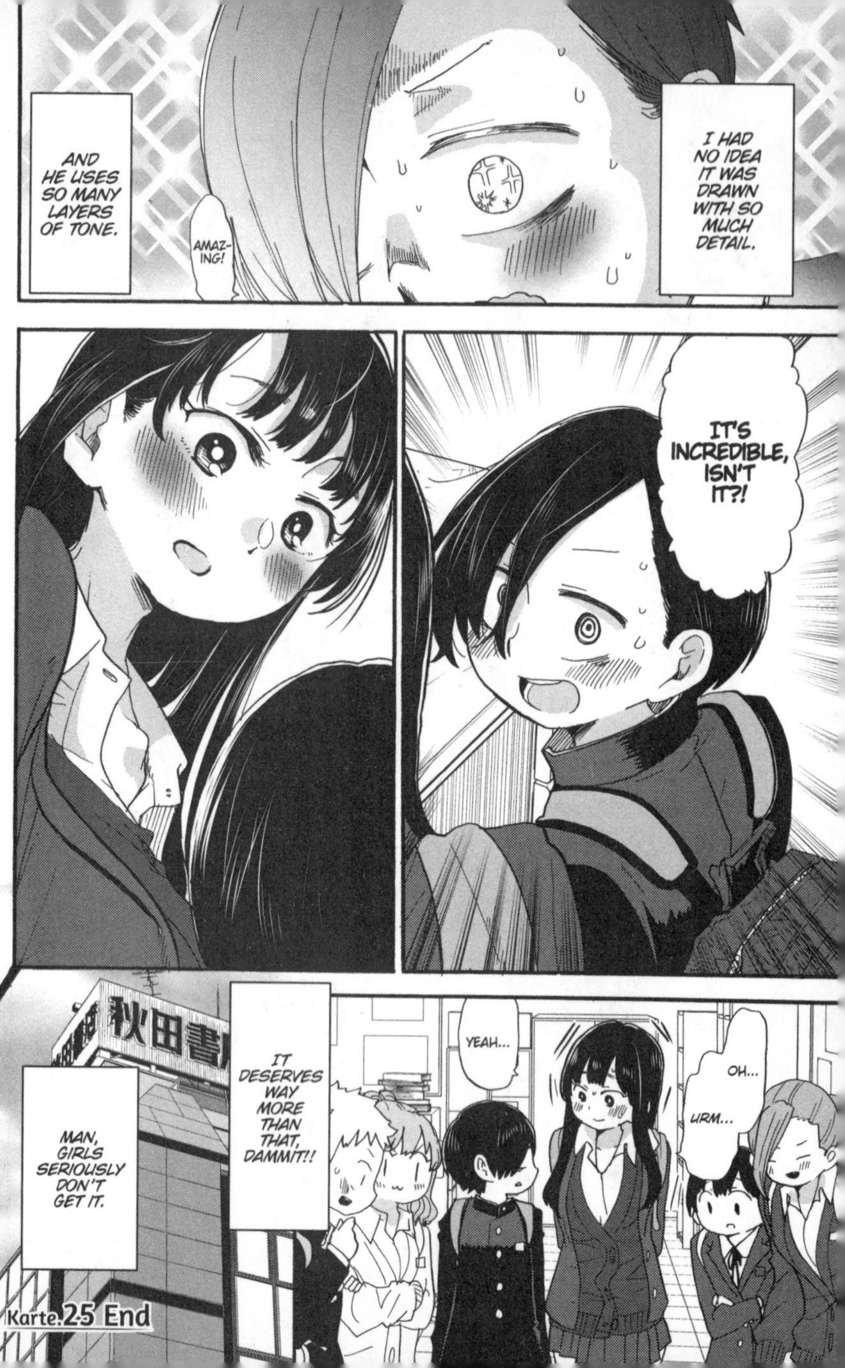
I HAD NO IDEA IT WAS DRAWN WITH SO MUCH DETAIL.
AMAZ-ING!
AND HE USES SO MANY LAYERS OF TONE.
IT'S INCREDIBLE, ISN'T IT?!
OH...
URM...
YEAH...
IT DESERVES WAY MORE THAN THAT, DAMMIT!!
秋田書
MAN, GIRLS SERIOUSLY DON'T GET IT.
Karte.25 End

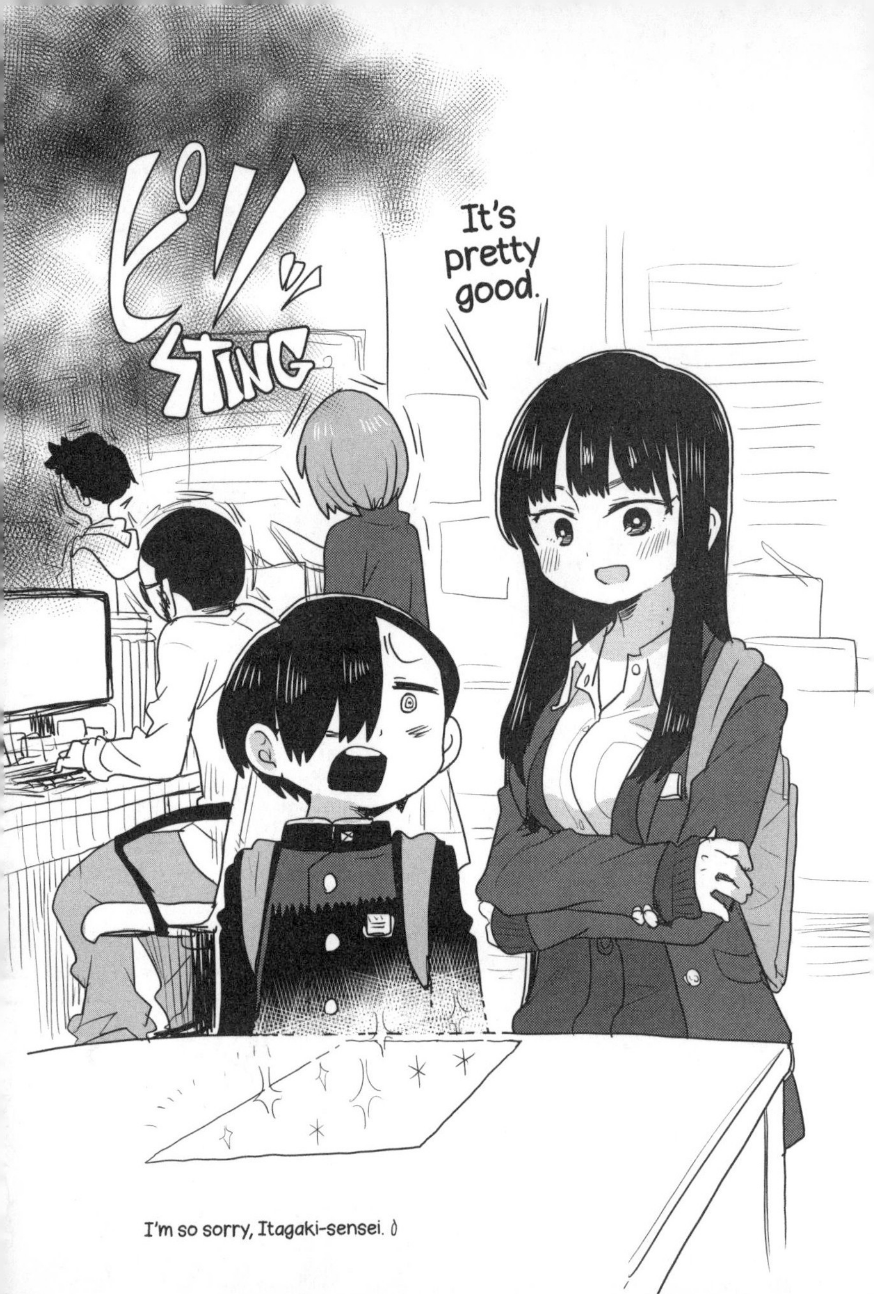
It's pretty good.
ピリ
STING
I'm so sorry, Itagaki-sensei.

The
Dangers
in My
Heart

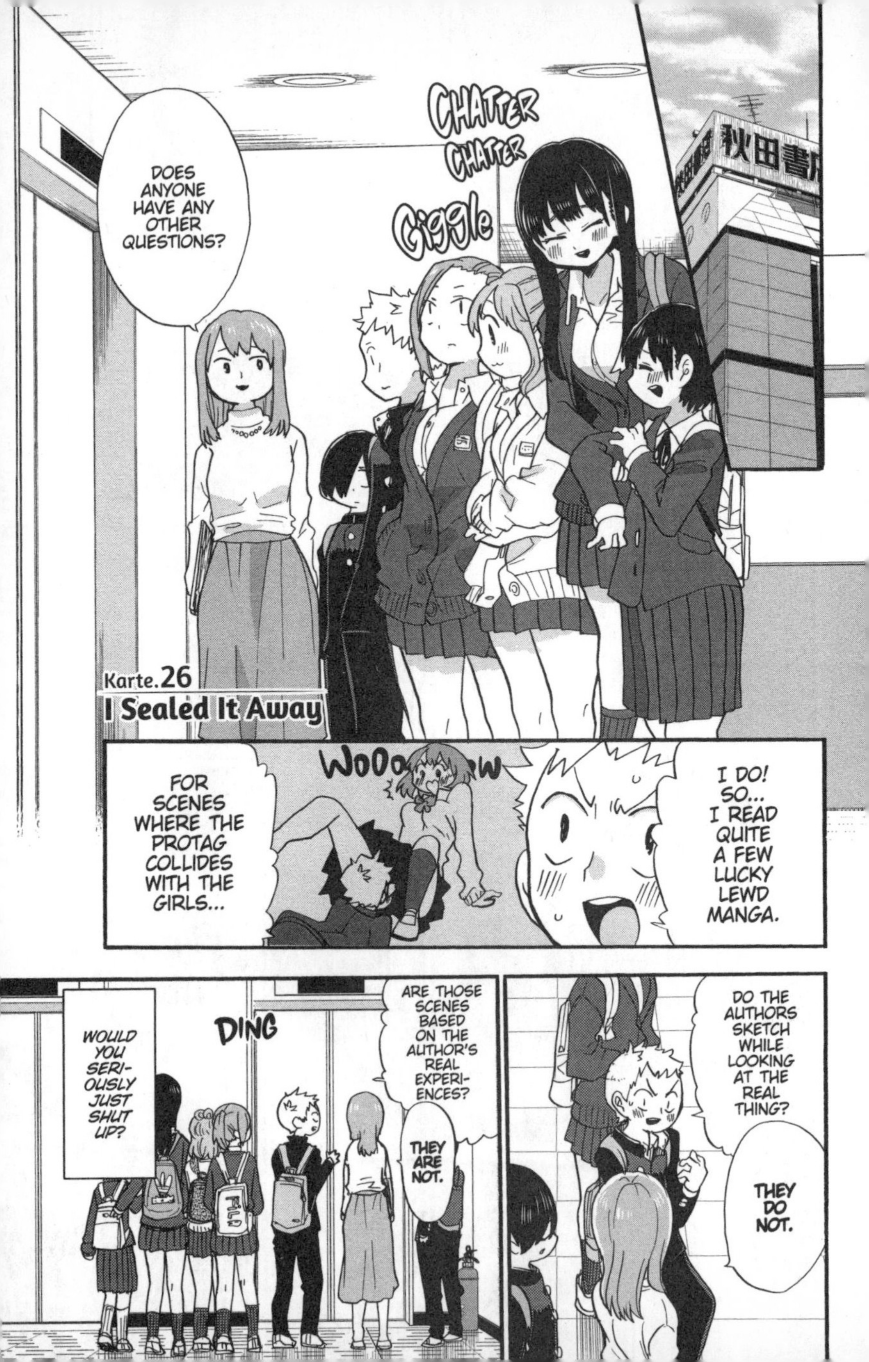
秋田書
CHATTER CHATTER
Giggle
DOES ANYONE HAVE ANY OTHER QUESTIONS?
Karte. 26
I Sealed It Away
I DO! SO... I READ QUITE A FEW LUCKY LEWD MANGA.
FOR SCENES WHERE THE PROTAG COLLIDES WITH THE GIRLS...
DO THE AUTHORS SKETCH WHILE LOOKING AT THE REAL THING?
THEY DO NOT.
ARE THOSE SCENES BASED ON THE AUTHOR'S REAL EXPERI-ENCES?
THEY ARE NOT.
DING
WOULD YOU SERIOUSLY JUST SHUT UP?

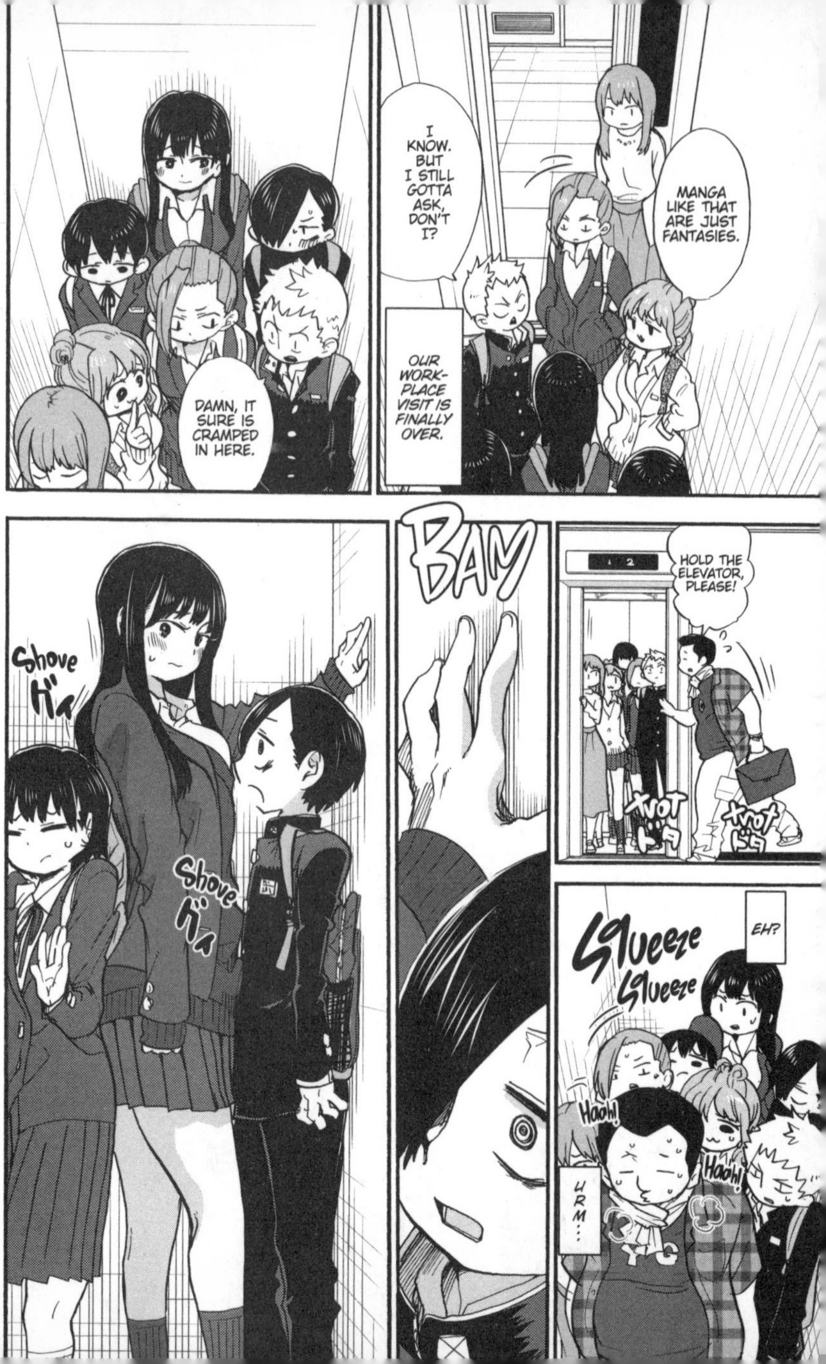
MANGA LIKE THAT ARE JUST FANTASIES.
I KNOW. BUT I STILL GOTTA ASK, DON'T I?
OUR WORK-PLACE VISIT IS FINALLY OVER.
DAMN, IT SURE IS CRAMPED IN HERE.
HOLD THE ELEVATOR, PLEASE!
Squeeze
Squeeze
EH?
Haah!
URM...
Haah!
BAM
Shove
Shove

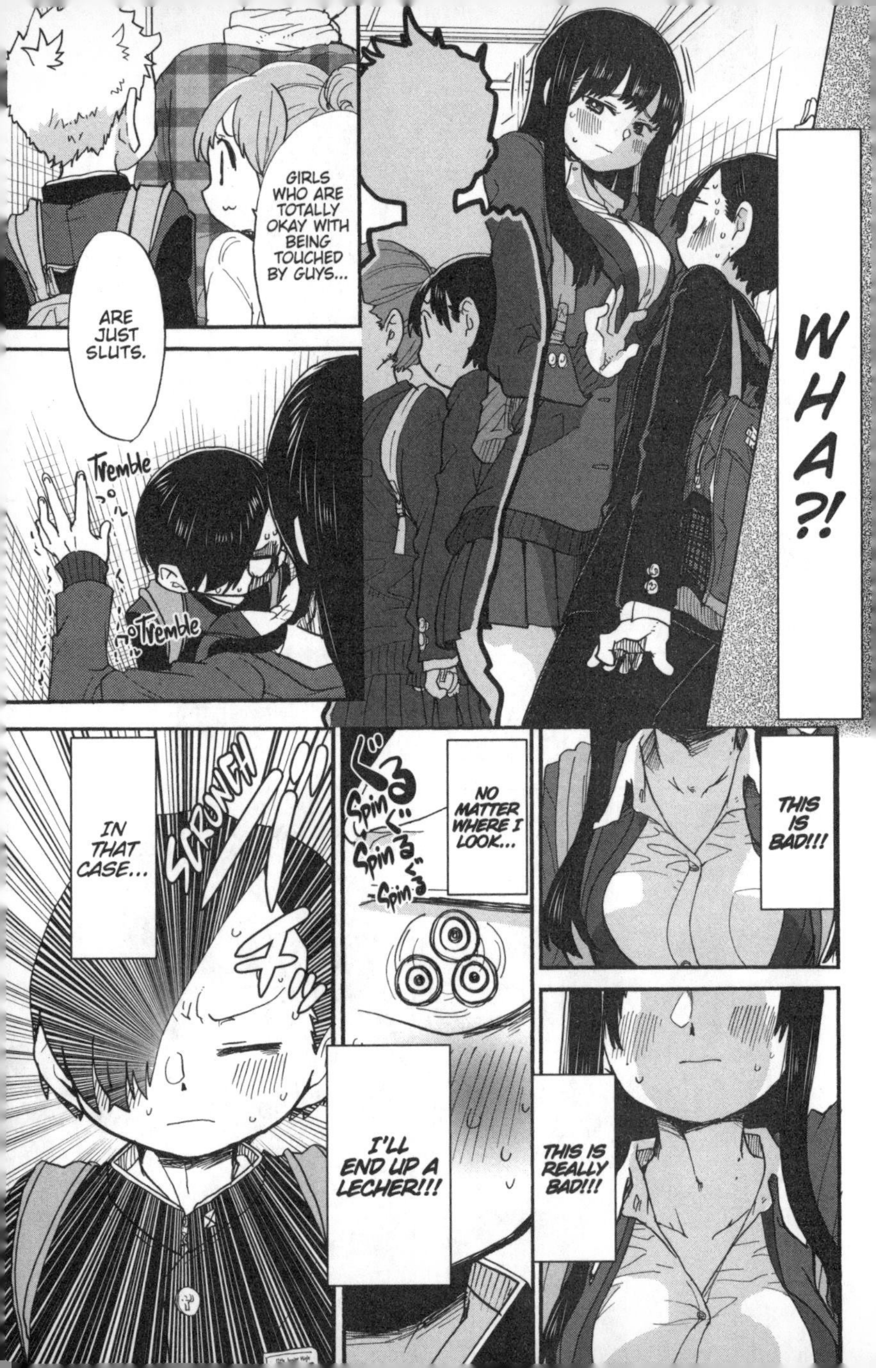
WHA?!
GIRLS WHO ARE TOTALLY OKAY WITH BEING TOUCHED BY GUYS...
ARE JUST SLUTS.
Tremble
Tremble
THIS IS BAD!!!
THIS IS REALLY BAD!!!
NO MATTER WHERE I LOOK...
Spin
Spin
Spin
I'LL END UP A LECHER!!!
IN THAT CASE...
SCRUNCH

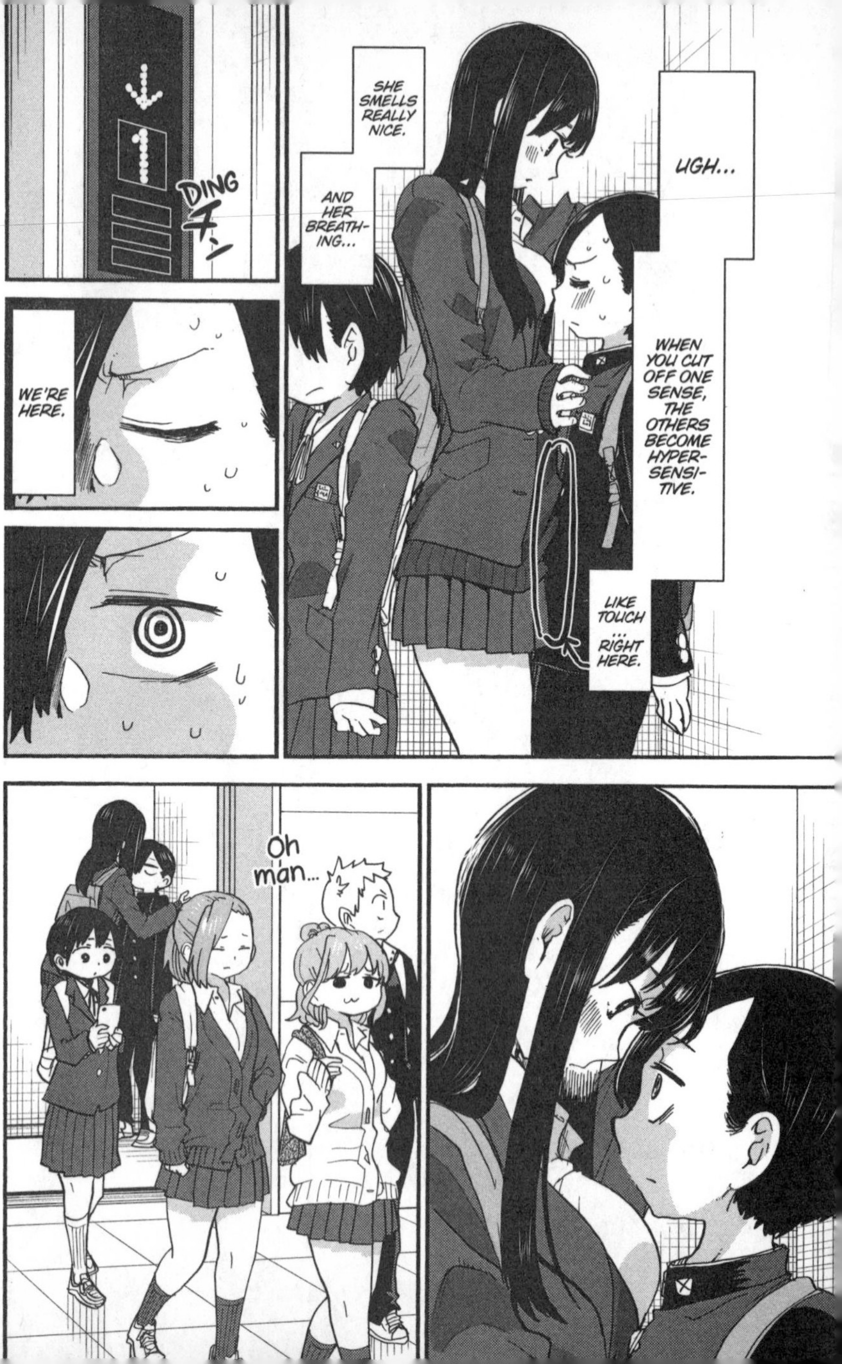
SHE SMELLS REALLY NICE.
AND HER BREATHING...
UGH...
WHEN YOU CUT OFF ONE SENSE, THE OTHERS BECOME HYPERSENSITIVE.
LIKE TOUCH... RIGHT HERE.
DING チン
WE'RE HERE.
Oh man...

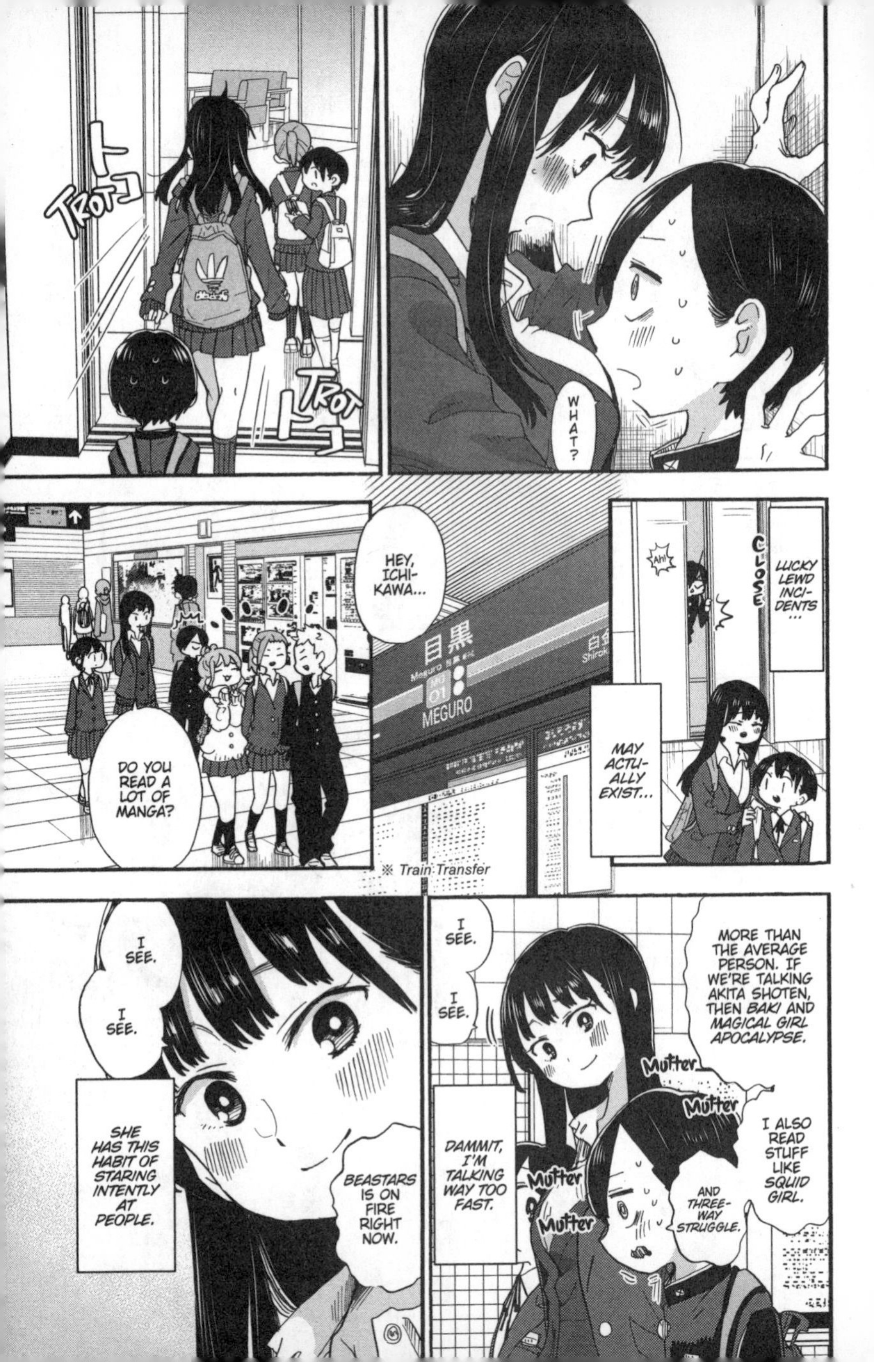
WHAT?
TROT
TROT
CLOSE
AH!
LUCKY LEWD INCIDENTS...
MAY ACTUALLY EXIST...
HEY, ICHIKAWA...
目黒
MEGURO
DO YOU READ A LOT OF MANGA?
※ Train Transfer
MORE THAN THE AVERAGE PERSON. IF WE'RE TALKING AKITA SHOTEN, THEN BAKI AND MAGICAL GIRL APOCALYPSE.
I SEE.
I SEE.
Mutter
Mutter
I ALSO READ STUFF LIKE SQUID GIRL.
AND THREE-WAY STRUGGLE.
Mutter
Mutter
DAMMIT, I'M TALKING WAY TOO FAST.
I SEE.
I SEE.
BEASTARS IS ON FIRE RIGHT NOW.
SHE HAS THIS HABIT OF STARING INTENTLY AT PEOPLE.

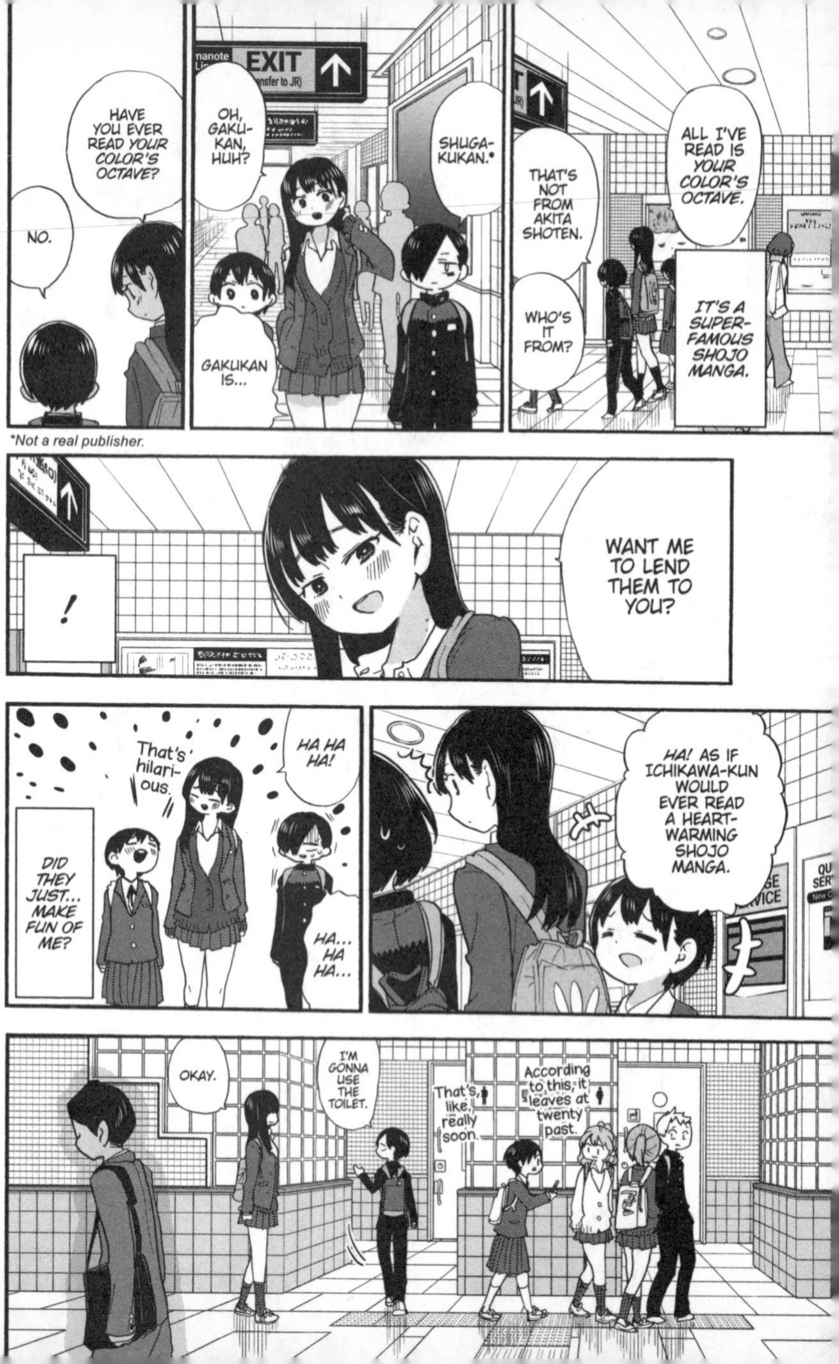
ALL I'VE READ IS *YOUR COLOR'S OCTAVE.*
THAT'S NOT FROM AKITA SHOTEN.
WHO'S IT FROM?
IT'S A SUPER-FAMOUS SHOJO MANGA.
SHUGA-KUKAN.*
OH, GAKU-KAN, HUH?
GAKUKAN IS...
HAVE YOU EVER READ *YOUR COLOR'S OCTAVE?*
NO.
*Not a real publisher.
WANT ME TO LEND THEM TO YOU?
!
HA! AS IF ICHIKAWA-KUN WOULD EVER READ A HEART-WARMING SHOJO MANGA.
HA HA HA!
That's hilari-ous.
HA... HA HA...
DID THEY JUST... MAKE FUN OF ME?
According to this, it leaves at twenty past.
That's, like, really soon.
I'M GONNA USE THE TOILET.
OKAY.

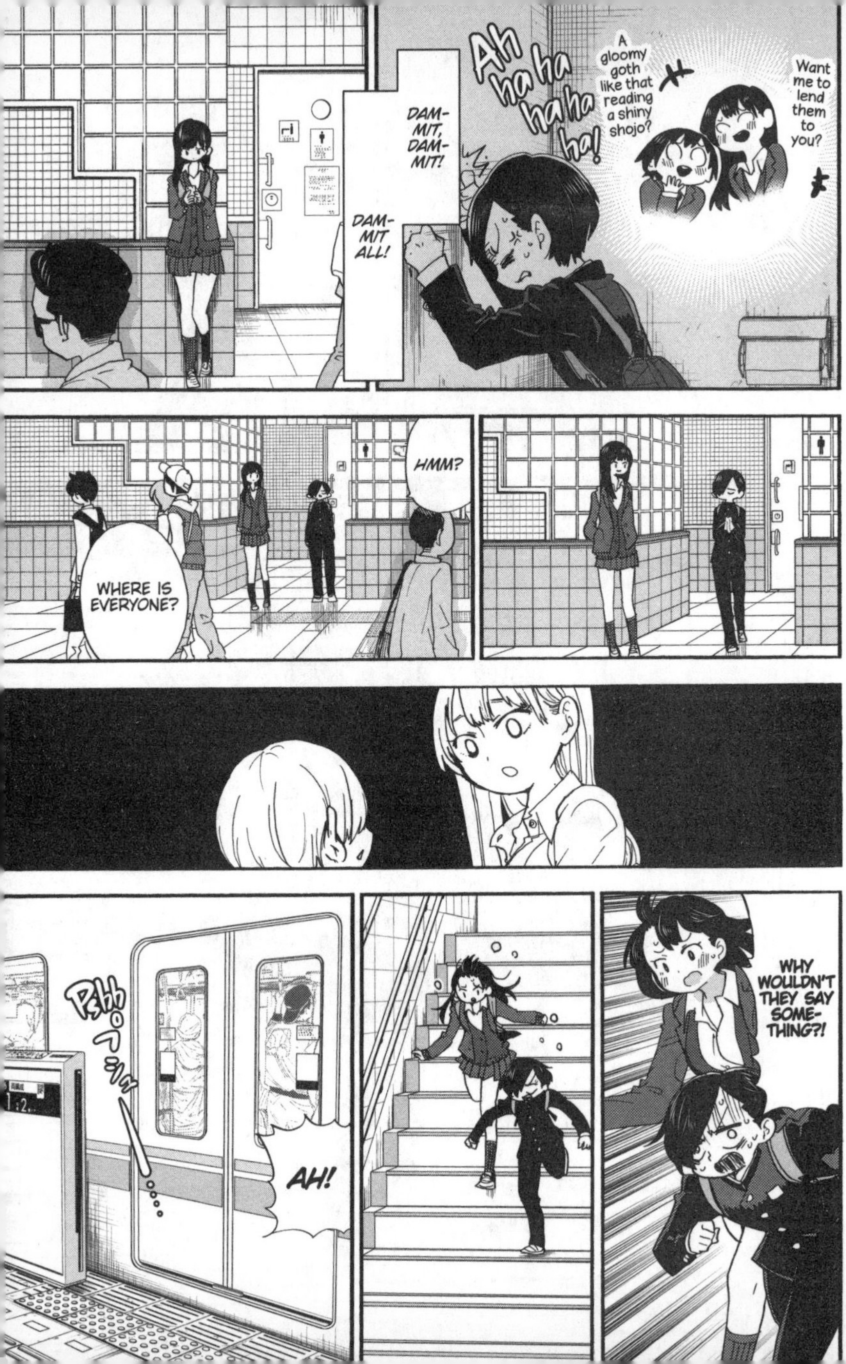

Want me to lend them to you?
A gloomy goth like that reading a shiny shojo?
Ah ha ha ha ha ha!
DAM-MIT, DAM-MIT!
DAM-MIT ALL!
HMM?
WHERE IS EVERYONE?
WHY WOULDN'T THEY SAY SOME-THING?!
Pshh
AH!

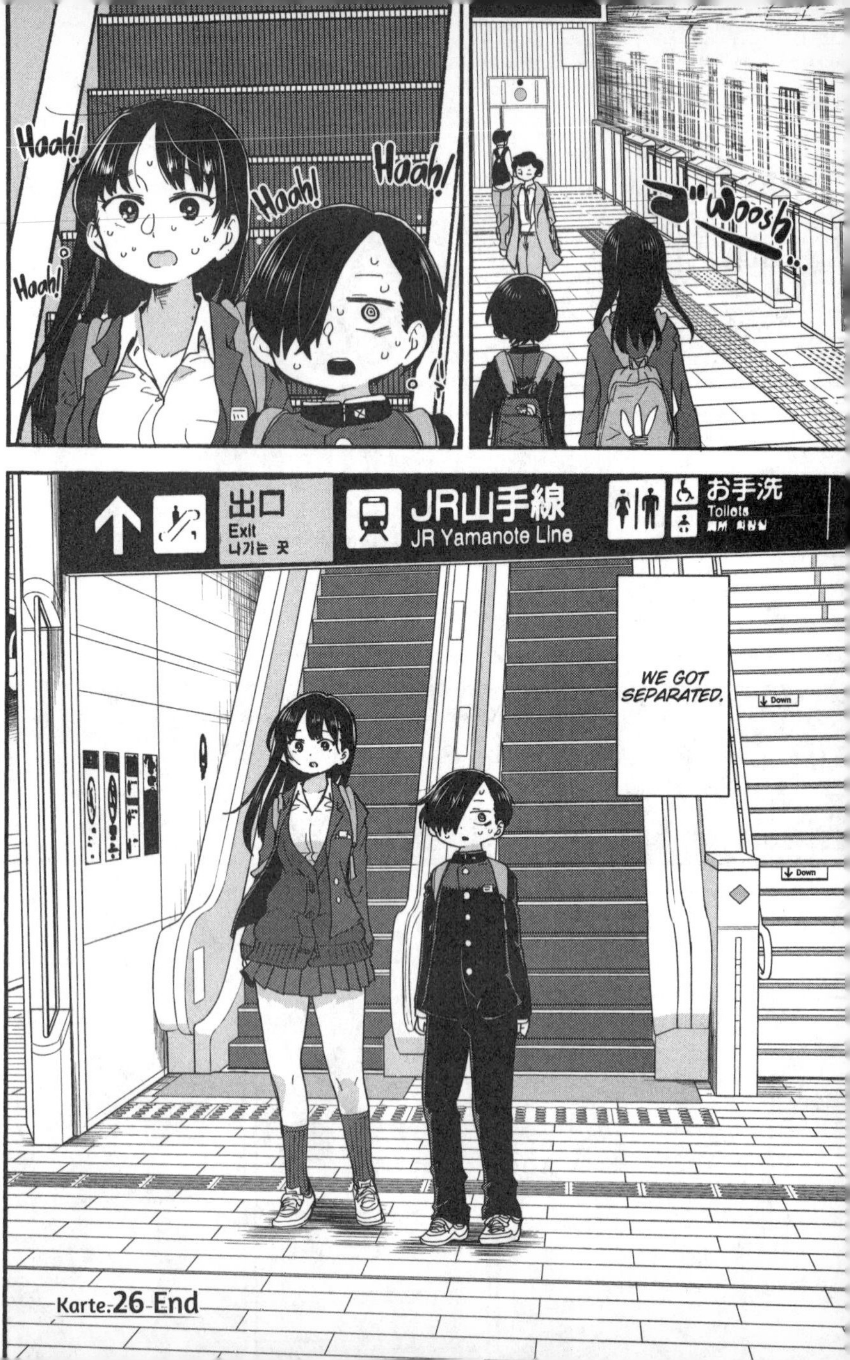
ゴWoosh...
Haah!
Haah!
Haah!
Haah!
出口
Exit
나가는 곳
JR山手線
JR Yamanote Line
お手洗
Toilets
WE GOT SEPARATED.
Down
Down
Karte.26 End

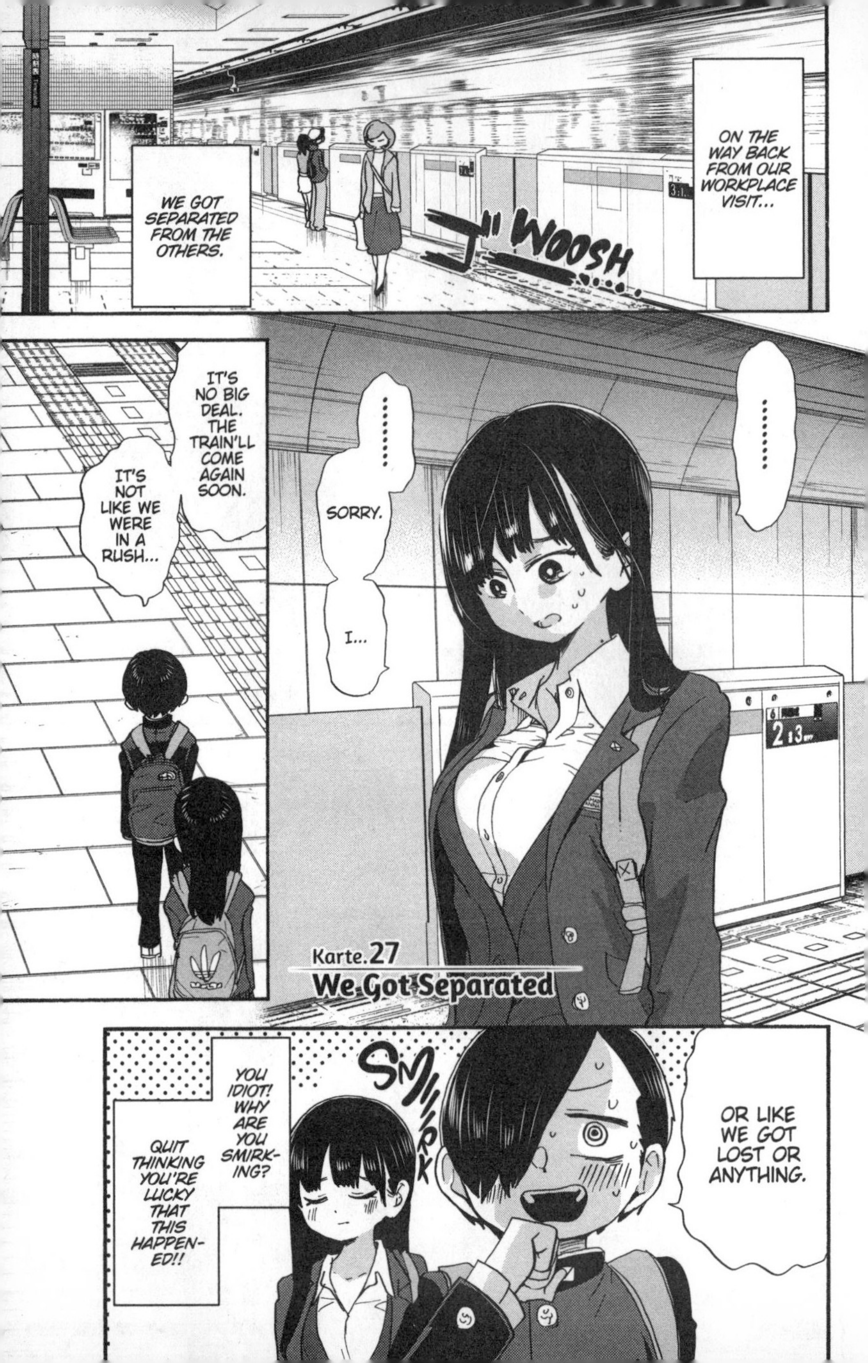
ON THE WAY BACK FROM OUR WORKPLACE VISIT...
WOOSH
WE GOT SEPARATED FROM THE OTHERS.
......
......
SORRY.
I...
Karte. 27
We Got Separated
IT'S NO BIG DEAL. THE TRAIN'LL COME AGAIN SOON.
IT'S NOT LIKE WE WERE IN A RUSH...
OR LIKE WE GOT LOST OR ANYTHING.
SMIRK
YOU IDIOT! WHY ARE YOU SMIRK-ING?
QUIT THINKING YOU'RE LUCKY THAT THIS HAPPEN-ED!!

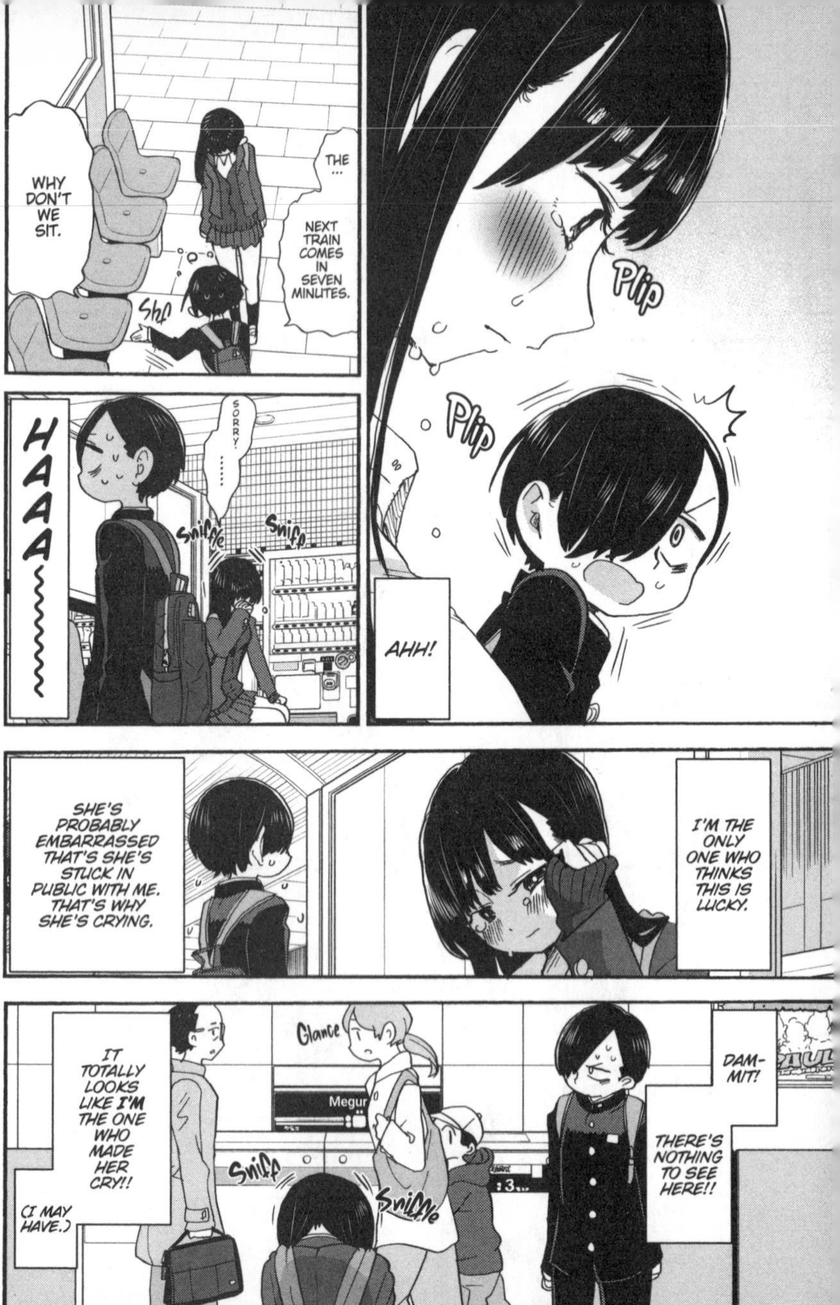
Plip
Plip
AHH!
THE... NEXT TRAIN COMES IN SEVEN MINUTES.
WHY DON'T WE SIT.
Shf
SORRY......
Sniff
Sniffle
HAAAA~
I'M THE ONLY ONE WHO THINKS THIS IS LUCKY.
SHE'S PROBABLY EMBARRASSED THAT'S SHE'S STUCK IN PUBLIC WITH ME. THAT'S WHY SHE'S CRYING.
DAM-MIT!
THERE'S NOTHING TO SEE HERE!!
Glance
Megur
IT TOTALLY LOOKS LIKE I'M THE ONE WHO MADE HER CRY!!
(I MAY HAVE.)
Sniffle
Sniff

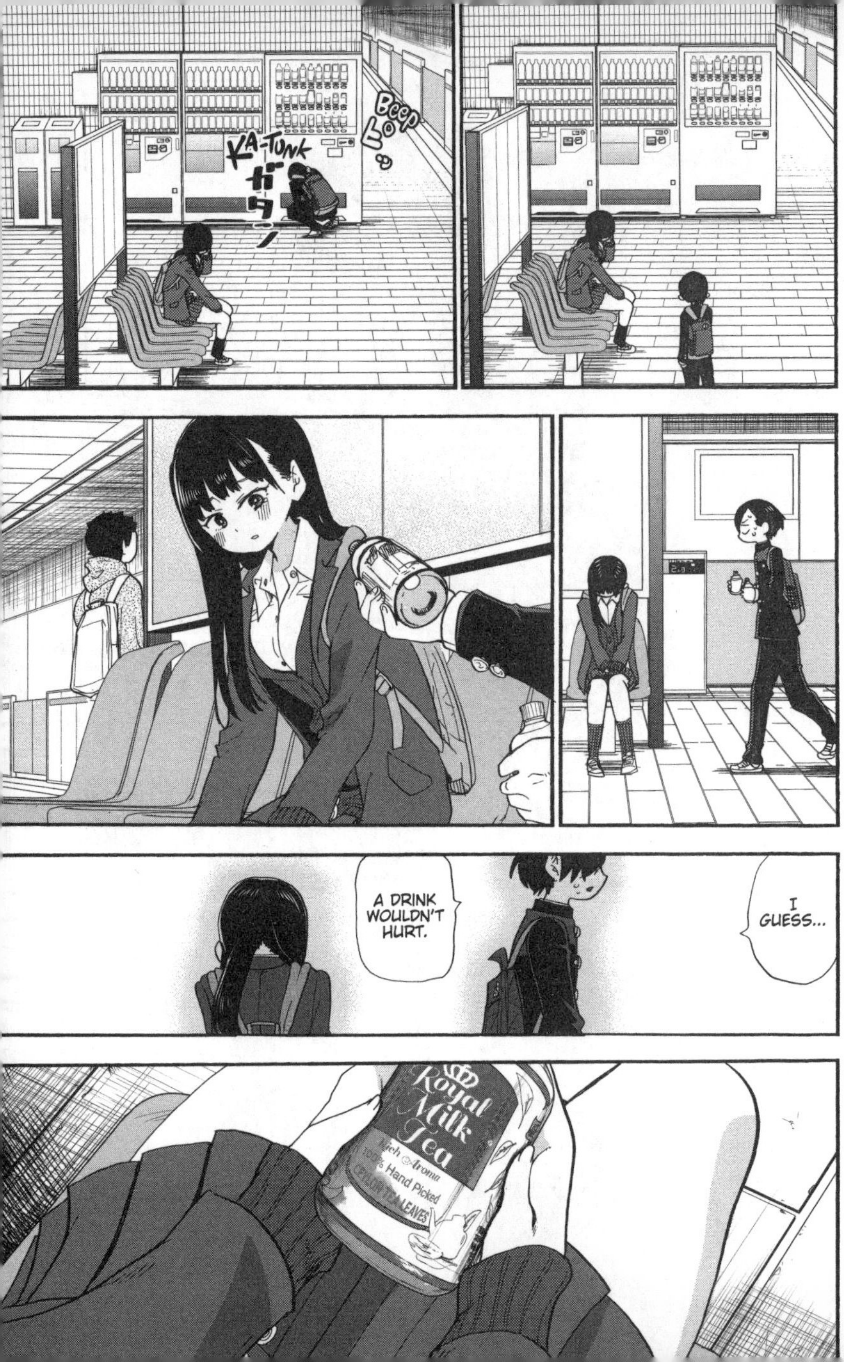
Beep
KA-TUNK
I GUESS...
A DRINK WOULDN'T HURT.
Royal Milk Tea
Rich Aroma
100% Hand Picked
CEYLON TEA LEAVES

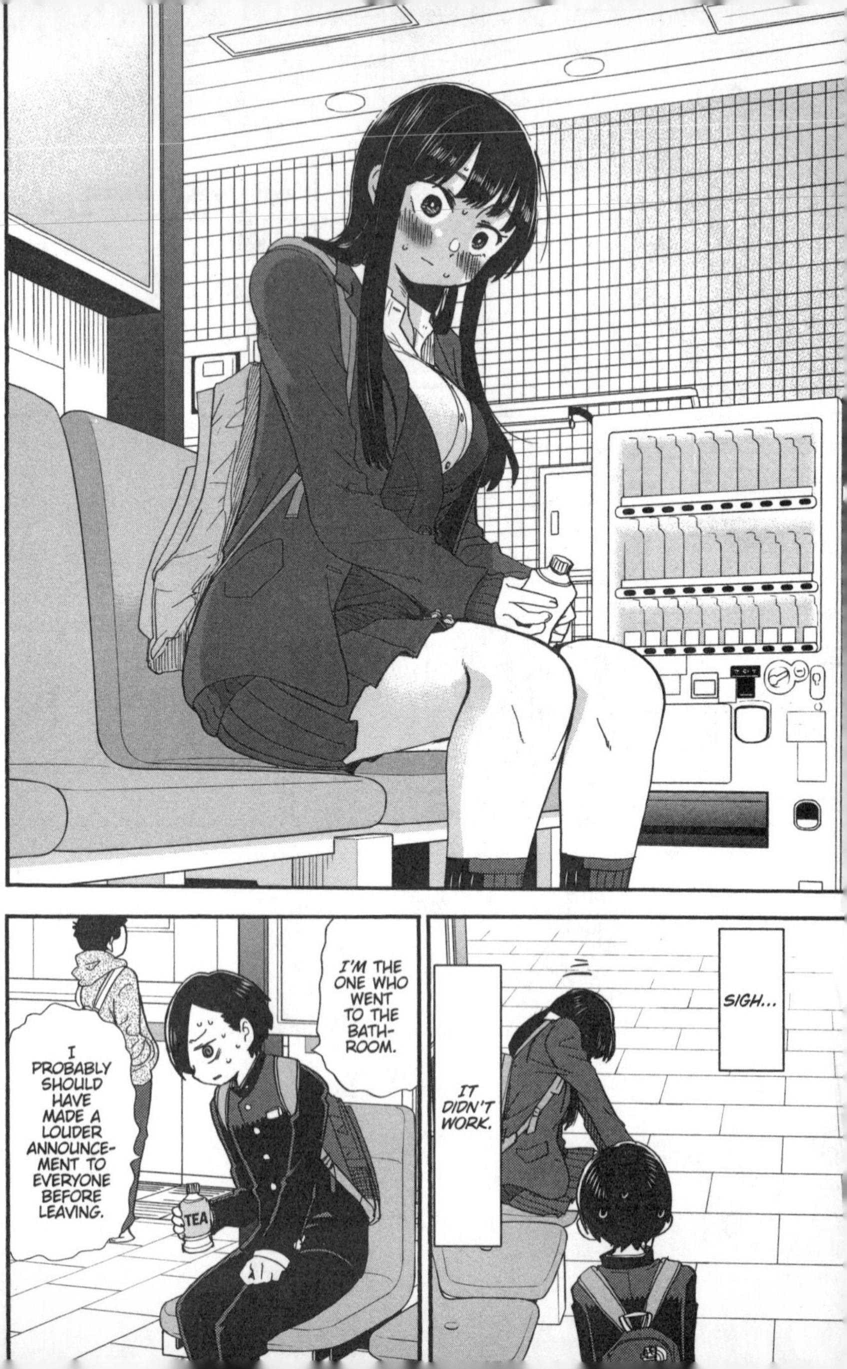
SIGH...
IT DIDN'T WORK.
I'M THE ONE WHO WENT TO THE BATHROOM.
I PROBABLY SHOULD HAVE MADE A LOUDER ANNOUNCEMENT TO EVERYONE BEFORE LEAVING.
TEA

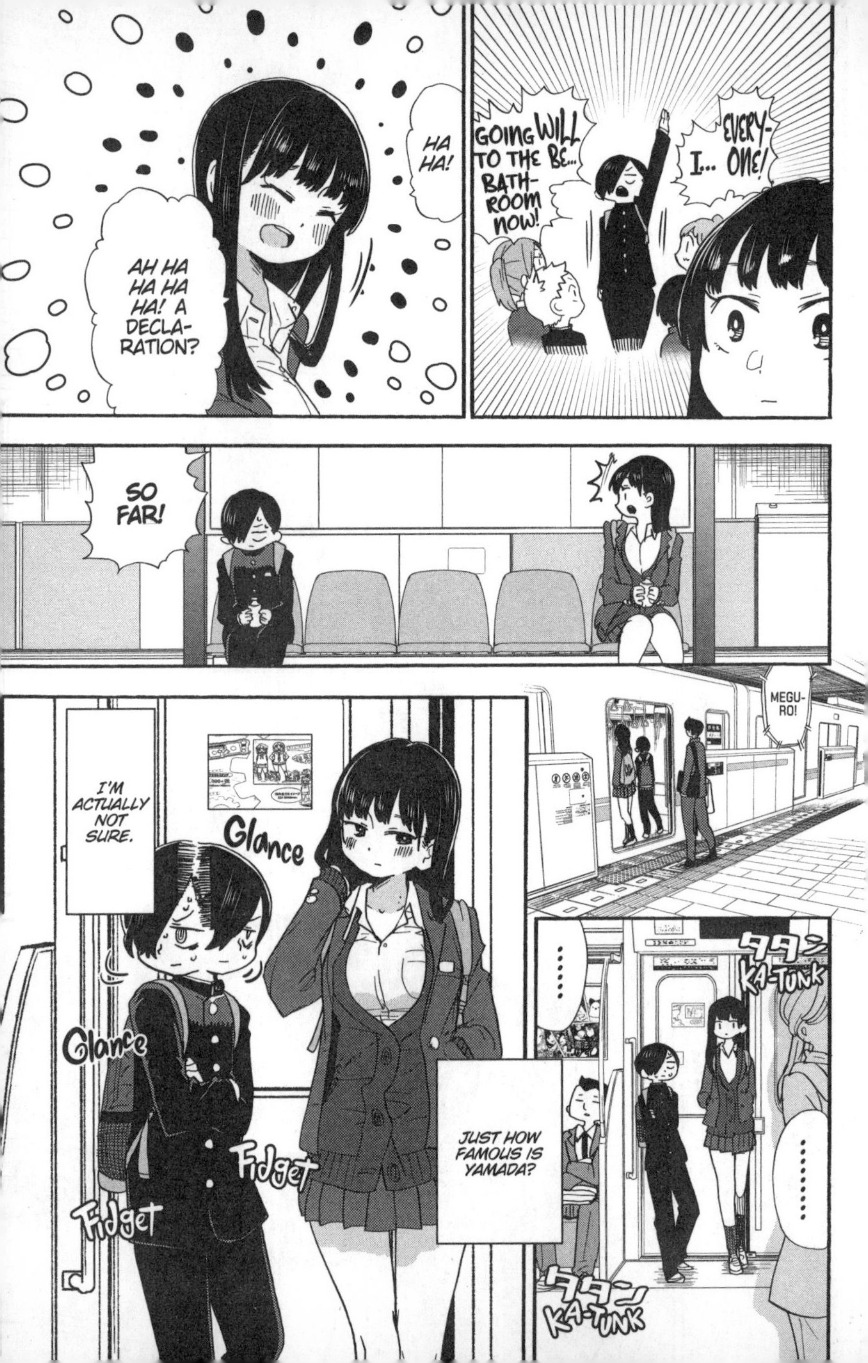
EVERY-ONE! I...
WILL BE... GOING TO THE BATH-ROOM NOW!
HA HA!
AH HA HA HA HA! A DECLA-RATION?
SO FAR!
MEGURO!
タタン KA-TUNK
......
......
タタン KA-TUNK
JUST HOW FAMOUS IS YAMADA?
I'M ACTUALLY NOT SURE.
Glance
Glance
Fidget
Fidget

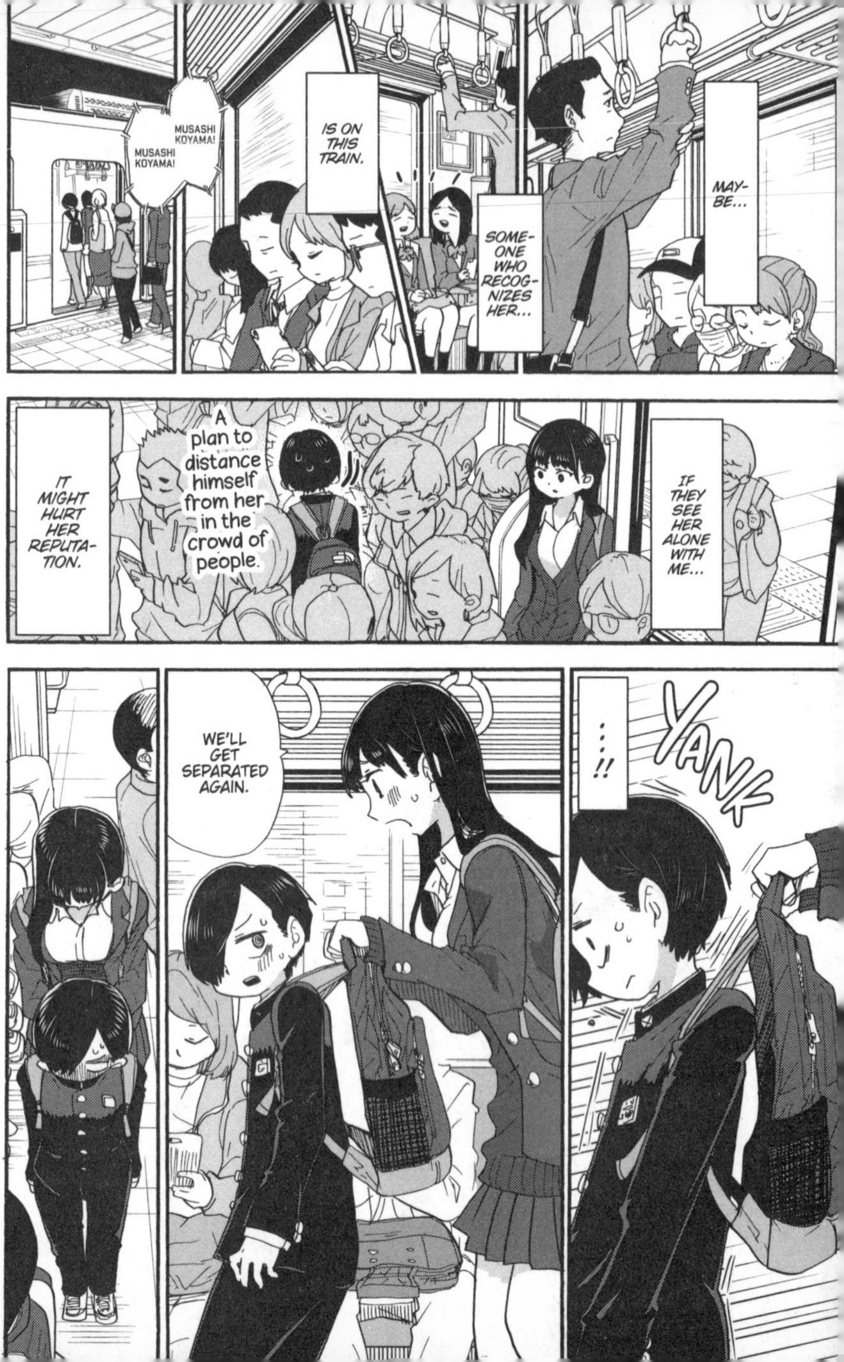
MAYBE...
SOMEONE WHO RECOGNIZES HER...
IS ON THIS TRAIN.
MUSASHI KOYAMA!
MUSASHI KOYAMA!
IF THEY SEE HER ALONE WITH ME...
A plan to distance himself from her in the crowd of people.
IT MIGHT HURT HER REPUTATION.
YANK
...!!
WE'LL GET SEPARATED AGAIN.

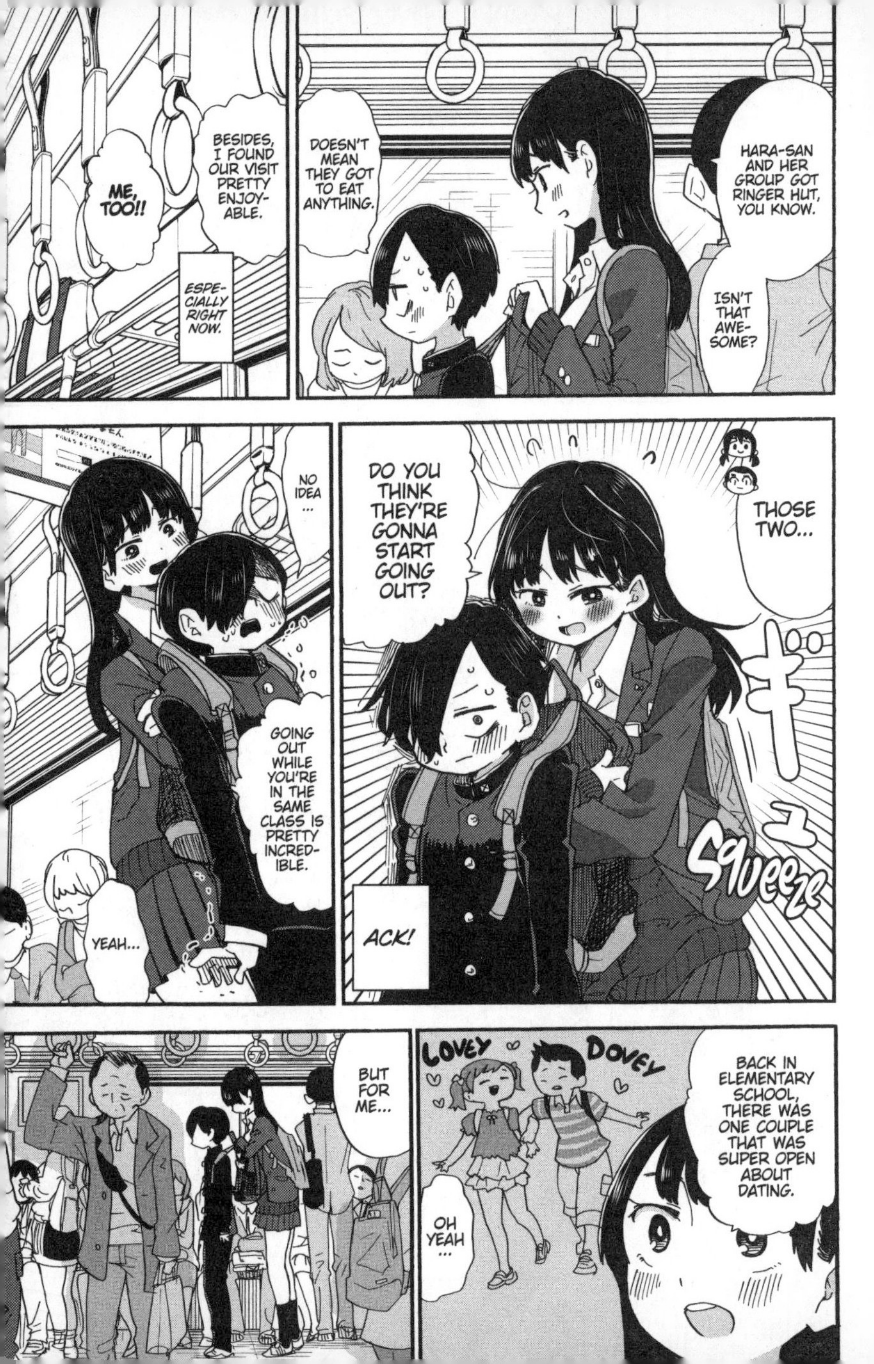
HARA-SAN AND HER GROUP GOT RINGER HUT, YOU KNOW.
ISN'T THAT AWE-SOME?
DOESN'T MEAN THEY GOT TO EAT ANYTHING.
BESIDES, I FOUND OUR VISIT PRETTY ENJOY-ABLE.
ESPE-CIALLY RIGHT NOW.
ME, TOO!!
THOSE TWO...
DO YOU THINK THEY'RE GONNA START GOING OUT?
ギュ
SQUEEZE
ACK!
NO IDEA...
GOING OUT WHILE YOU'RE IN THE SAME CLASS IS PRETTY INCRED-IBLE.
YEAH...
BACK IN ELEMENTARY SCHOOL, THERE WAS ONE COUPLE THAT WAS SUPER OPEN ABOUT DATING.
LOVEY DOVEY
OH YEAH...
BUT FOR ME...

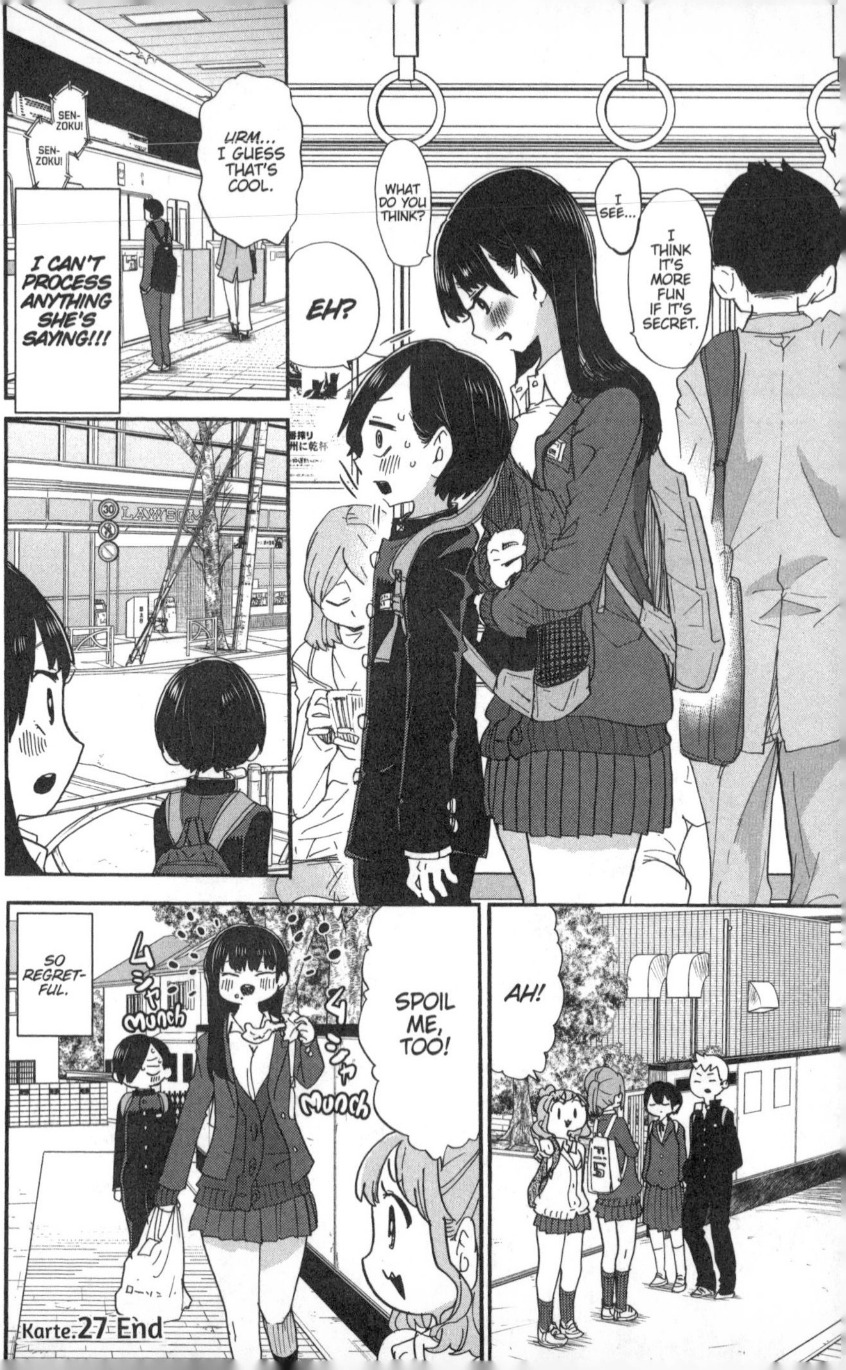
I SEE...
I THINK IT'S MORE FUN IF IT'S SECRET.
WHAT DO YOU THINK?
EH?
URM... I GUESS THAT'S COOL.
SEN-ZOKU!
SEN-ZOKU!
I CAN'T PROCESS ANYTHING SHE'S SAYING!!!
AH!
SPOIL ME, TOO!
Munch
SO REGRETFUL.
Munch
Karte. 27 End

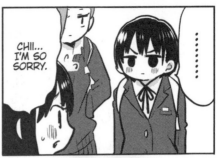

....
CHII... I'M SO SORRY.
I'M THE ONE WHO OUGHT TO BE SORRY!!
I'M GROUP LEADER, AND I THOUGHT WE HAD TO STAY ON SCHEDULE NO MATTER WHAT.
Sob Sob
I WAS SO OBSESSED WITH BEING ON TIME...
THAT I LOST SIGHT OF EVERY-THING ELSE.
IT'S ALL RIGHT. EVERYONE MAKES MISTAKES.
WHO THE HELL DO YOU THINK YOU ARE?!

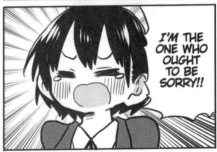

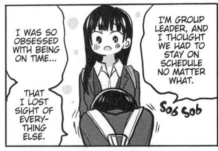

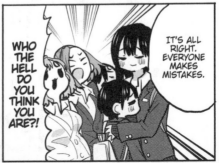

The
Dangers
in My
Heart

Karte.28 I'm Enjoying School

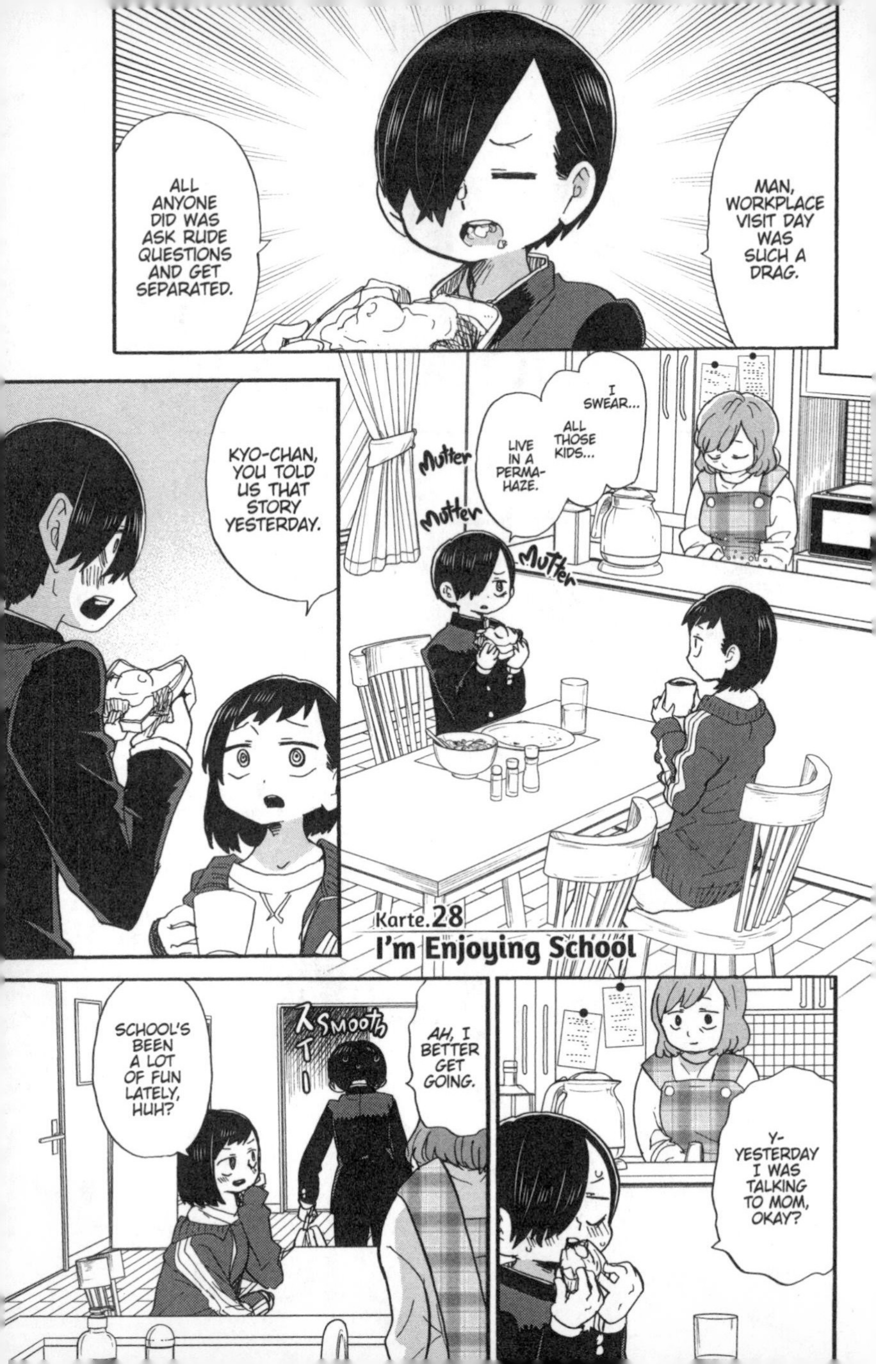
MAN, WORKPLACE VISIT DAY WAS SUCH A DRAG.
ALL ANYONE DID WAS ASK RUDE QUESTIONS AND GET SEPARATED.
I SWEAR...
ALL THOSE KIDS...
LIVE IN A PERMA-HAZE.
Mutter
Mutter
Mutter
KYO-CHAN, YOU TOLD US THAT STORY YESTERDAY.
Y-YESTERDAY I WAS TALKING TO MOM, OKAY?
AH, I BETTER GET GOING.
スィー SMOOTH
SCHOOL'S BEEN A LOT OF FUN LATELY, HUH?

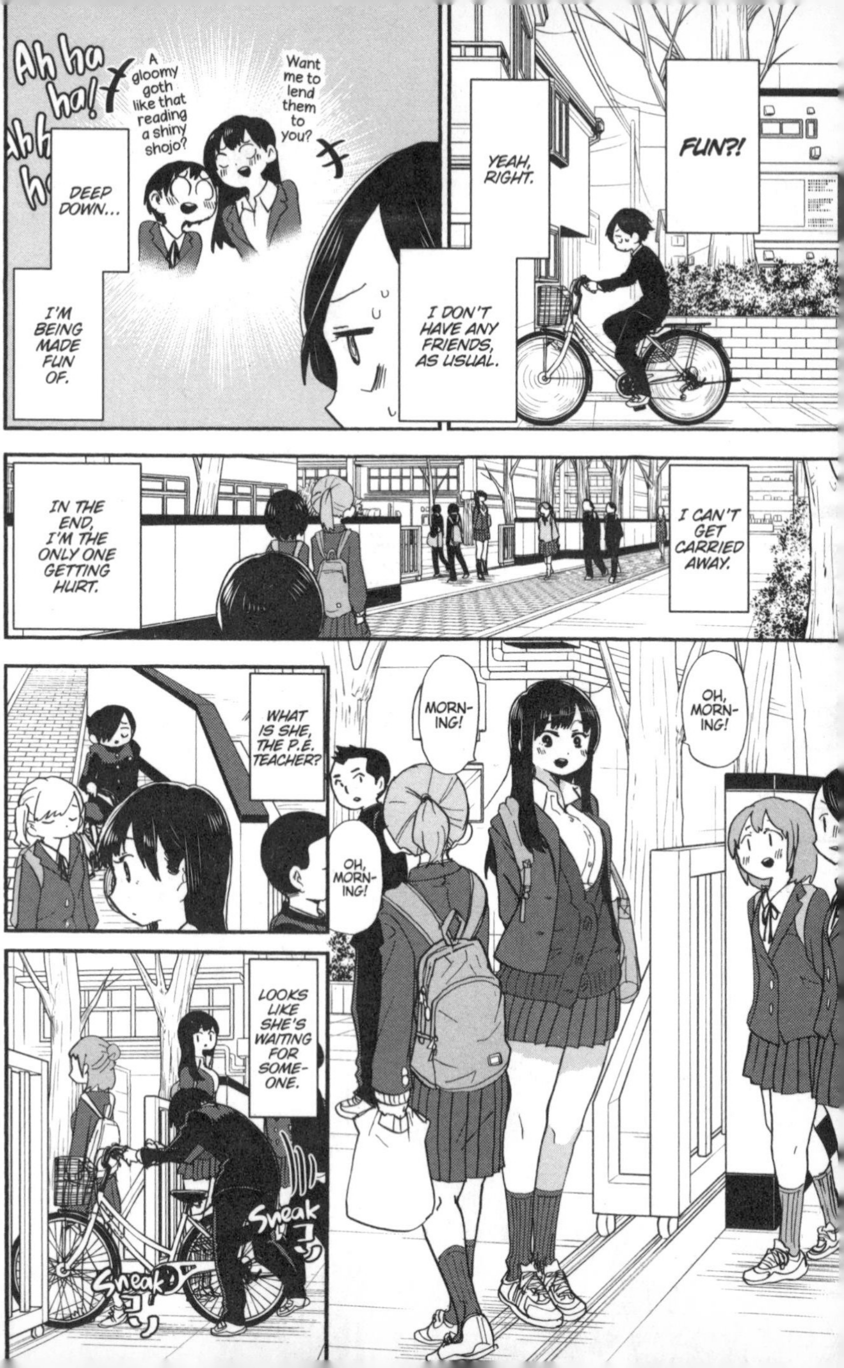

FUN?!
YEAH, RIGHT.
I DON'T HAVE ANY FRIENDS, AS USUAL.
Want me to lend them to you?
A gloomy goth like that reading a shiny shojo?
Ah ha ha!
DEEP DOWN...
I'M BEING MADE FUN OF.
I CAN'T GET CARRIED AWAY.
IN THE END, I'M THE ONLY ONE GETTING HURT.
OH, MORNING!
MORN-ING!
OH, MORN-ING!
WHAT IS SHE, THE P.E. TEACHER?
LOOKS LIKE SHE'S WAITING FOR SOME-ONE.
Sneak
Sneak

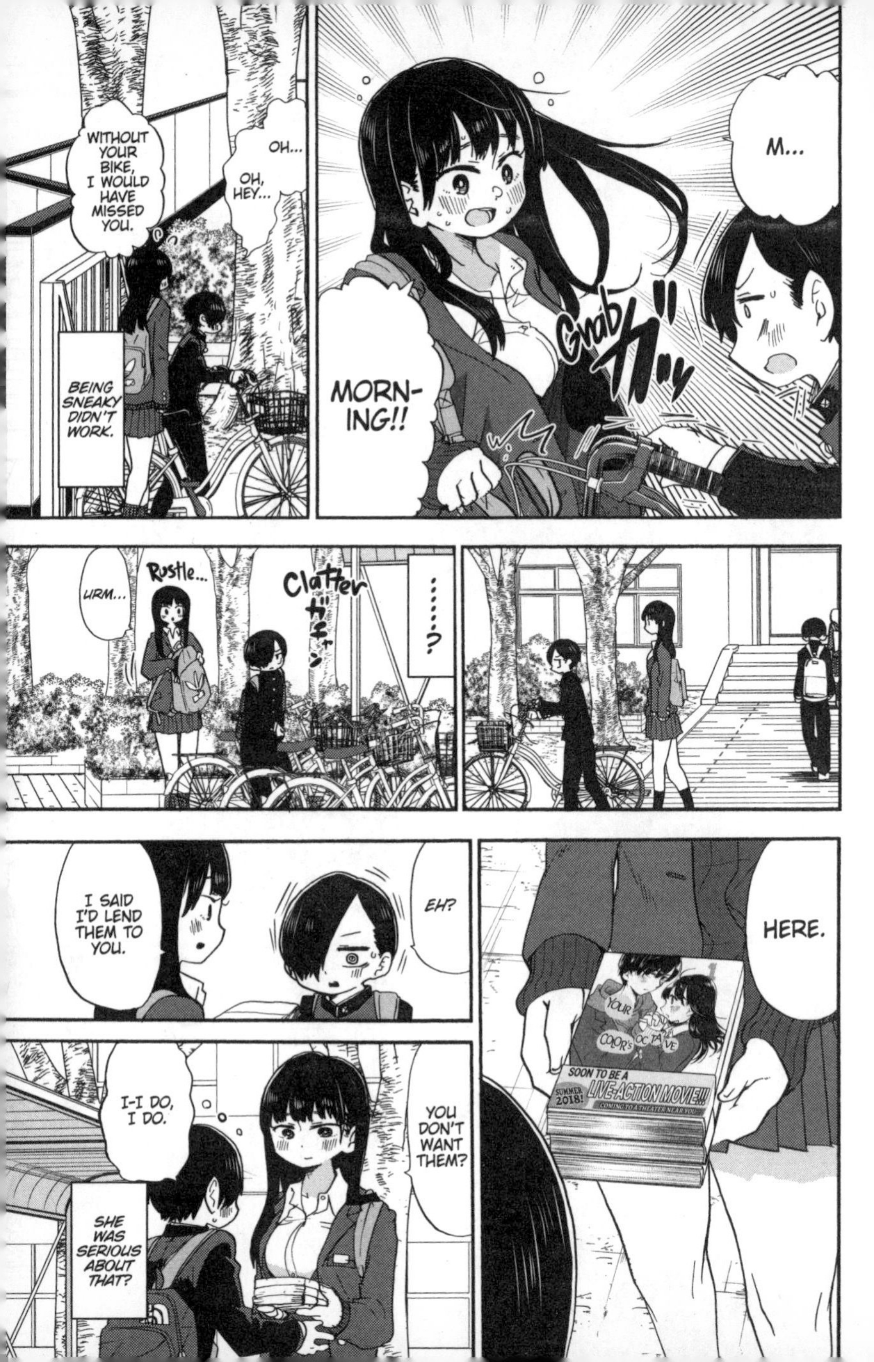
M...
Grab ガッ
MORNING!!
OH...
OH, HEY...
WITHOUT YOUR BIKE, I WOULD HAVE MISSED YOU.
BEING SNEAKY DIDN'T WORK.
......?
Clatter ガチャン
Rustle...
URM...
HERE.
YOUR COLOR'S OCTAVE
SOON TO BE A LIVE-ACTION MOVIE!!!
SUMMER 2018!
COMING TO A THEATER NEAR YOU
EH?
I SAID I'D LEND THEM TO YOU.
YOU DON'T WANT THEM?
I-I DO, I DO.
SHE WAS SERIOUS ABOUT THAT?

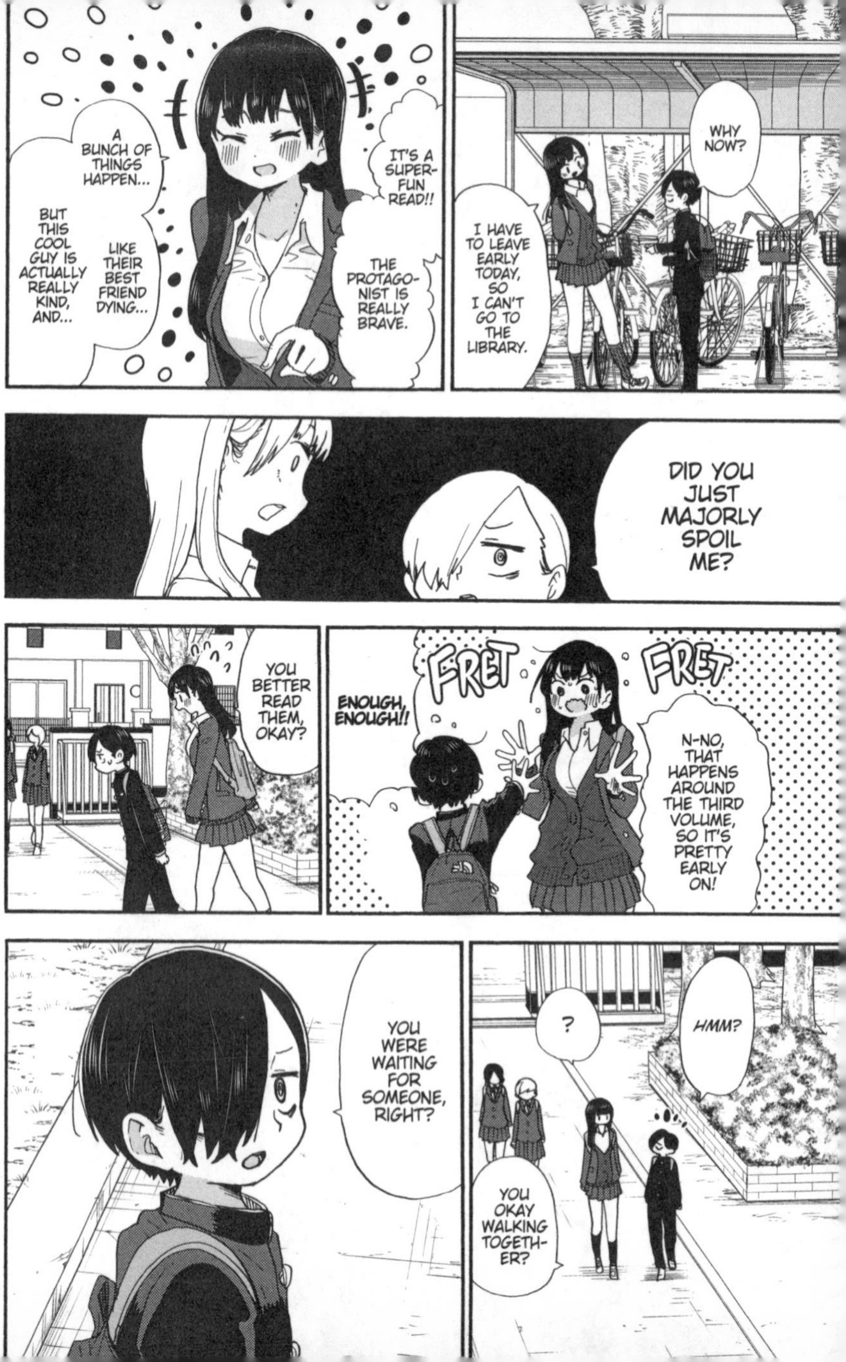
WHY NOW?
I HAVE TO LEAVE EARLY TODAY, SO I CAN'T GO TO THE LIBRARY.
IT'S A SUPER-FUN READ!!
THE PROTAGONIST IS REALLY BRAVE.
A BUNCH OF THINGS HAPPEN...
LIKE THEIR BEST FRIEND DYING...
BUT THIS COOL GUY IS ACTUALLY REALLY KIND, AND...
DID YOU JUST MAJORLY SPOIL ME?
FRET
FRET
N-NO, THAT HAPPENS AROUND THE THIRD VOLUME, SO IT'S PRETTY EARLY ON!
ENOUGH, ENOUGH!!
YOU BETTER READ THEM, OKAY?
HMM?
?
YOU OKAY WALKING TOGETHER?
YOU WERE WAITING FOR SOMEONE, RIGHT?

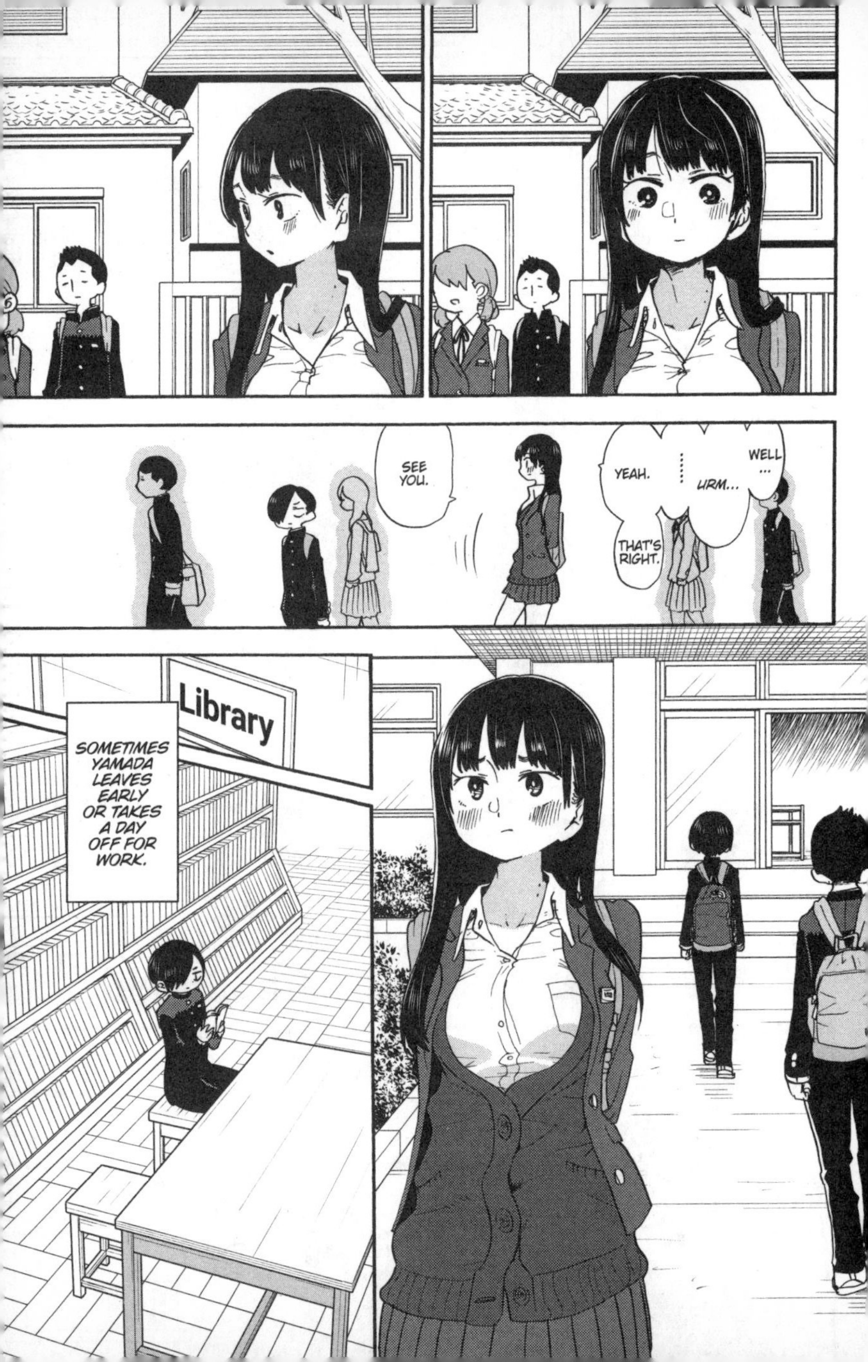
WELL ...
URM...
......
YEAH.
THAT'S RIGHT.
SEE YOU.
Library
SOMETIMES YAMADA LEAVES EARLY OR TAKES A DAY OFF FOR WORK.

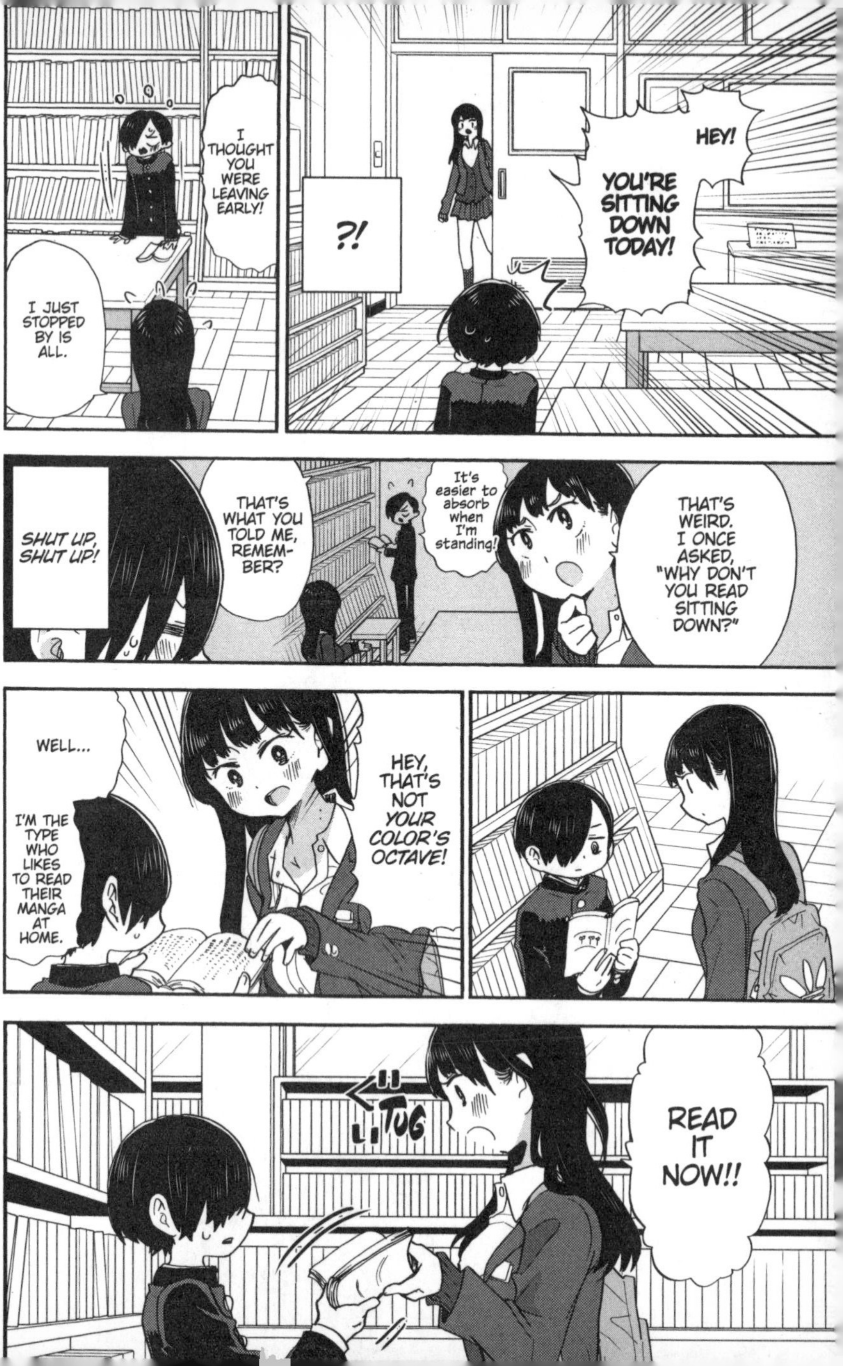
HEY!
YOU'RE SITTING DOWN TODAY!
?!
I THOUGHT YOU WERE LEAVING EARLY!
I JUST STOPPED BY IS ALL.
THAT'S WEIRD. I ONCE ASKED, "WHY DON'T YOU READ SITTING DOWN?"
It's easier to absorb when I'm standing!
THAT'S WHAT YOU TOLD ME, REMEMBER?
SHUT UP, SHUT UP!
HEY, THAT'S NOT YOUR COLOR'S OCTAVE!
WELL...
I'M THE TYPE WHO LIKES TO READ THEIR MANGA AT HOME.
READ IT NOW!!
TUG

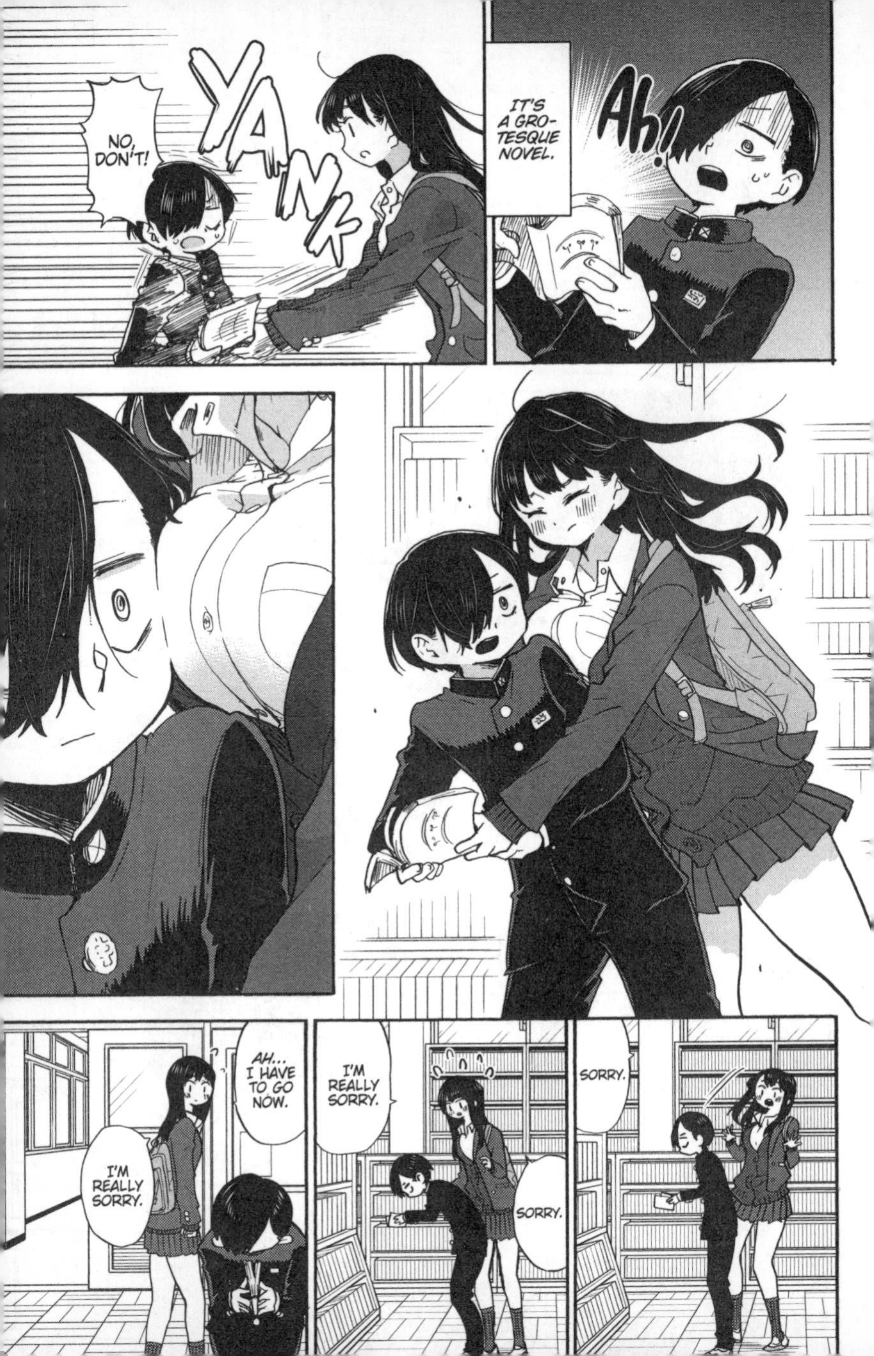
IT'S A GRO-TESQUE NOVEL.
Ah!!
YANK
NO, DON'T!
SORRY.
I'M REALLY SORRY.
SORRY.
AH... I HAVE TO GO NOW.
I'M REALLY SORRY.

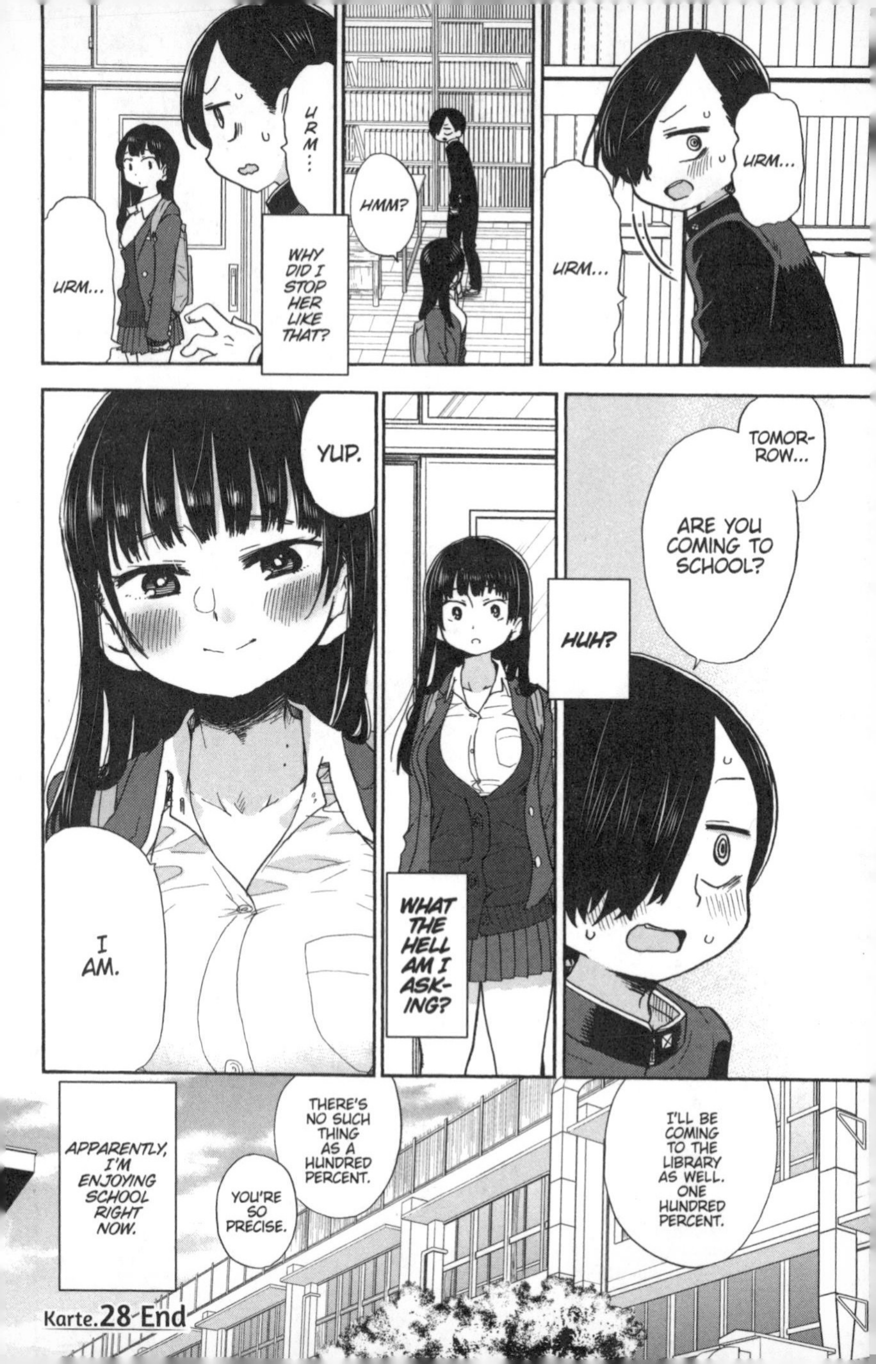
URM...
URM...
HMM?
WHY DID I STOP HER LIKE THAT?
URM...
URM...
TOMORROW...
ARE YOU COMING TO SCHOOL?
HUH?
WHAT THE HELL AM I ASKING?
YUP.
I AM.
I'LL BE COMING TO THE LIBRARY AS WELL. ONE HUNDRED PERCENT.
THERE'S NO SUCH THING AS A HUNDRED PERCENT.
YOU'RE SO PRECISE.
APPARENTLY, I'M ENJOYING SCHOOL RIGHT NOW.
Karte.28 End

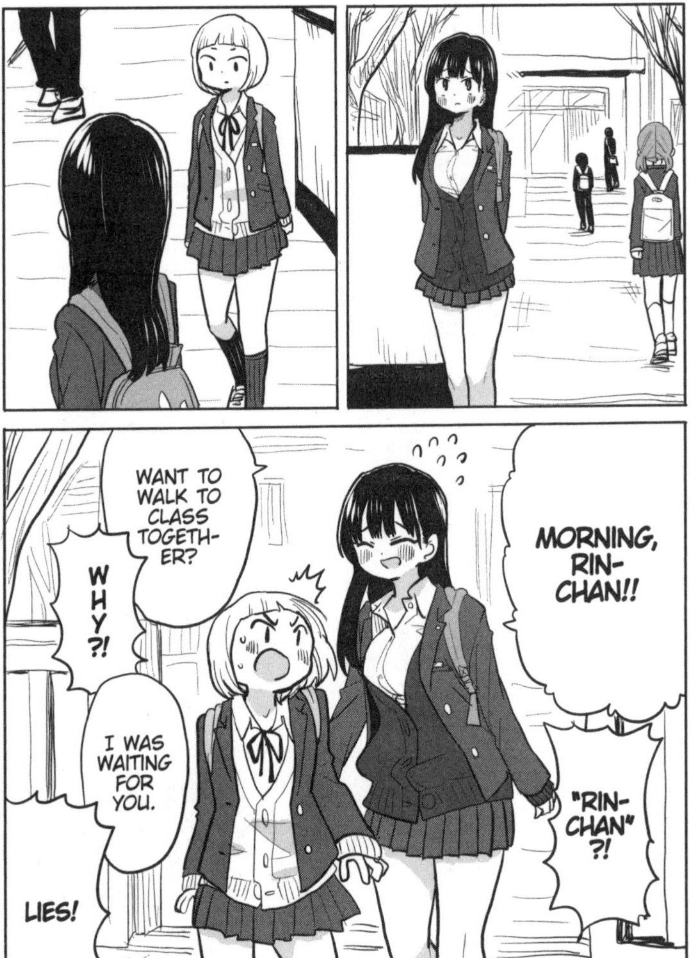
MORNING, RIN-CHAN!!
"RIN-CHAN"?!
WANT TO WALK TO CLASS TOGETH-ER?
WHY?!
I WAS WAITING FOR YOU.
LIES!

The
Dangers
in My
Heart

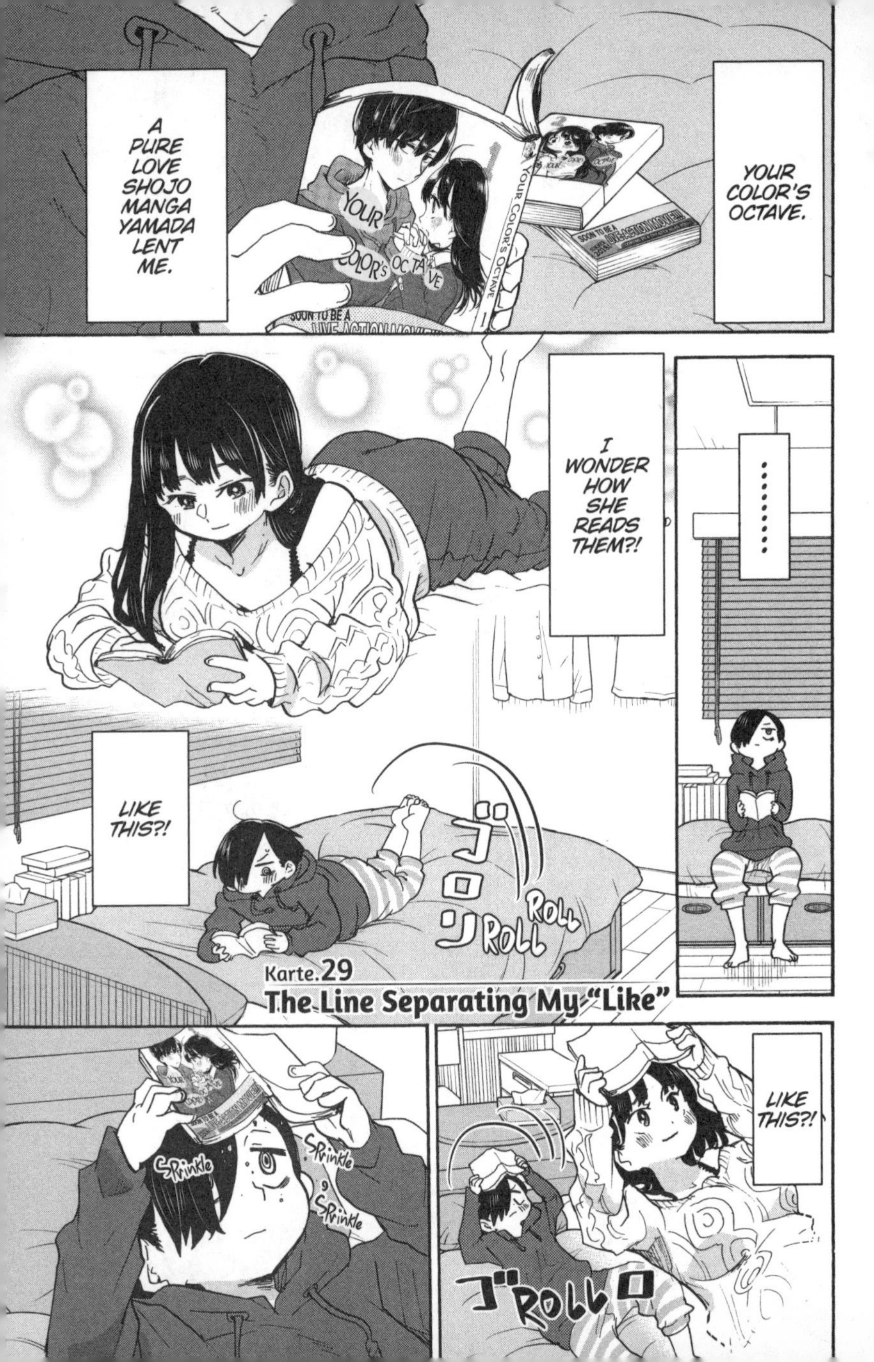
YOUR COLOR'S OCTAVE.
A PURE LOVE SHOJO MANGA YAMADA LENT ME.
YOUR COLOR'S OCTAVE
……
I WONDER HOW SHE READS THEM?!
ゴロン ROLL ROLL
LIKE THIS?!
Karte. 29
The Line Separating My "Like"
LIKE THIS?!
ゴロ ROLL
SPRINKLE
SPRINKLE SPRINKLE

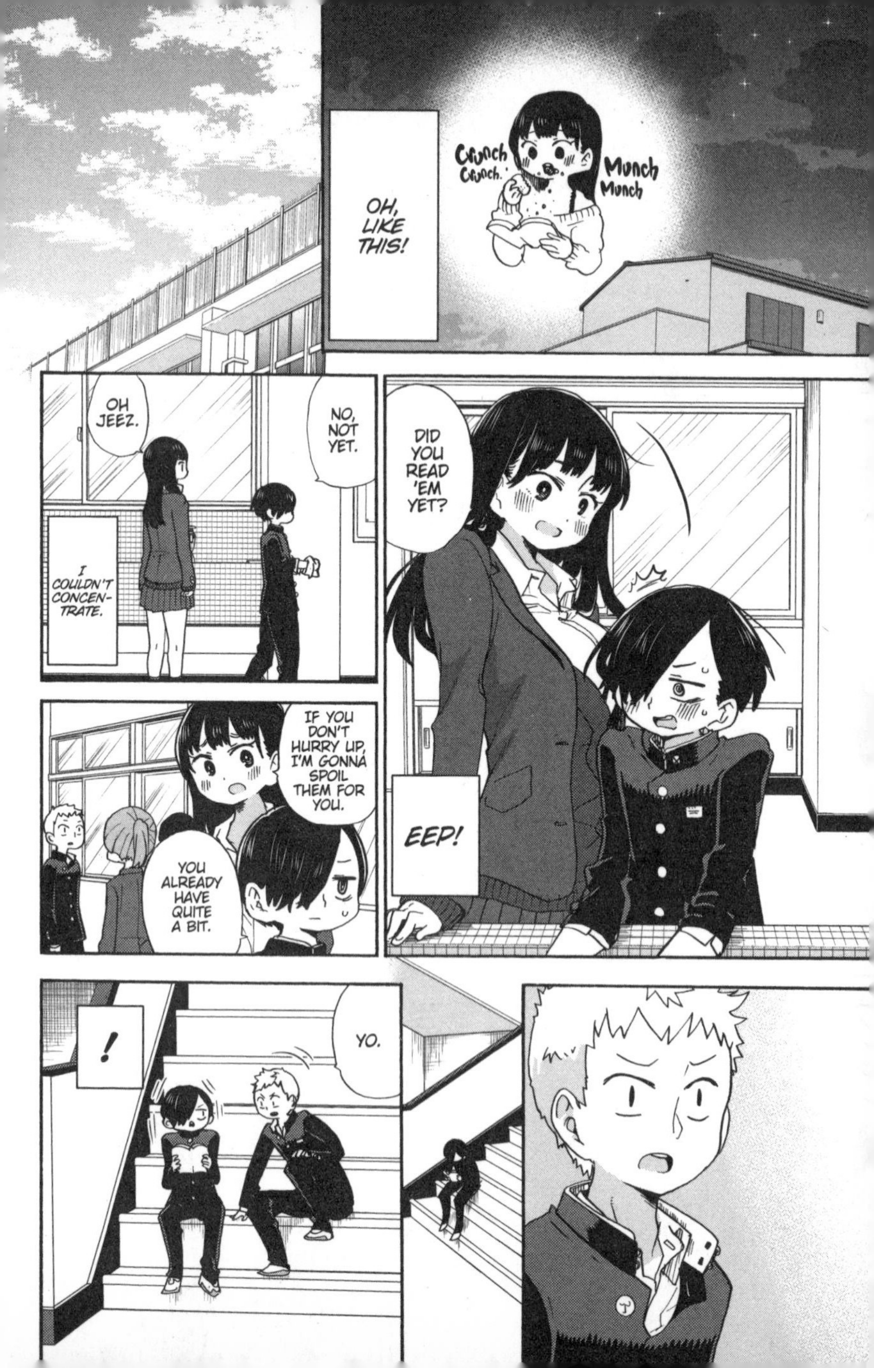
Munch Munch
Crunch Crunch.
OH, LIKE THIS!
DID YOU READ 'EM YET?
EEP!
NO, NOT YET.
OH JEEZ.
I COULDN'T CONCENTRATE.
IF YOU DON'T HURRY UP, I'M GONNA SPOIL THEM FOR YOU.
YOU ALREADY HAVE QUITE A BIT.
YO.
!

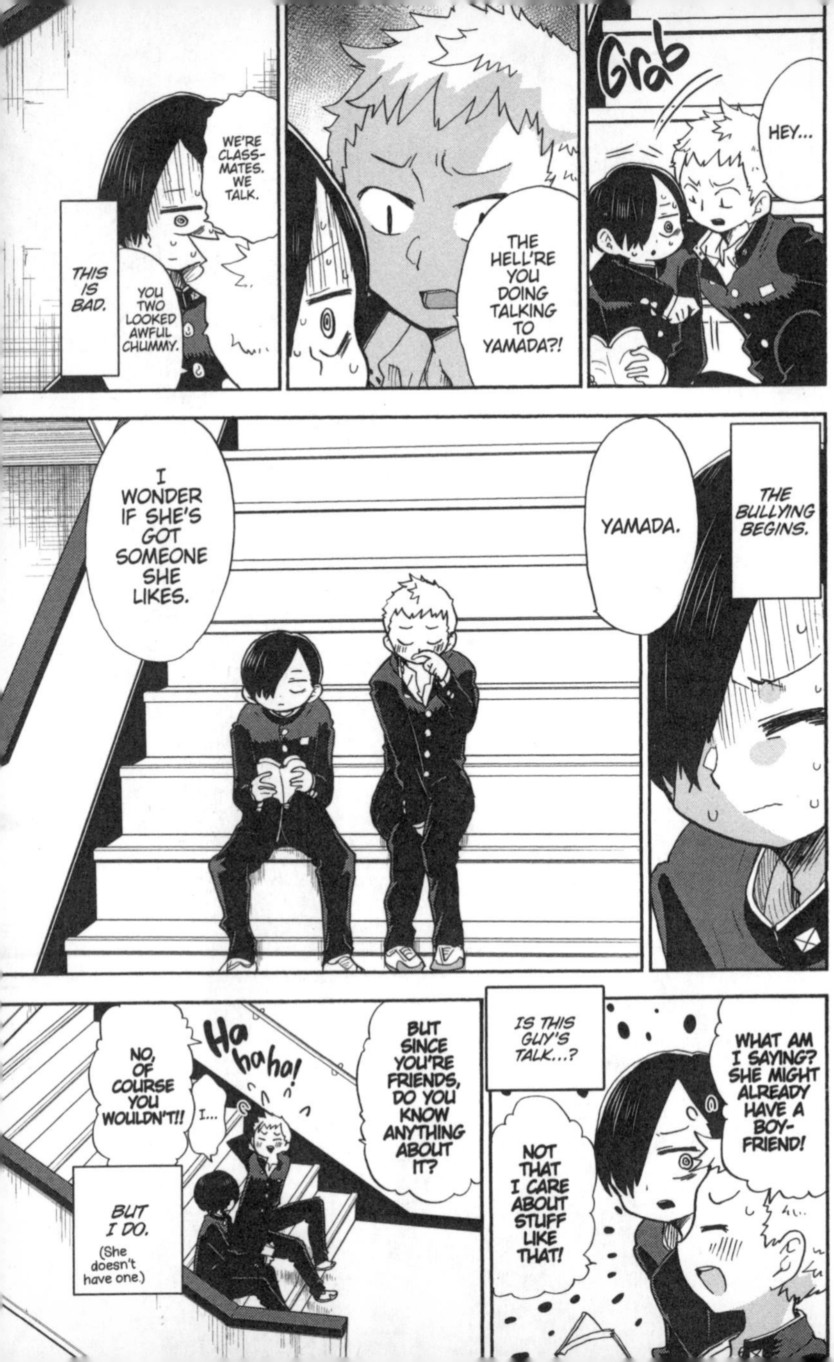
Grab
HEY...
THE HELL'RE YOU DOING TALKING TO YAMADA?!
WE'RE CLASSMATES. WE TALK.
THIS IS BAD.
YOU TWO LOOKED AWFUL CHUMMY.
THE BULLYING BEGINS.
YAMADA.
I WONDER IF SHE'S GOT SOMEONE SHE LIKES.
WHAT AM I SAYING? SHE MIGHT ALREADY HAVE A BOY-FRIEND!
IS THIS GUY'S TALK...?
NOT THAT I CARE ABOUT STUFF LIKE THAT!
BUT SINCE YOU'RE FRIENDS, DO YOU KNOW ANYTHING ABOUT IT?
Ha haha!
NO, OF COURSE YOU WOULDN'T!!
I...
BUT I DO.
(She doesn't have one.)

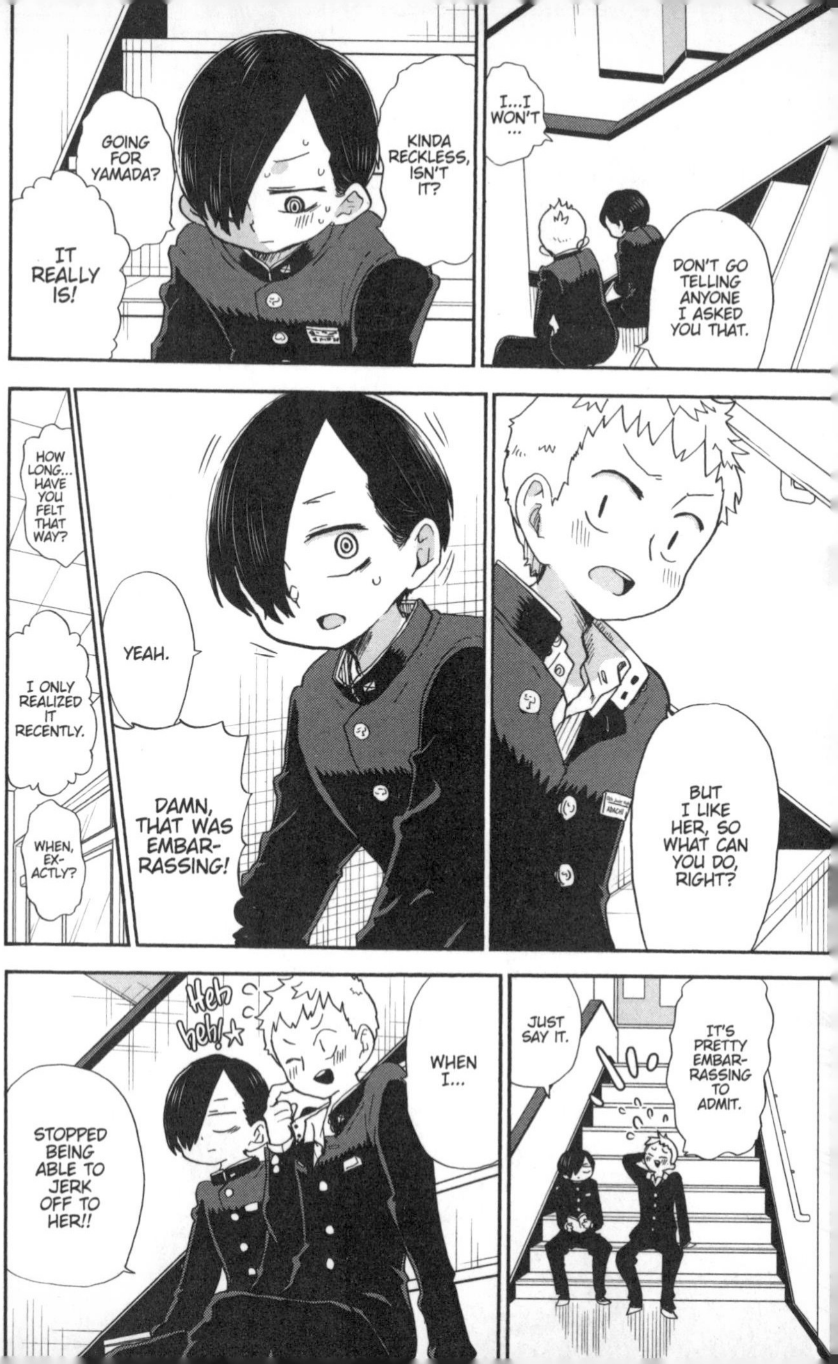
I...I WON'T ...
DON'T GO TELLING ANYONE I ASKED YOU THAT.
KINDA RECKLESS, ISN'T IT?
GOING FOR YAMADA?
IT REALLY IS!
BUT I LIKE HER, SO WHAT CAN YOU DO, RIGHT?
HOW LONG... HAVE YOU FELT THAT WAY?
YEAH.
I ONLY REALIZED IT RECENTLY.
DAMN, THAT WAS EMBARRASSING!
WHEN, EXACTLY?
IT'S PRETTY EMBARRASSING TO ADMIT.
JUST SAY IT.
WHEN I...
Heh heh!★
STOPPED BEING ABLE TO JERK OFF TO HER!!

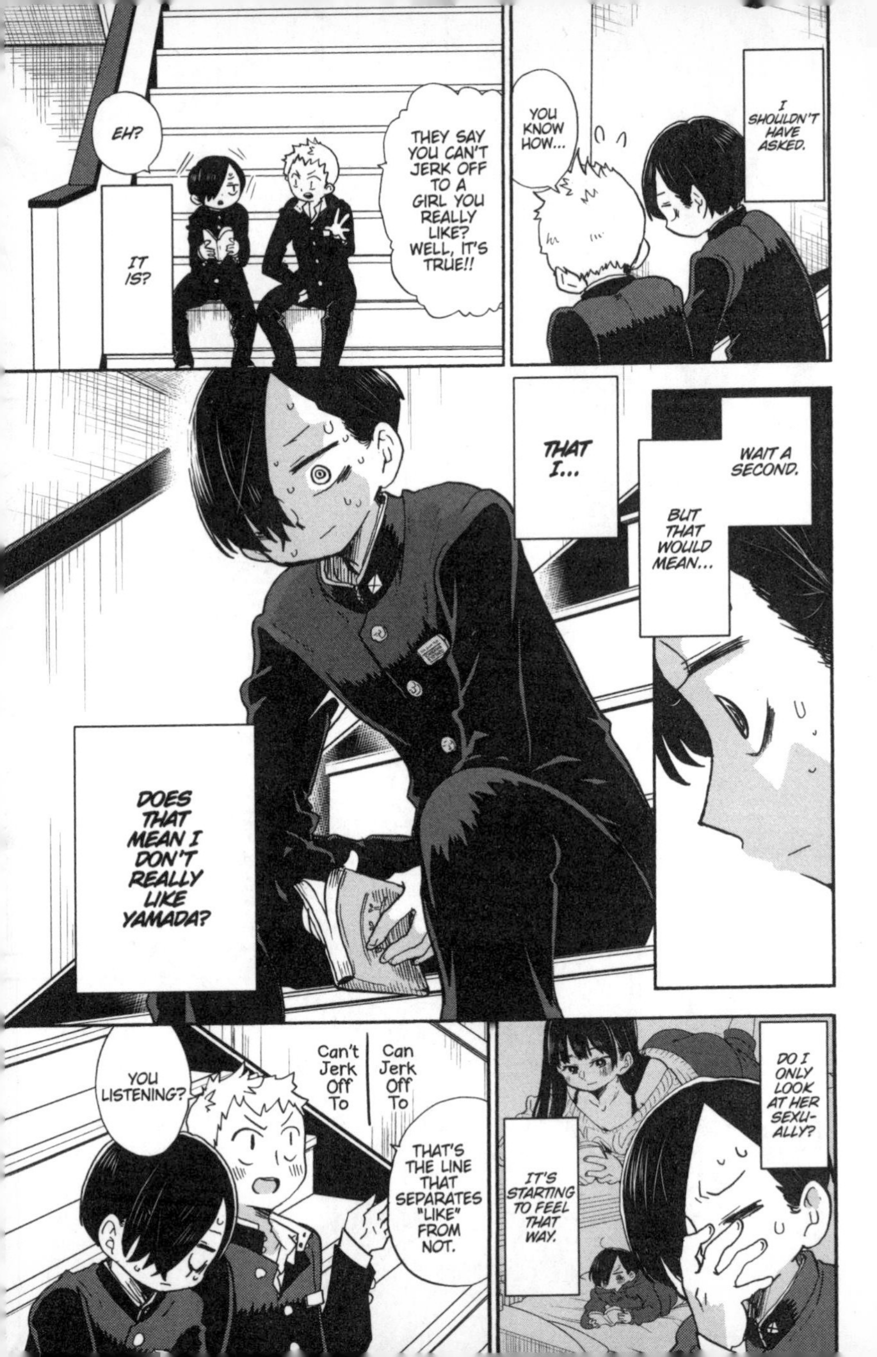
I SHOULDN'T HAVE ASKED.
YOU KNOW HOW...
THEY SAY YOU CAN'T JERK OFF TO A GIRL YOU REALLY LIKE? WELL, IT'S TRUE!!
EH?
IT IS?
WAIT A SECOND.
BUT THAT WOULD MEAN...
THAT I...
DOES THAT MEAN I DON'T REALLY LIKE YAMADA?
DO I ONLY LOOK AT HER SEXU-ALLY?
IT'S STARTING TO FEEL THAT WAY.
Can Jerk Off To
Can't Jerk Off To
YOU LISTENING?
THAT'S THE LINE THAT SEPARATES "LIKE" FROM NOT.

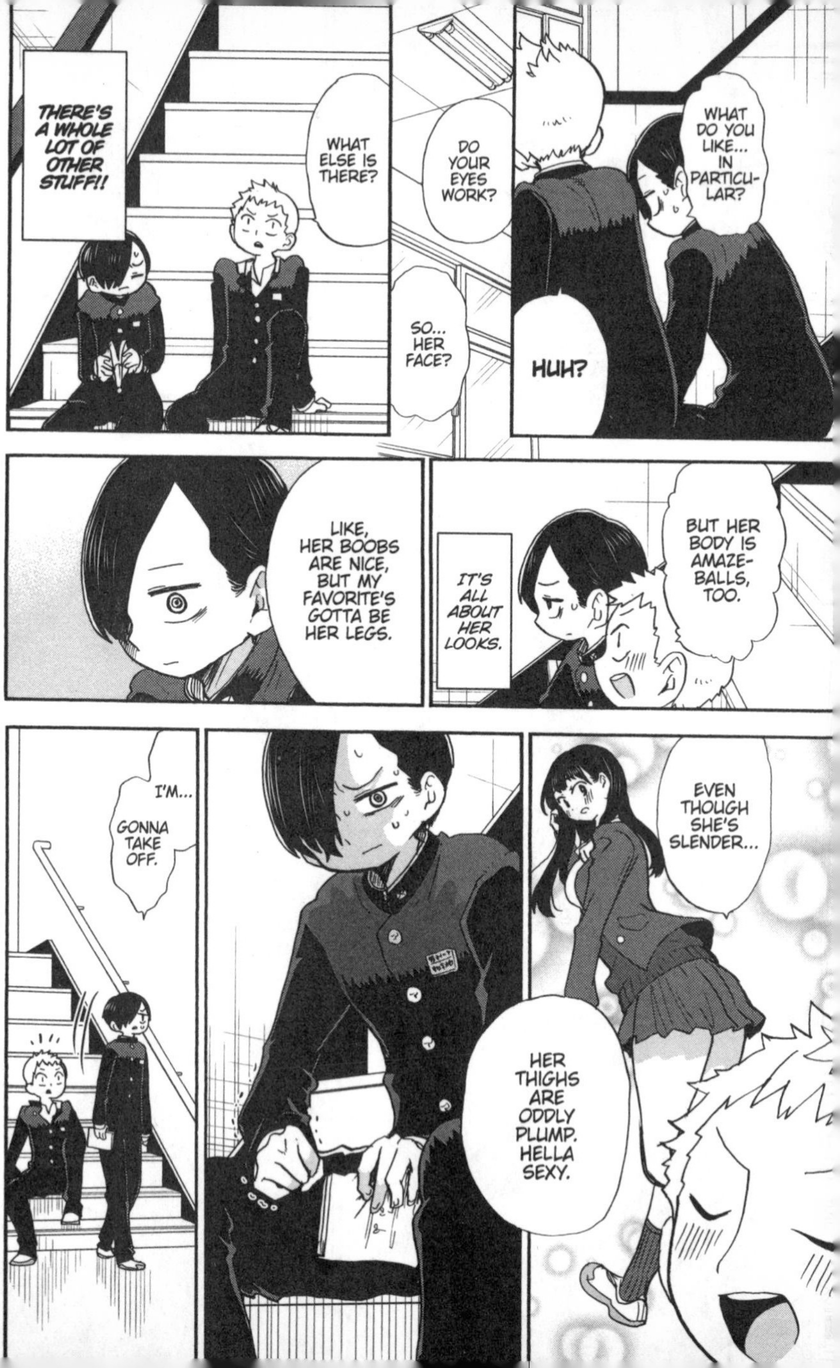
WHAT DO YOU LIKE... IN PARTICULAR?
HUH?
DO YOUR EYES WORK?
SO... HER FACE?
WHAT ELSE IS THERE?
THERE'S A WHOLE LOT OF OTHER STUFF!!
BUT HER BODY IS AMAZE-BALLS, TOO.
IT'S ALL ABOUT HER LOOKS.
LIKE, HER BOOBS ARE NICE, BUT MY FAVORITE'S GOTTA BE HER LEGS.
EVEN THOUGH SHE'S SLENDER...
HER THIGHS ARE ODDLY PLUMP. HELLA SEXY.
I'M...
GONNA TAKE OFF.

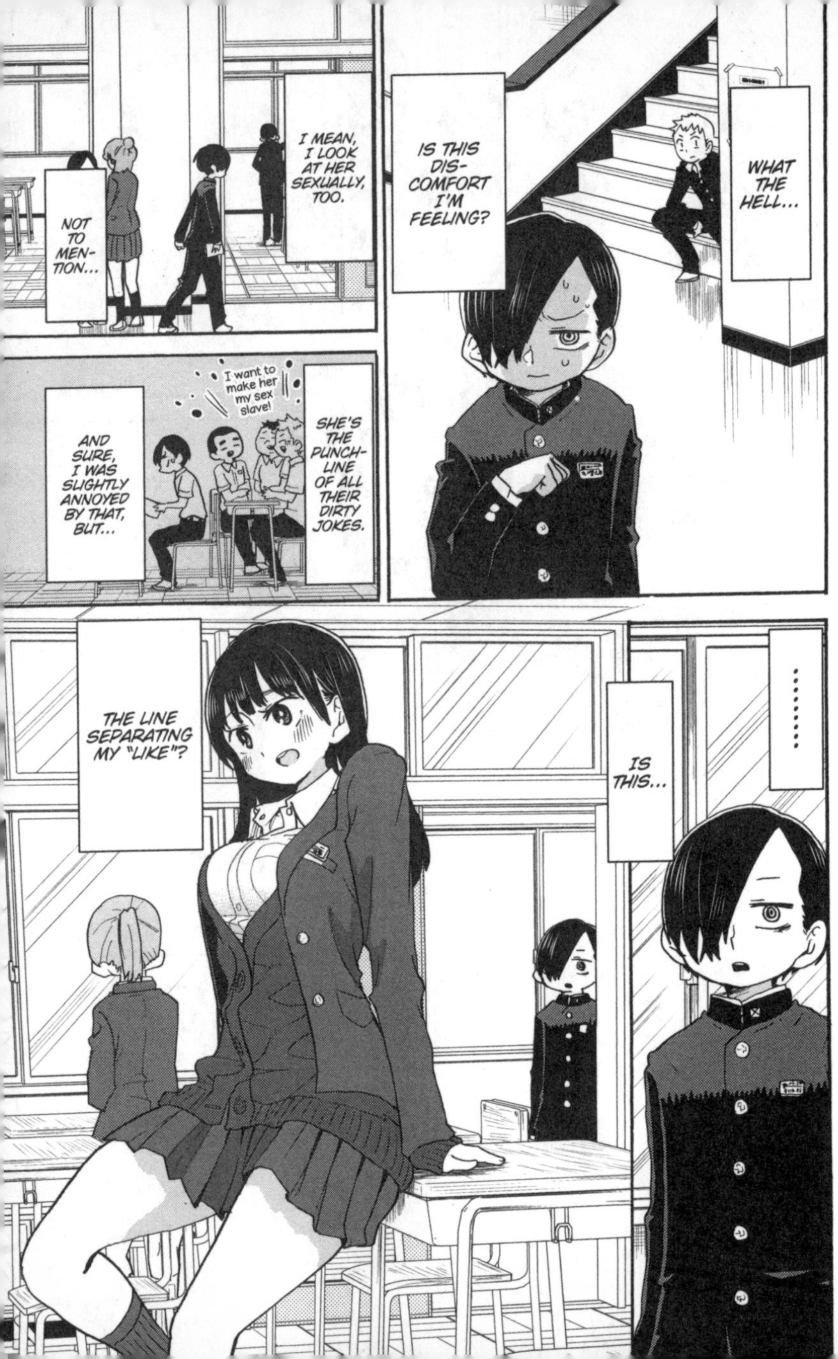
WHAT THE HELL...
IS THIS DIS-COMFORT I'M FEELING?
I MEAN, I LOOK AT HER SEXUALLY, TOO.
NOT TO MEN-TION...
SHE'S THE PUNCH-LINE OF ALL THEIR DIRTY JOKES.
I want to make her my sex slave!
AND SURE, I WAS SLIGHTLY ANNOYED BY THAT, BUT...
....
IS THIS...
THE LINE SEPARATING MY "LIKE"?

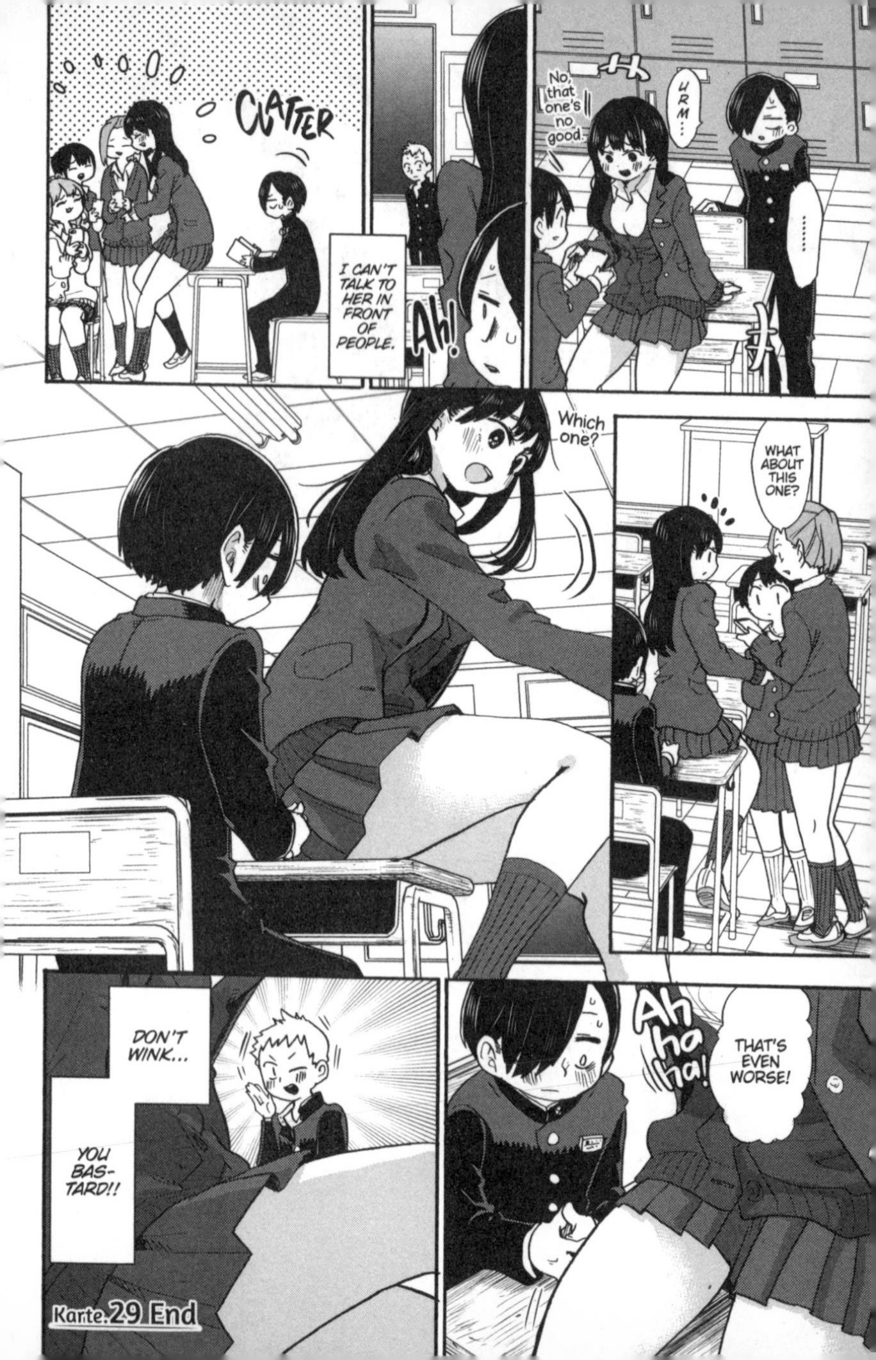
URM...
No, that one's no good.
......
I CAN'T TALK TO HER IN FRONT OF PEOPLE.
Ah!
CLATTER
WHAT ABOUT THIS ONE?
Which one?
Ahahaha!
THAT'S EVEN WORSE!
DON'T WINK...
YOU BASTARD!!
Karte.29 End

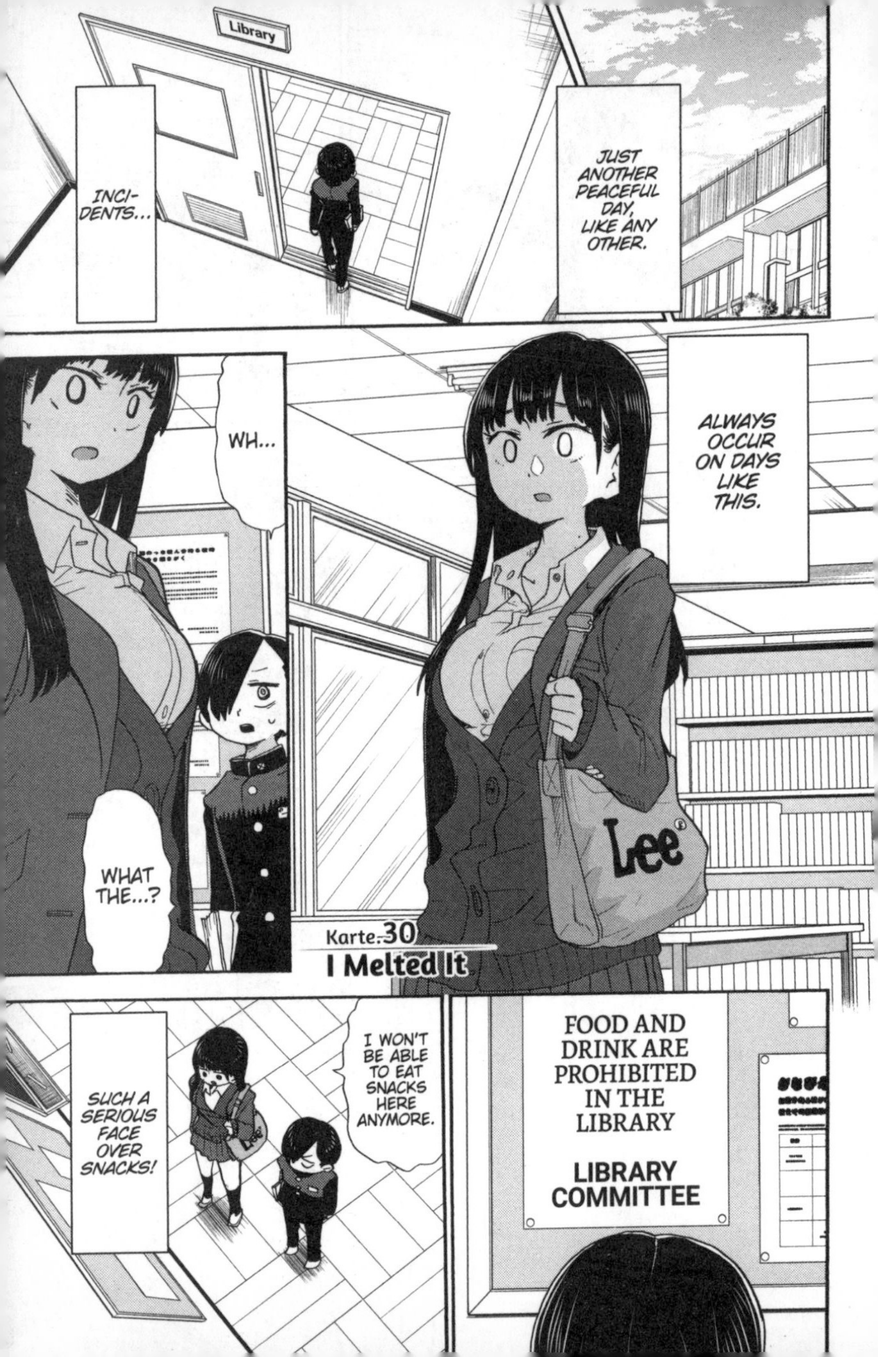
JUST ANOTHER PEACEFUL DAY, LIKE ANY OTHER.
Library
INCI-DENTS...
ALWAYS OCCUR ON DAYS LIKE THIS.
Karte.30
I Melted It
WH...
WHAT THE...?
FOOD AND DRINK ARE PROHIBITED IN THE LIBRARY
LIBRARY COMMITTEE
I WON'T BE ABLE TO EAT SNACKS HERE ANYMORE.
SUCH A SERIOUS FACE OVER SNACKS!
Lee

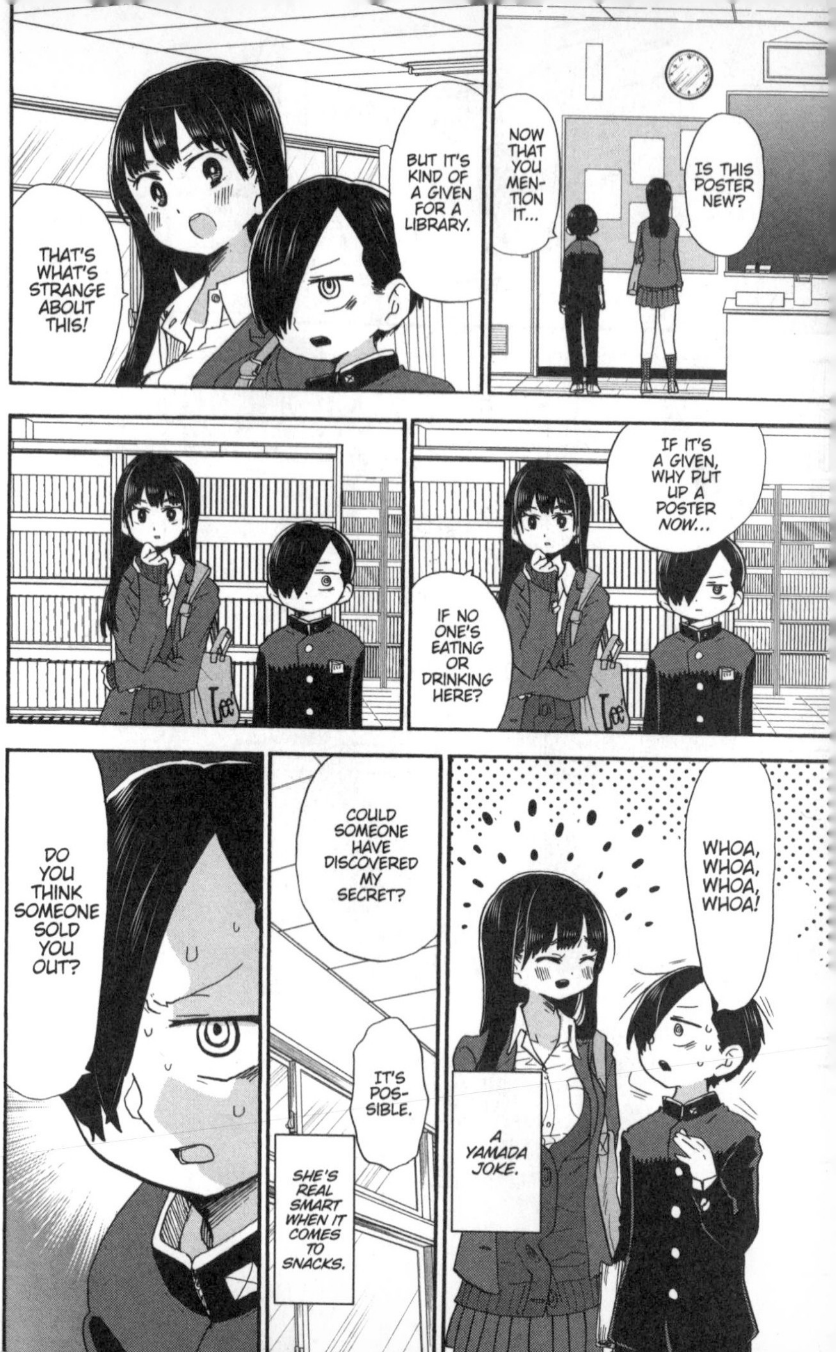

IS THIS POSTER NEW?
NOW THAT YOU MEN-TION IT...
BUT IT'S KIND OF A GIVEN FOR A LIBRARY.
THAT'S WHAT'S STRANGE ABOUT THIS!
IF IT'S A GIVEN, WHY PUT UP A POSTER *NOW*...
IF NO ONE'S EATING OR DRINKING HERE?
WHOA, WHOA, WHOA, WHOA!
A YAMADA JOKE.
COULD SOMEONE HAVE DISCOVERED MY SECRET?
IT'S POS-SIBLE.
SHE'S REAL SMART WHEN IT COMES TO SNACKS.
DO YOU THINK SOMEONE SOLD YOU OUT?

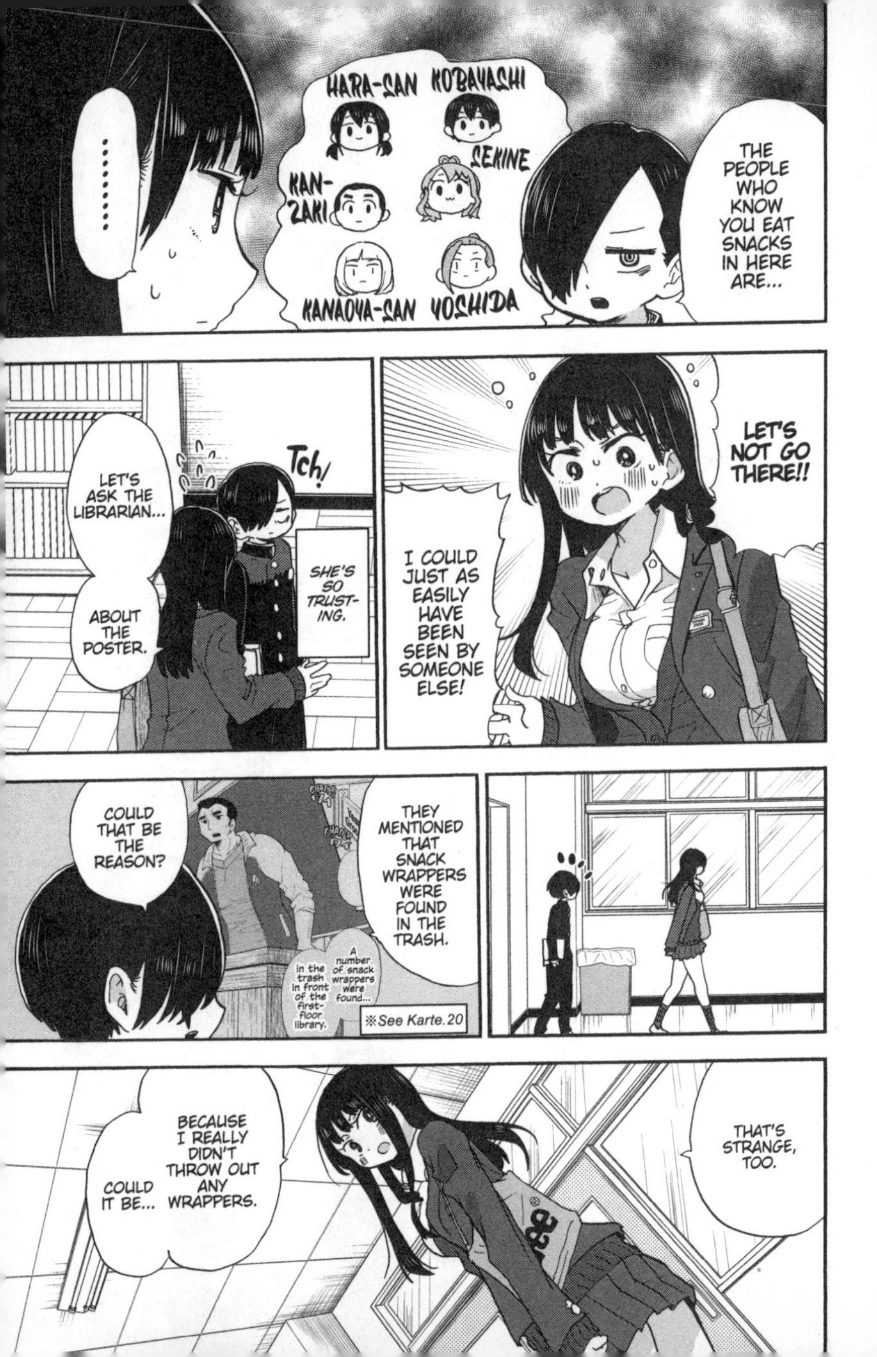
THE PEOPLE WHO KNOW YOU EAT SNACKS IN HERE ARE...
KOBAYASHI
HARA-SAN
SEKINE
KAN-ZAKI
YOSHIDA
KANAOYA-SAN
......
LET'S NOT GO THERE!!
I COULD JUST AS EASILY HAVE BEEN SEEN BY SOMEONE ELSE!
Tch!
SHE'S SO TRUSTING.
LET'S ASK THE LIBRARIAN...
ABOUT THE POSTER.
THEY MENTIONED THAT SNACK WRAPPERS WERE FOUND IN THE TRASH.
A number of snack wrappers were found...
in the trash in front of the first-floor library.
※See Karte.20
COULD THAT BE THE REASON?
THAT'S STRANGE, TOO.
BECAUSE I REALLY DIDN'T THROW OUT ANY WRAPPERS.
COULD IT BE...

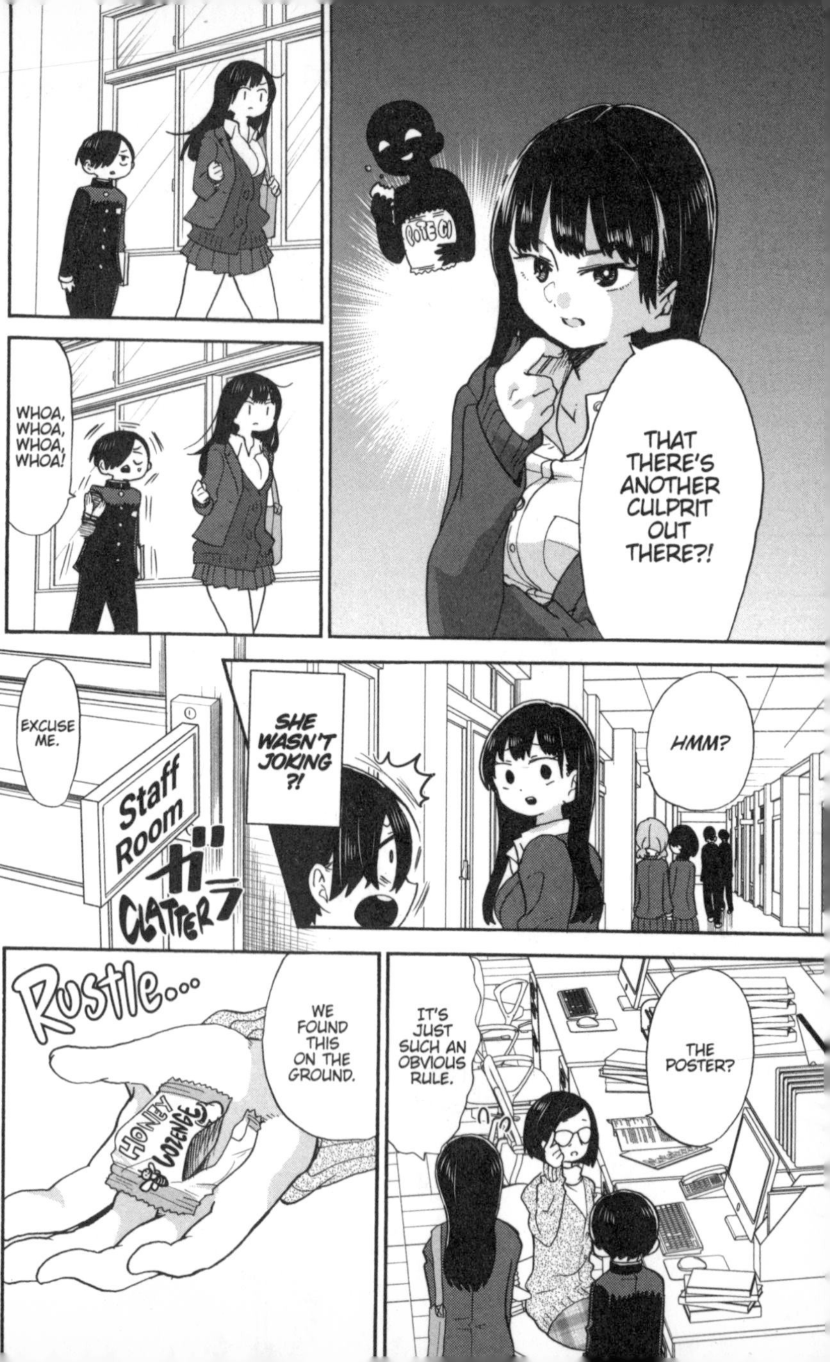

POTE CHI
THAT THERE'S ANOTHER CULPRIT OUT THERE?!
WHOA, WHOA, WHOA, WHOA!
HMM?
SHE WASN'T JOKING?!
EXCUSE ME.
Staff Room
CLATTER
THE POSTER?
IT'S JUST SUCH AN OBVIOUS RULE.
WE FOUND THIS ON THE GROUND.
Rustle...
HONEY LOZENGE

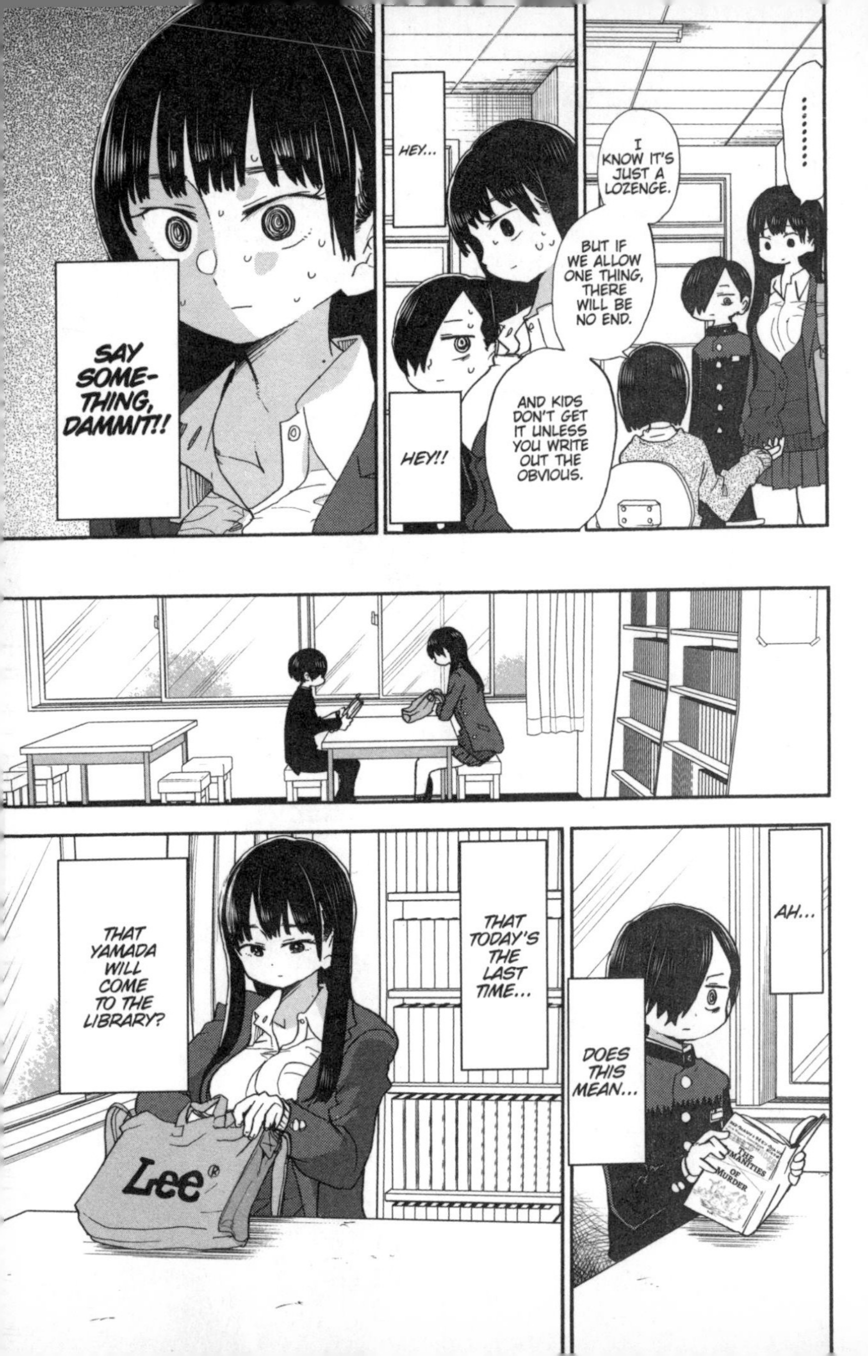
......
I KNOW IT'S JUST A LOZENGE.
BUT IF WE ALLOW ONE THING, THERE WILL BE NO END.
AND KIDS DON'T GET IT UNLESS YOU WRITE OUT THE OBVIOUS.
HEY...
HEY!!
SAY SOME-THING, DAMMIT!!
AH...
DOES THIS MEAN...
THAT TODAY'S THE LAST TIME...
THAT YAMADA WILL COME TO THE LIBRARY?
Lee

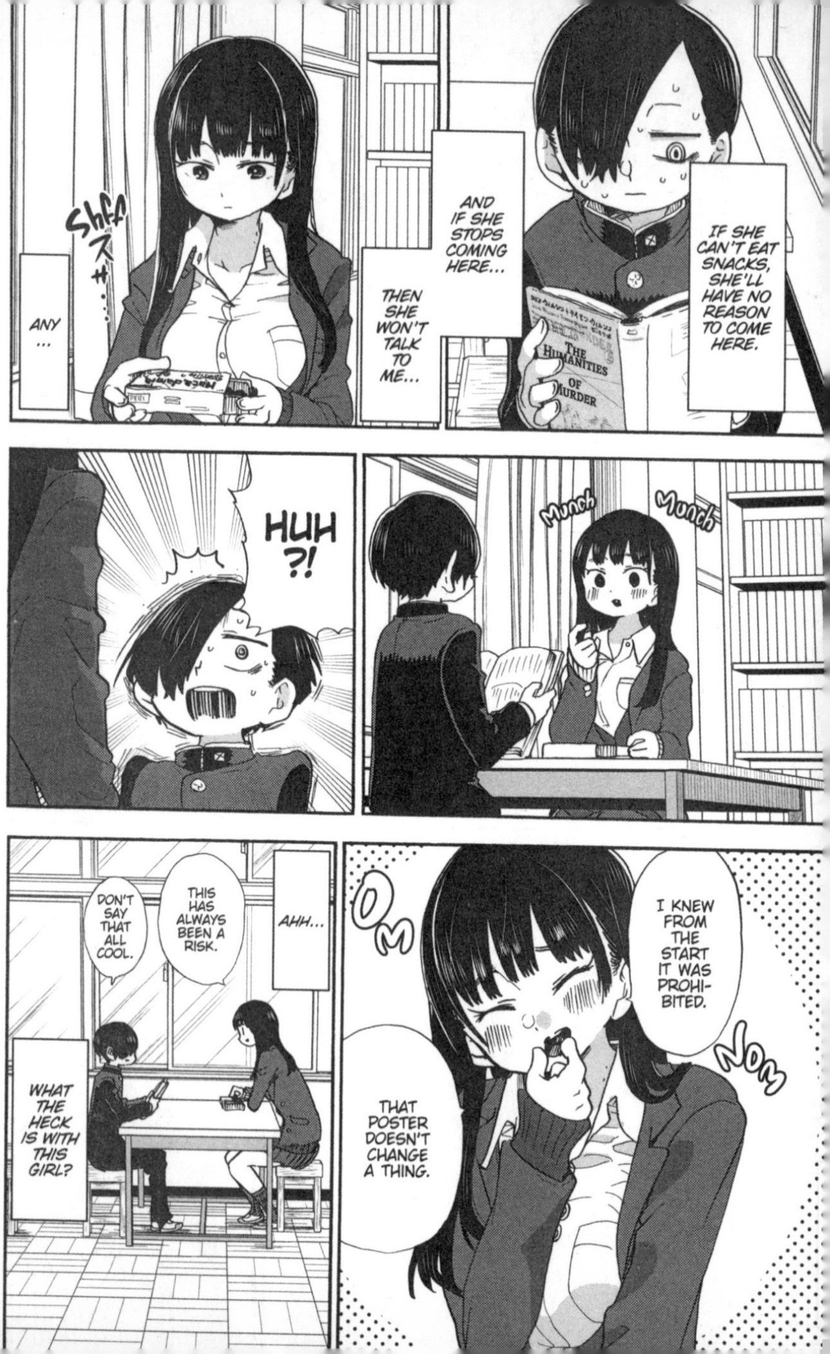
IF SHE CAN'T EAT SNACKS, SHE'LL HAVE NO REASON TO COME HERE.
THE HUMANITIES OF MURDER
AND IF SHE STOPS COMING HERE...
THEN SHE WON'T TALK TO ME...
Shff
ズサ…
ANY ...
Munch
Munch
HUH ?!
OM
I KNEW FROM THE START IT WAS PROHIBITED.
NOM
THAT POSTER DOESN'T CHANGE A THING.
AHH...
THIS HAS ALWAYS BEEN A RISK.
DON'T SAY THAT ALL COOL.
WHAT THE HECK IS WITH THIS GIRL?

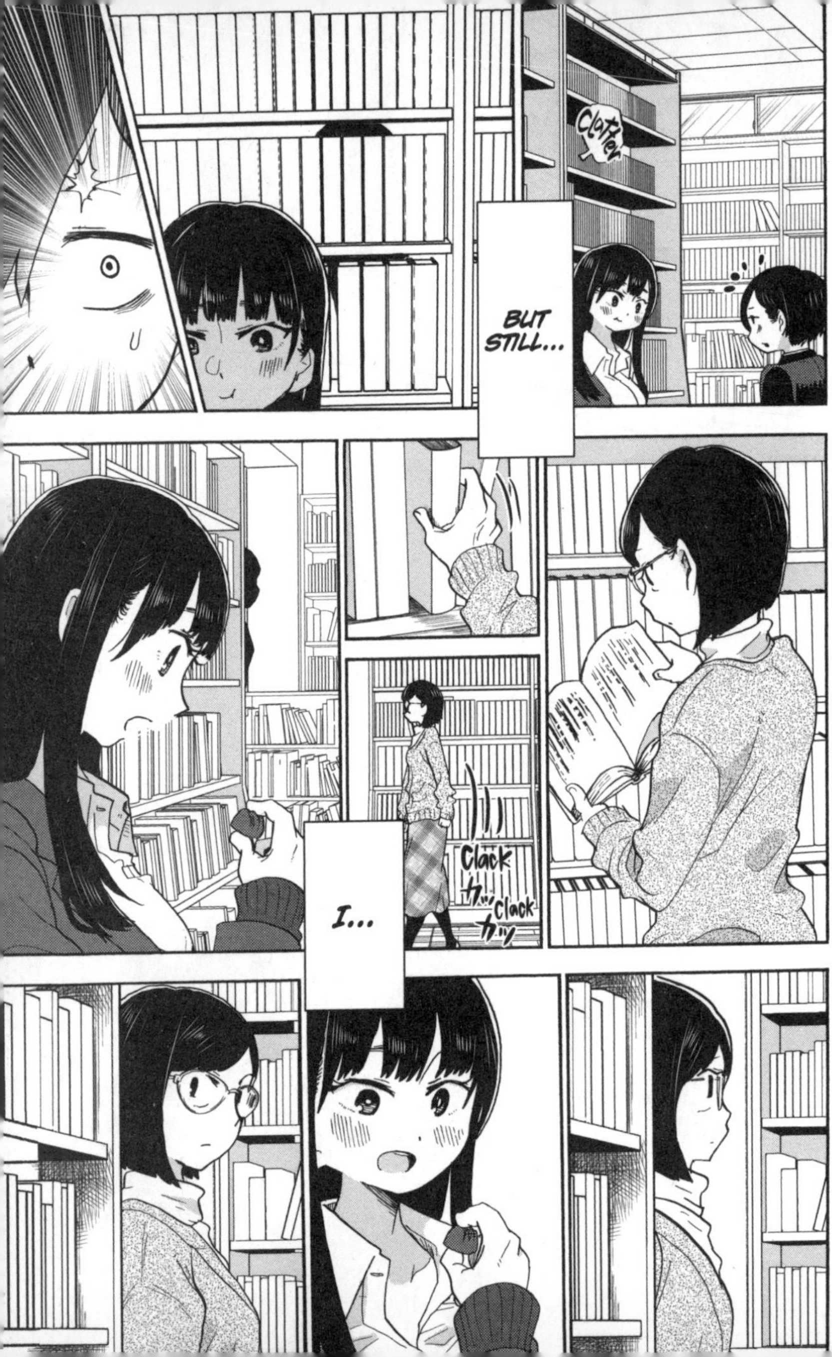
Clatter
BUT STILL...
Clack
カッ
Clack
カッ
I...

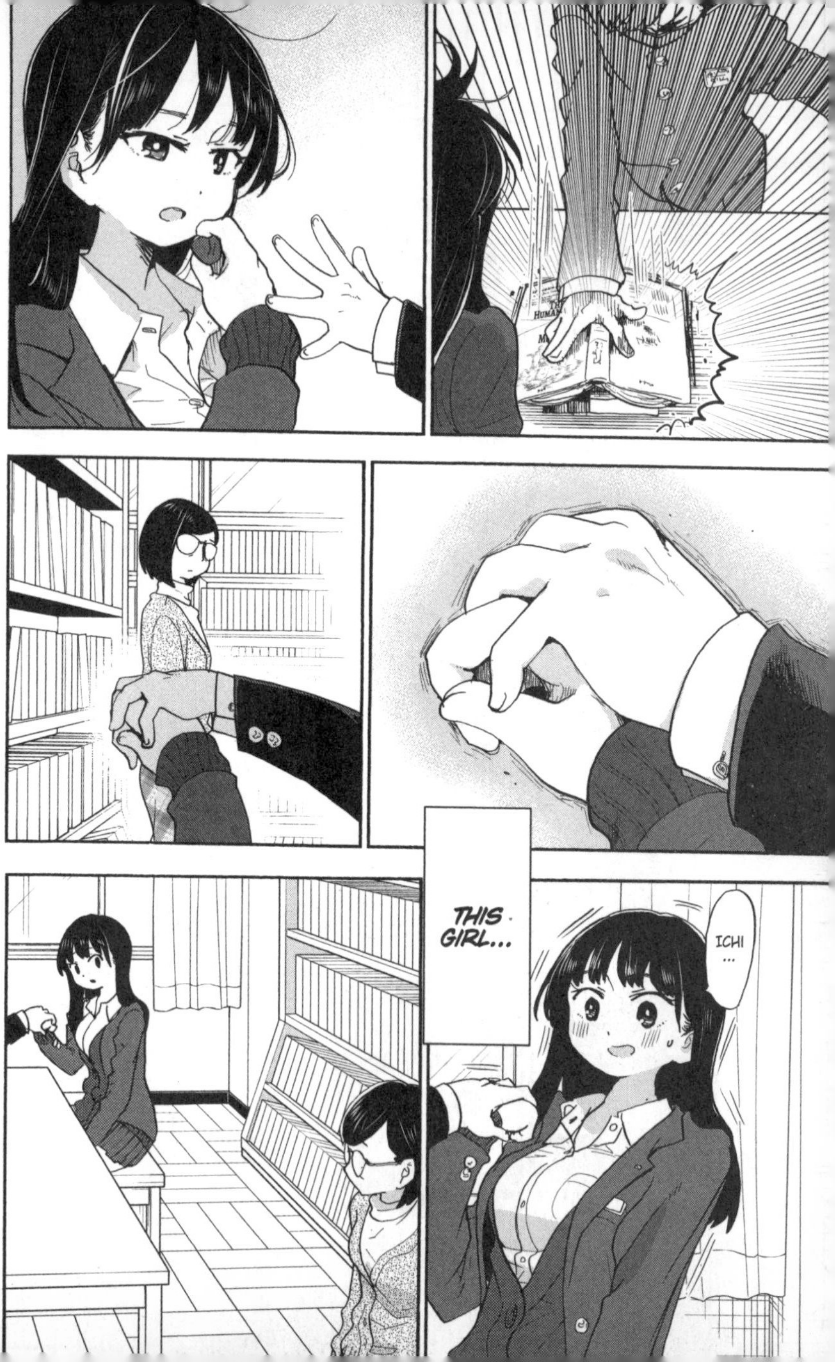
ICHI ...
THIS GIRL...

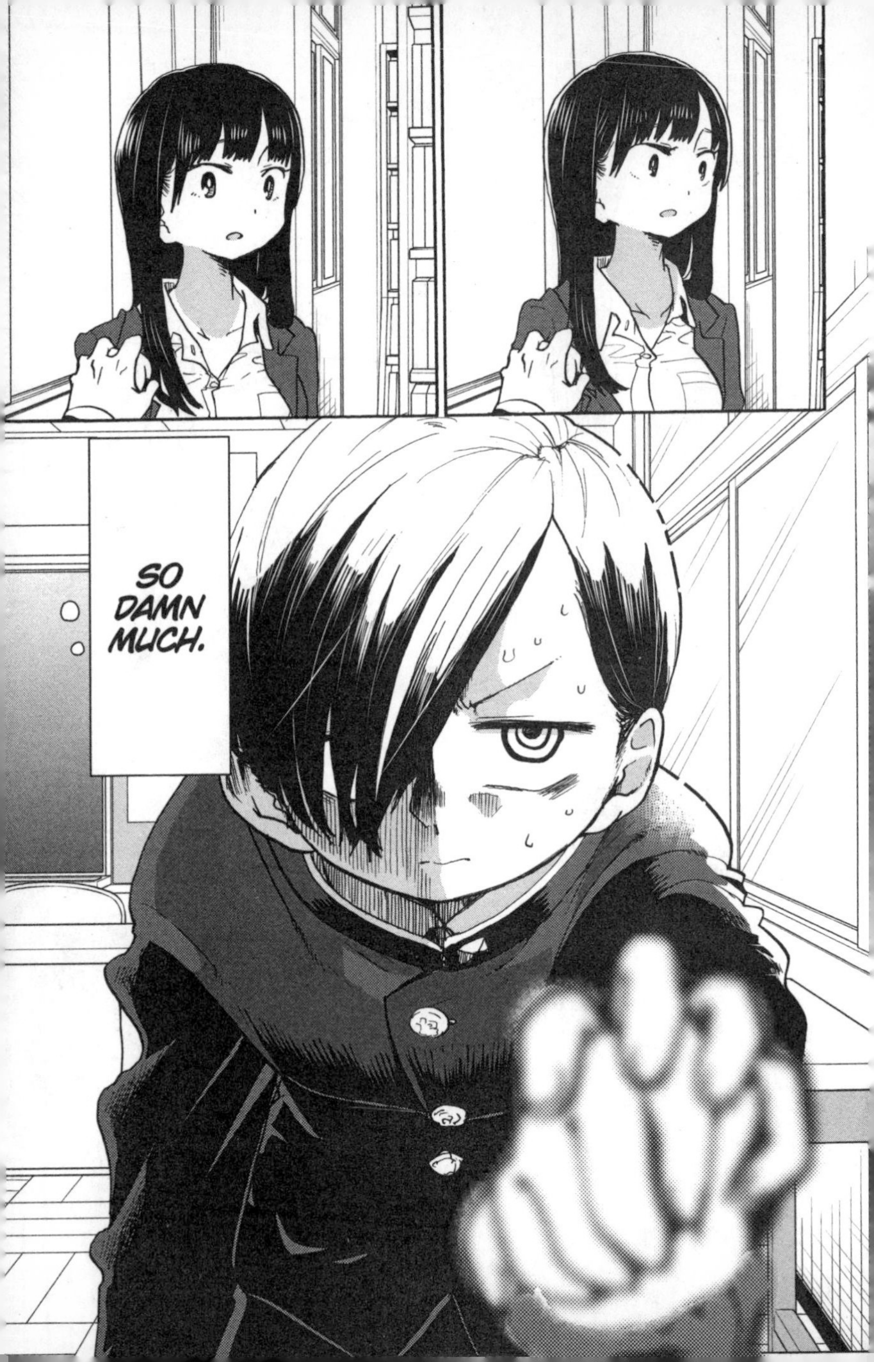
SO
DAMN
MUCH.

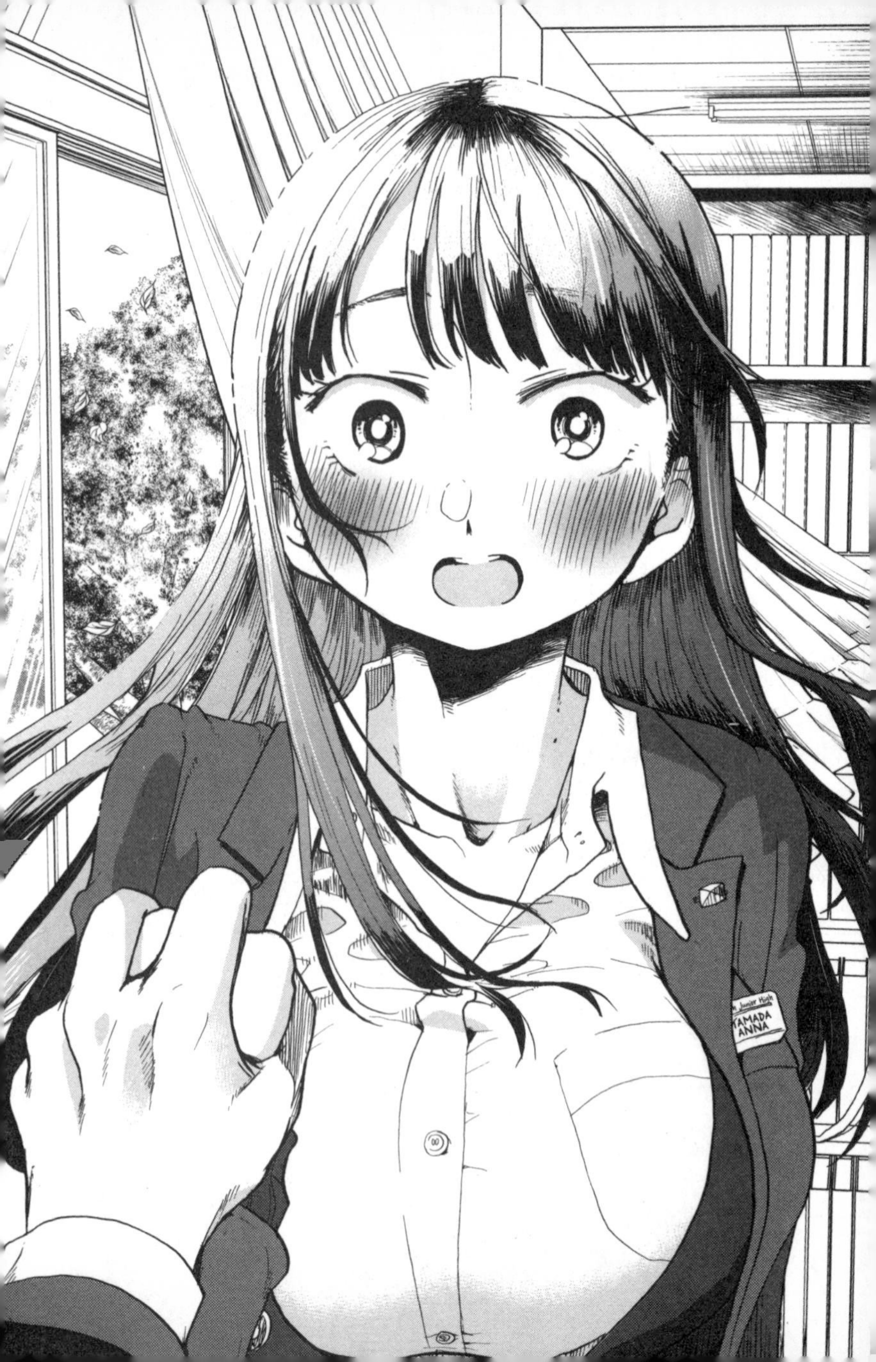
Junior High
YAMADA
ANNA

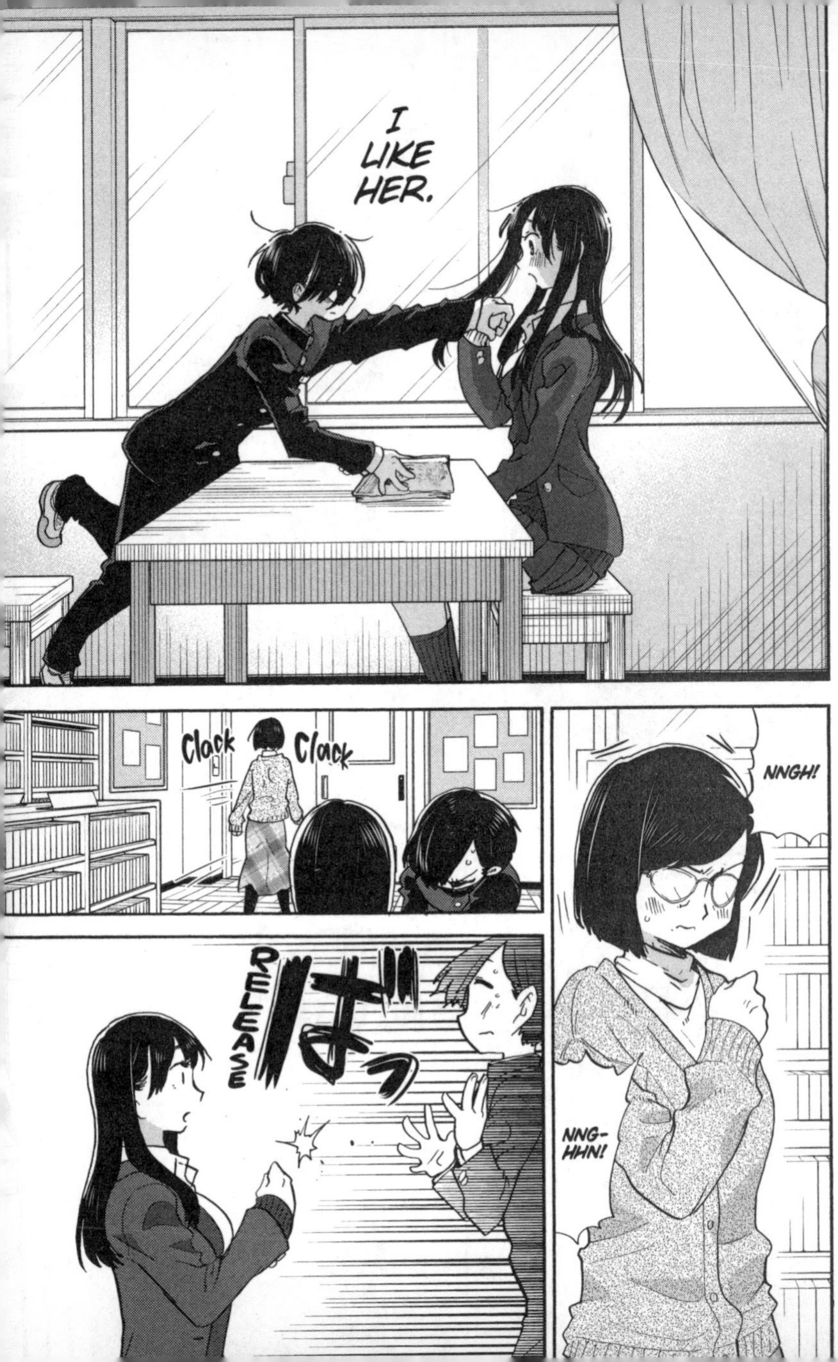
I LIKE HER.
NNGH!
NNG-HHN!
Clack
Clack
RELEASE
ぱっ
...

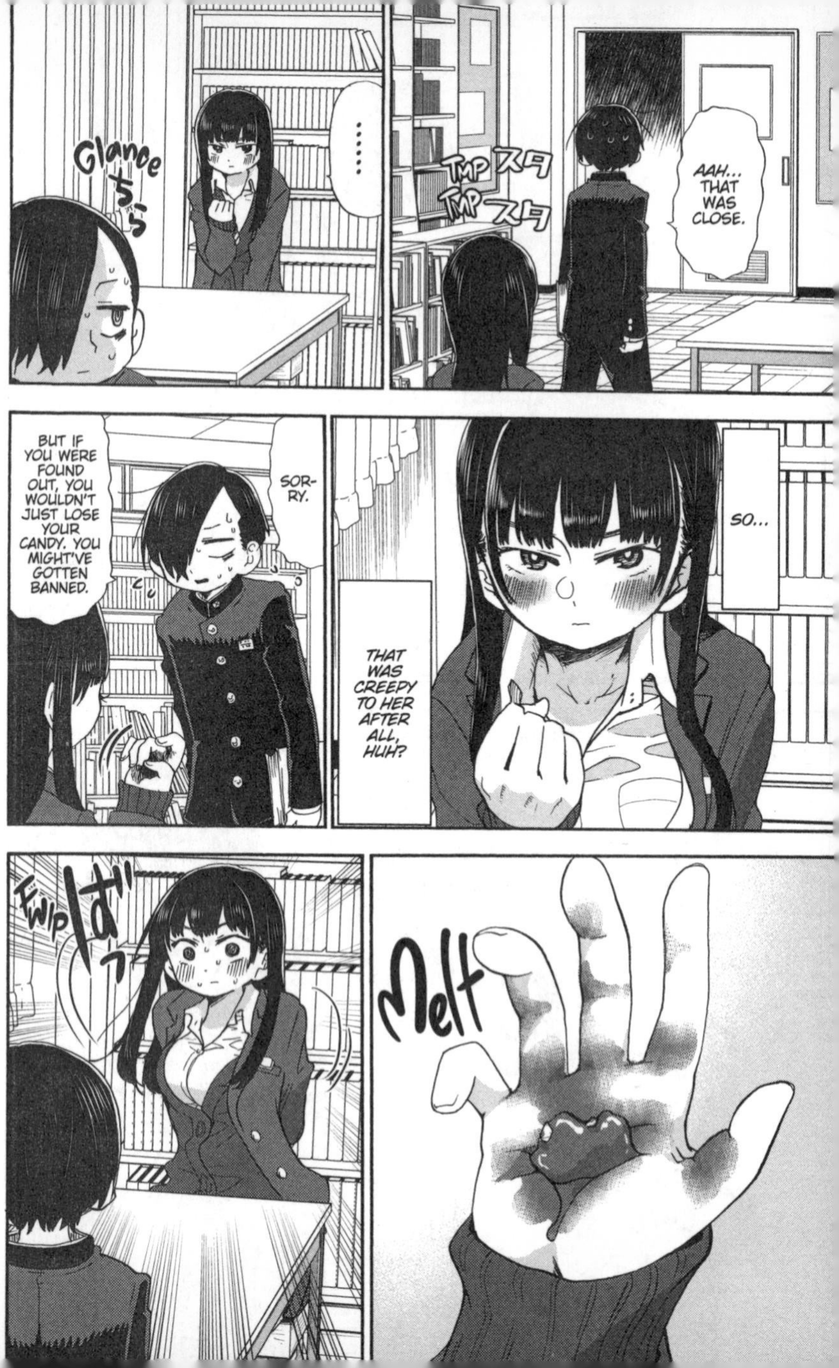
TMP スタ
TMP スタ
AAH... THAT WAS CLOSE.
......
Glance ちら
SO...
THAT WAS CREEPY TO HER AFTER ALL, HUH?
SOR-RY.
BUT IF YOU WERE FOUND OUT, YOU WOULDN'T JUST LOSE YOUR CANDY. YOU MIGHT'VE GOTTEN BANNED.
Melt
FWIP ばっ

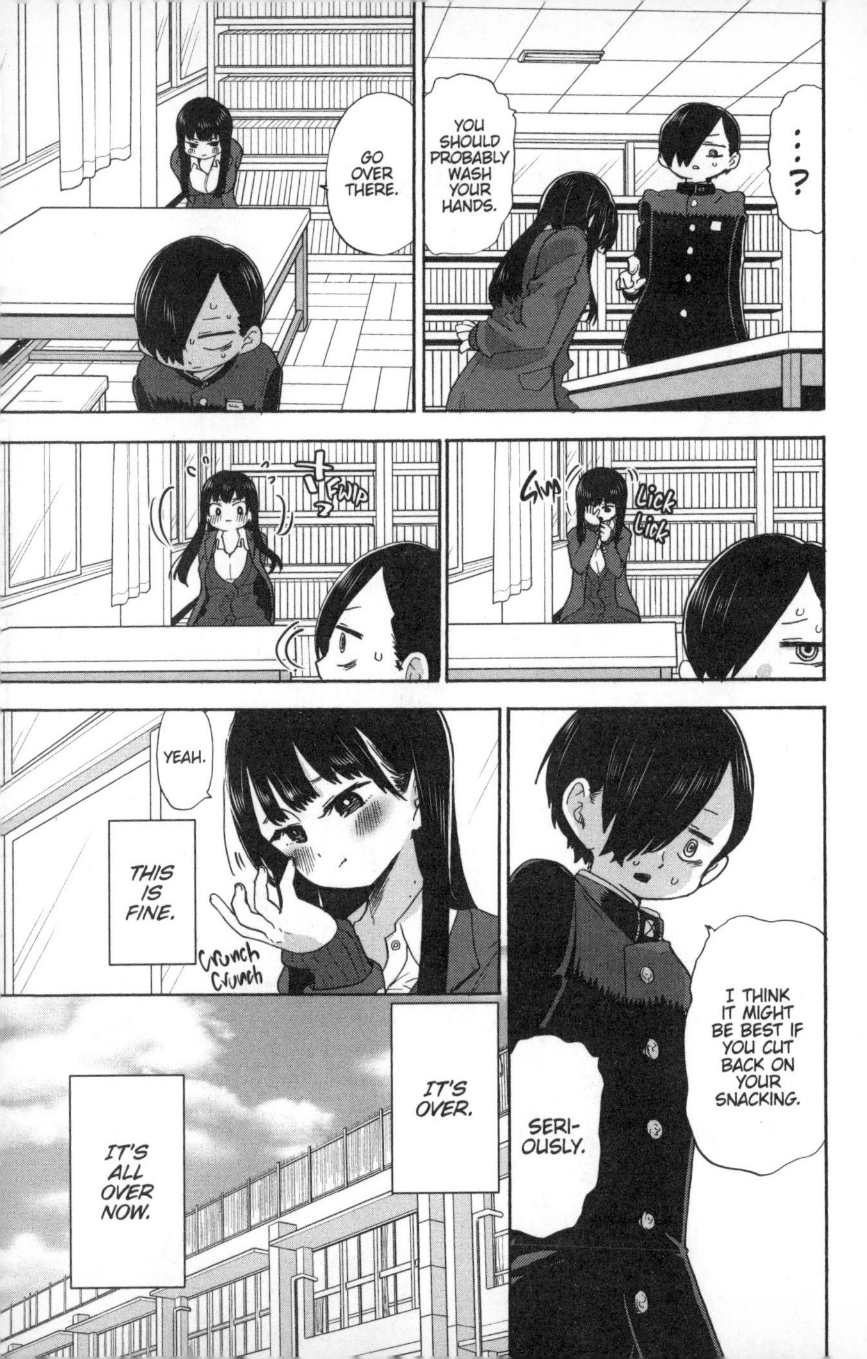
...?
YOU SHOULD PROBABLY WASH YOUR HANDS.
GO OVER THERE.
Slup
Lick Lick
FWIP
I THINK IT MIGHT BE BEST IF YOU CUT BACK ON YOUR SNACKING.
SERI-OUSLY.
YEAH.
THIS IS FINE.
Crunch Crunch
IT'S OVER.
IT'S ALL OVER NOW.

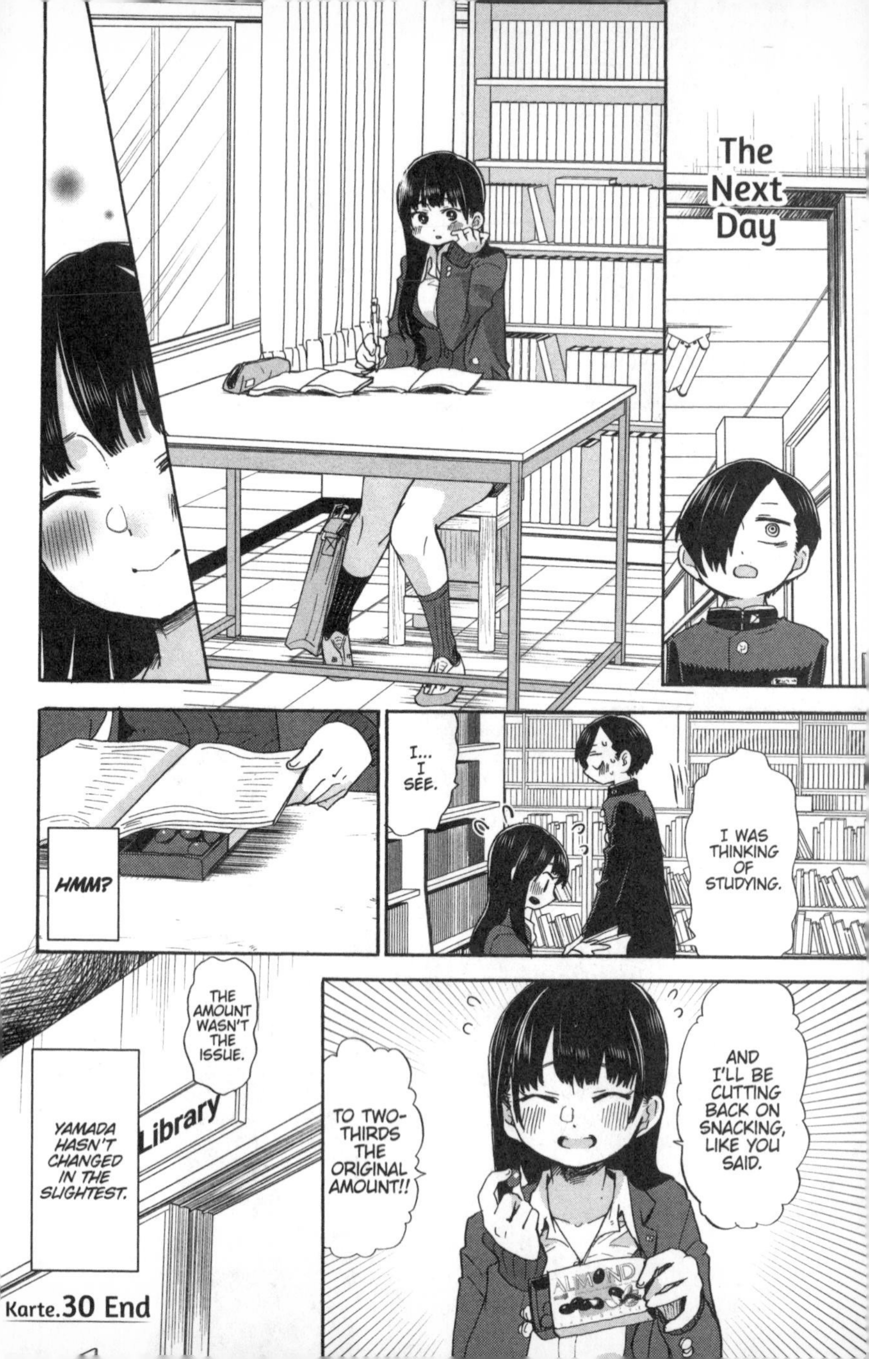
The Next Day
I WAS THINKING OF STUDYING.
I... I SEE.
HMM?
AND I'LL BE CUTTING BACK ON SNACKING, LIKE YOU SAID.
TO TWO-THIRDS THE ORIGINAL AMOUNT!!
ALMOND
THE AMOUNT WASN'T THE ISSUE.
Library
YAMADA HASN'T CHANGED IN THE SLIGHTEST.
Karte.30 End

Unsolved

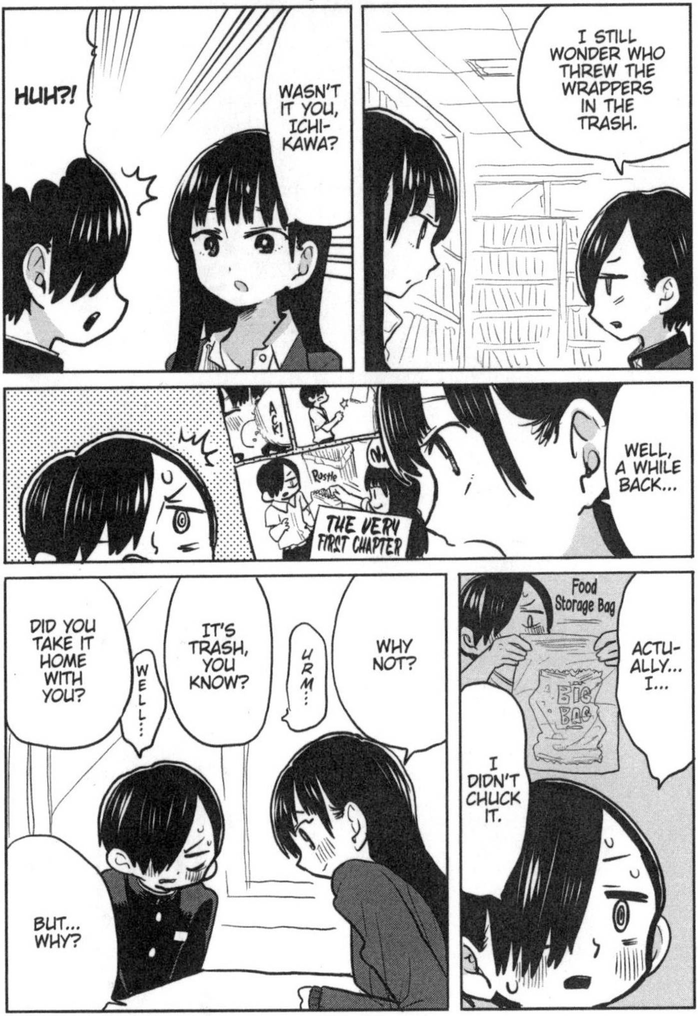
I STILL WONDER WHO THREW THE WRAPPERS IN THE TRASH.
WASN'T IT YOU, ICHI-KAWA?
HUH?!
WELL, A WHILE BACK...
ACK!
Rustle
THE VERY FIRST CHAPTER
Food Storage Bag
BIG BAG
ACTU-ALLY... I...
I DIDN'T CHUCK IT.
WHY NOT?
URM...
IT'S TRASH, YOU KNOW?
WELL...
DID YOU TAKE IT HOME WITH YOU?
BUT... WHY?

The
Dangers
in My
Heart

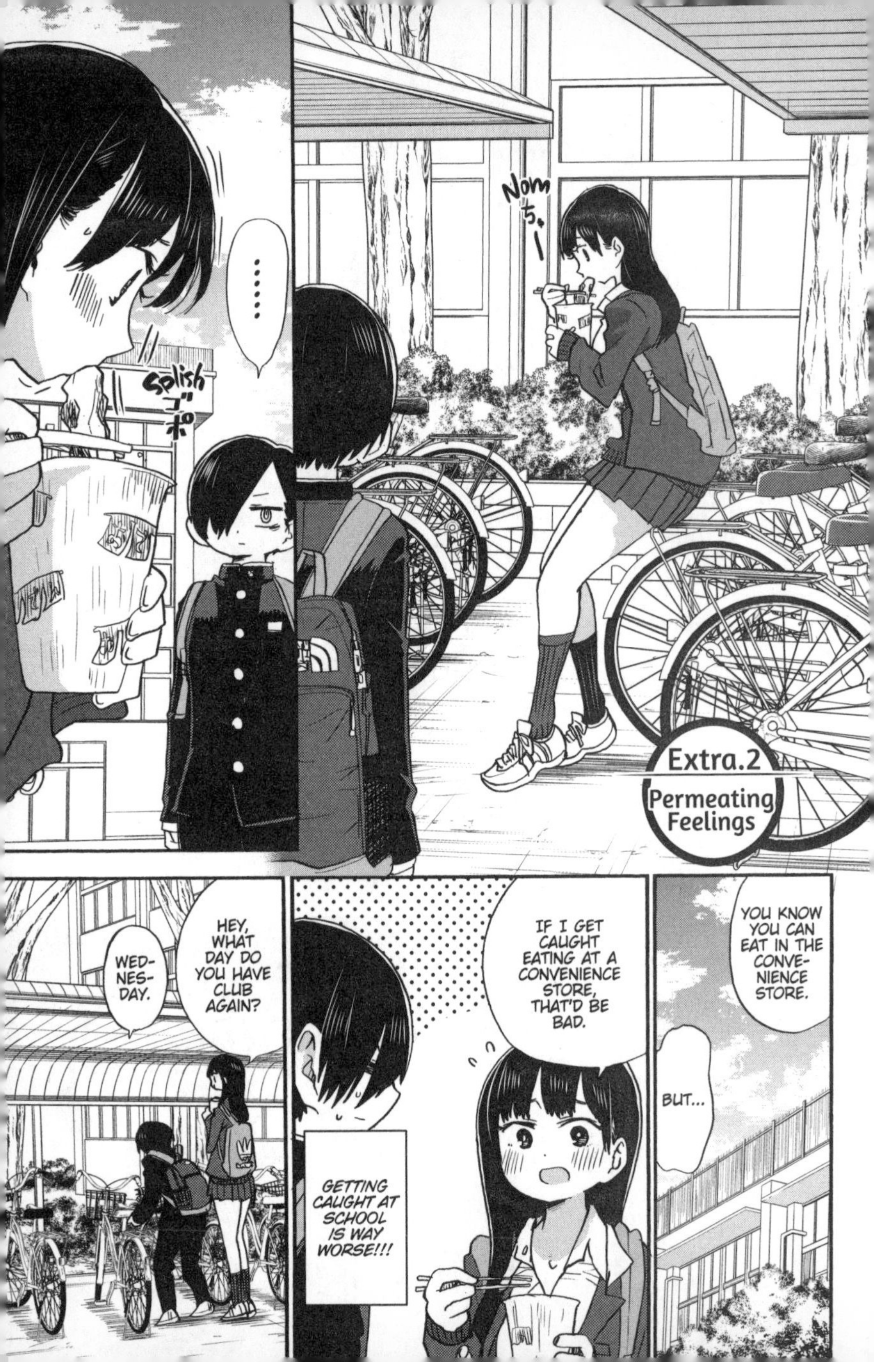
Nom
ちゅ
Extra.2
Permeating Feelings
......
Splish
ゴポ
YOU KNOW YOU CAN EAT IN THE CONVENIENCE STORE.
BUT...
IF I GET CAUGHT EATING AT A CONVENIENCE STORE, THAT'D BE BAD.
GETTING CAUGHT AT SCHOOL IS WAY WORSE!!!
HEY, WHAT DAY DO YOU HAVE CLUB AGAIN?
WEDNESDAY.

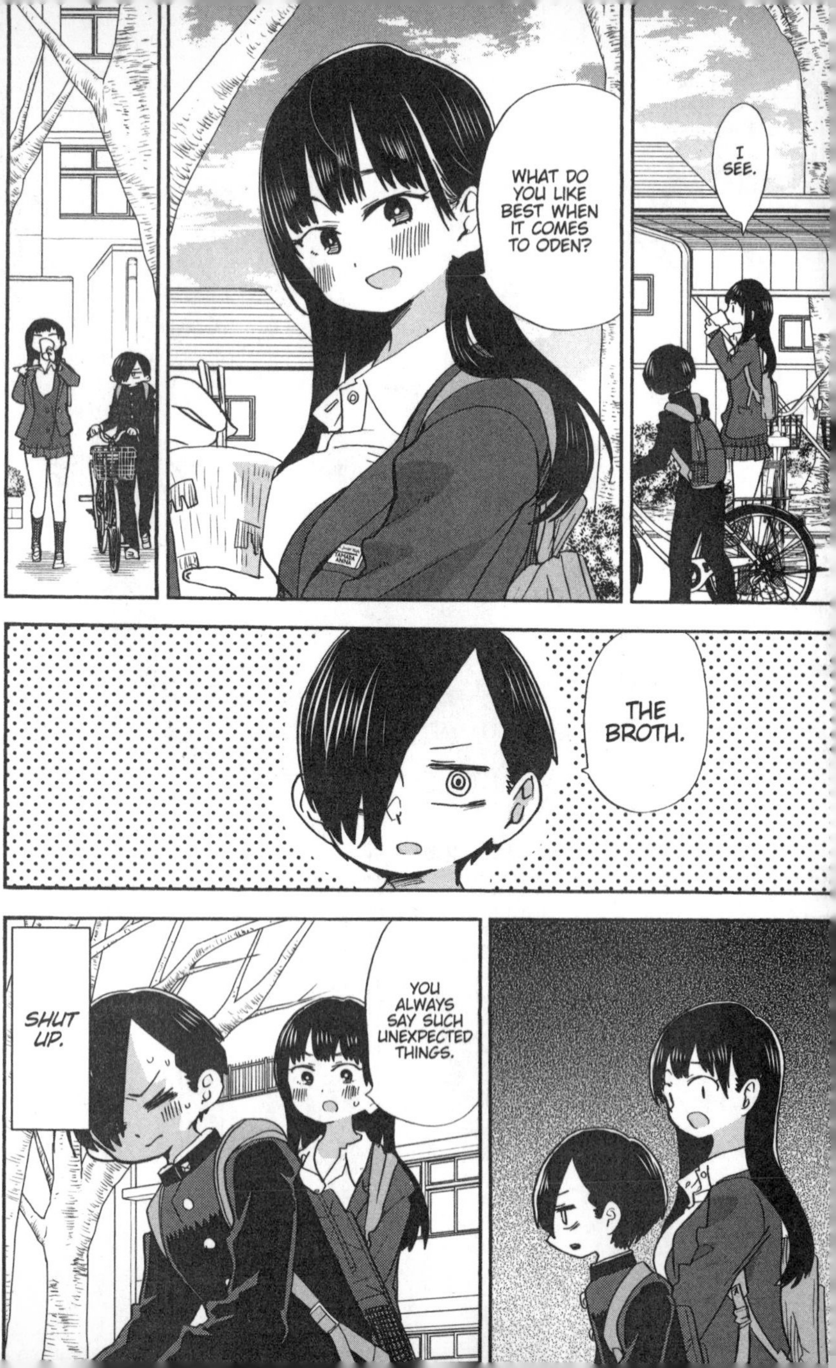
I SEE.
WHAT DO YOU LIKE BEST WHEN IT COMES TO ODEN?
THE BROTH.
YOU ALWAYS SAY SUCH UNEXPECTED THINGS.
SHUT UP.

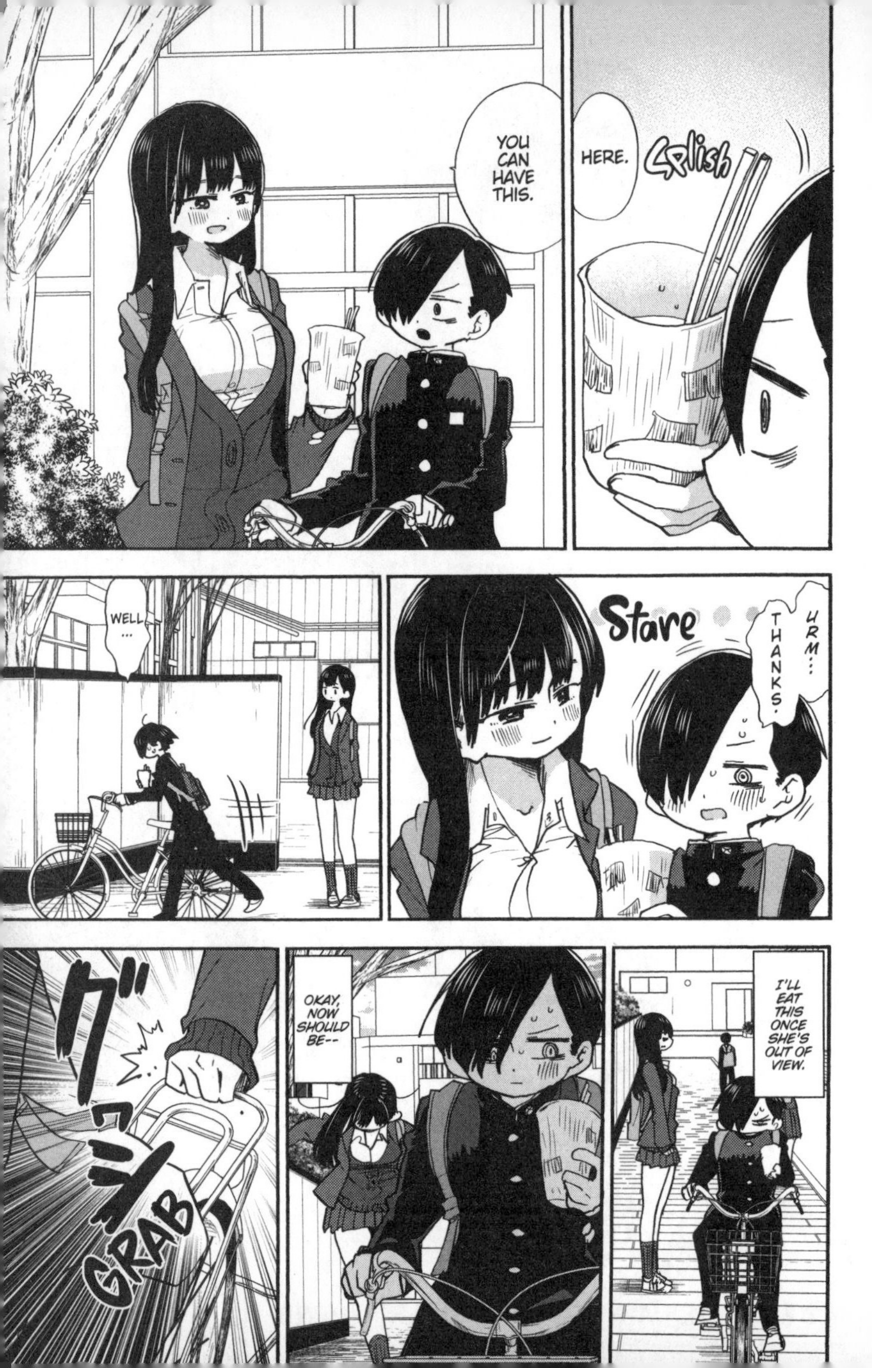

HERE.
Splish
YOU CAN HAVE THIS.
Stare
URM... THANKS.
WELL ...
I'LL EAT THIS ONCE SHE'S OUT OF VIEW.
OKAY, NOW SHOULD BE--
グッ
GRAB

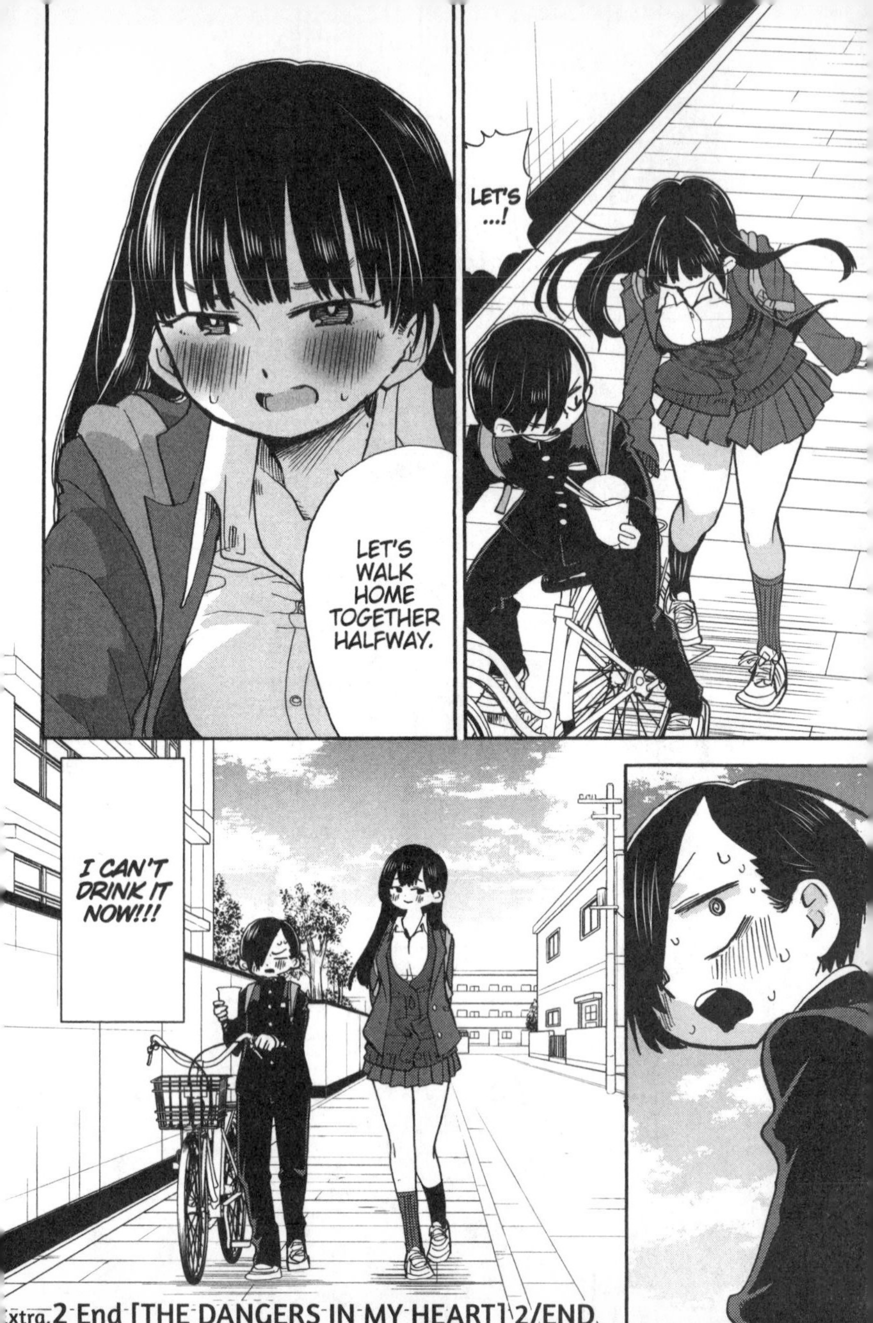
LET'S ...!
LET'S WALK HOME TOGETHER HALFWAY.
I CAN'T DRINK IT NOW!!!

Extra.2 End [THE DANGERS IN MY HEART] 2/END

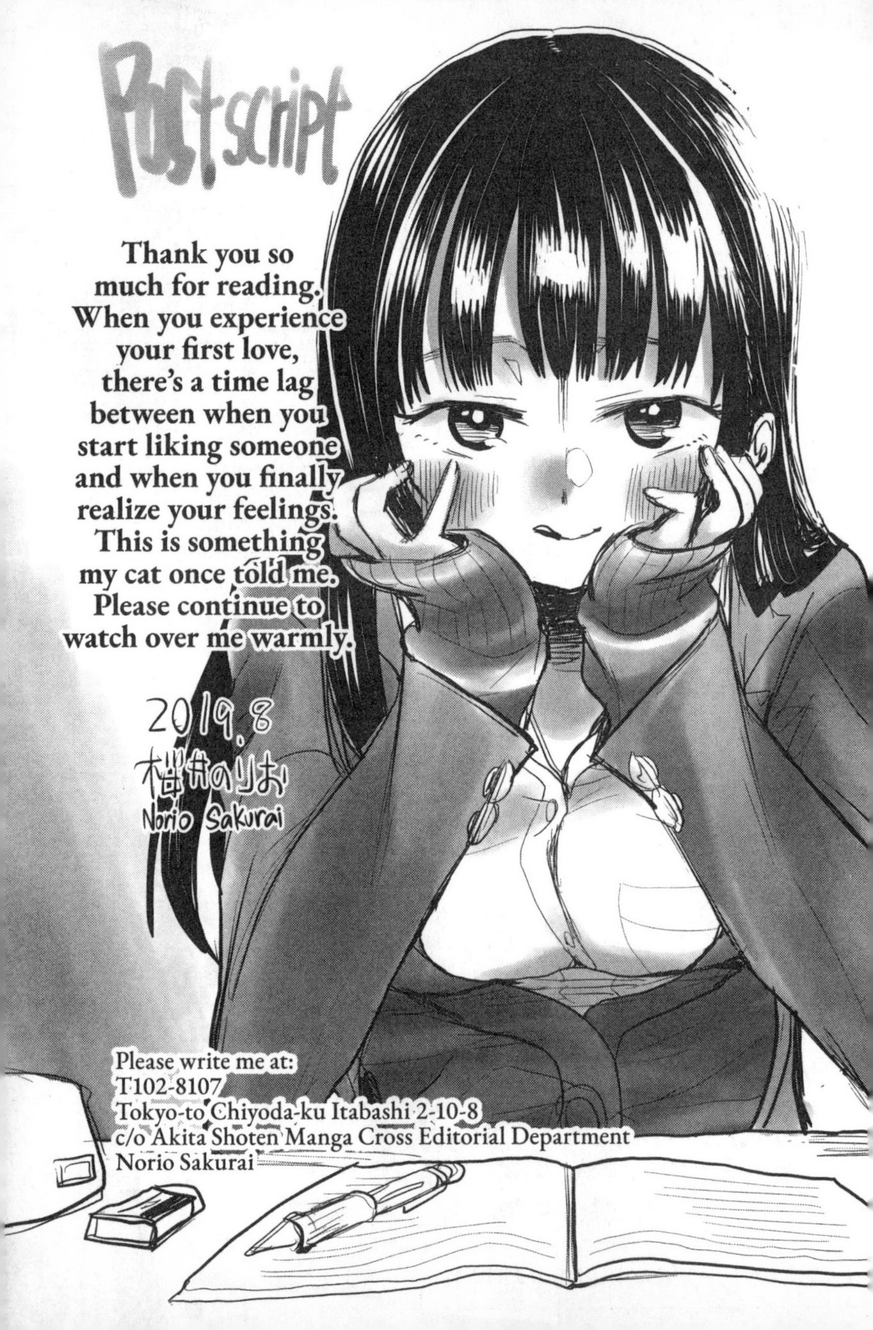

Postscript

Thank you so much for reading. When you experience your first love, there's a time lag between when you start liking someone and when you finally realize your feelings. This is something my cat once told me. Please continue to watch over me warmly.

2019.8
櫻井のりお
Norio Sakurai

Please write me at:
T102-8107
Tokyo-to Chiyoda-ku Itabashi 2-10-8
c/o Akita Shoten Manga Cross Editorial Department
Norio Sakurai

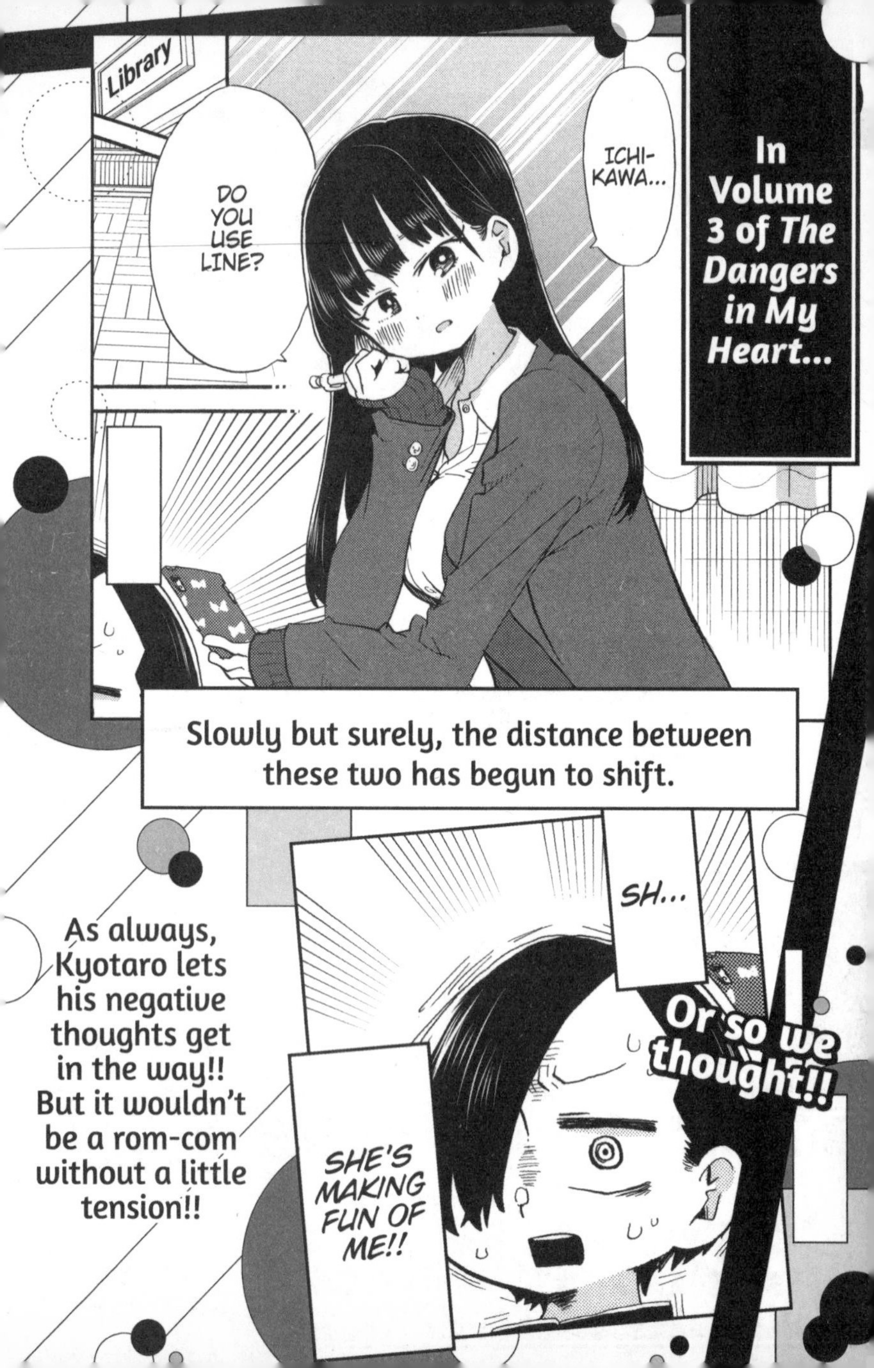
In Volume 3 of *The Dangers in My Heart*...
ICHI-KAWA...
DO YOU USE LINE?
Library
Slowly but surely, the distance between these two has begun to shift.
Or so we thought!!
SH...
SHE'S MAKING FUN OF ME!!
As always, Kyotaro lets his negative thoughts get in the way!! But it wouldn't be a rom-com without a little tension!!